Memory and History

How does the historian approach memory and how do historians use different sources to analyse how history and memory interact and impact on each other?

Memory and History explores the different aspects of the study of this field. Taking examples from Europe, Australia, the USA and Japan and treating periods beyond living memory as well as the recent past, the volume highlights the contours of the current vogue for memory among historians while demonstrating the diversity and imagination of the field.

Each chapter looks at a set of key historical and historiographical questions through research-based case studies:

- How does engaging with memory as either source or subject help to illuminate the past?
- What are the theoretical, ethical and/or methodological challenges that are encountered by historians engaging with memory in this way, and how might they be managed?
- How can the reading of a particular set of sources illuminate both of these questions?

This book will be essential reading for students of history and memory, providing an accessible guide to the historical study of memory through a focus on varied source materials.

Joan Tumblety teaches History at the University of Southampton. Her previous publications include *Remaking the Male Body: Masculinity and the Uses of Physical Culture in Interwar and Vichy France* (OUP, 2012) and she is currently working on health cures in early to mid-twentieth-century France.

The Routledge Guides to Using Historical Sources

How does the historian approach primary sources? How do interpretations differ? How can such sources be used to write history?

The *Routledge Guides to Using Historical Sources* series introduces students to different sources and illustrates how historians use them. Titles in the series offer a broad spectrum of primary sources and, using specific examples, examine the historical context of these sources and the different approaches that can be used to interpret them.

Reading Primary Sources, Miriam Dobson and Benjamin Ziemann
History Beyond the Text, Sarah Barber and Corinna Penniston-Bird
History and Material Culture, Karen Harvey
Understanding Medieval Primary Sources, Joel Rosenthal

Memory and History

Understanding memory as source and subject

Edited by
Joan Tumblety

 Routledge
Taylor & Francis Group

LONDON AND NEW YORK

First published 2013
by Routledge
2 Park Square, Milton Park, Abingdon, Oxon OX14 4RN

Simultaneously published in the USA and Canada by Routledge
711 Third Avenue, New York, NY 10017

Routledge is an imprint of the Taylor & Francis Group, an informa business

British Library Cataloguing in Publication Data
A catalogue record for this book is available from the British Library

Library of Congress Cataloging in Publication Data
Memory and history : understanding memory as source and subject / edited
by Joan Tumblety.
pages cm -- (The Routledge guides to using historical sources)
"Simultaneously published in the USA and Canada"--Title page verso.
Includes bibliographical references and index.
1. Oral history. 2. Memory. 3. Collective memory. 4. Memorials.
5. Historiography--Methodology. I. Tumblety, Joan.
D16.14.M45 2013
907.2--dc23
2012039801

ISBN: 978-0-415-67711-0 (hbk)
ISBN: 978-0-415-67712-7 (pbk)
ISBN: 978-0-203-55249-0 (ebk)

Typeset in Times New Roman
by Taylor & Francis Books

MIX
Paper from
responsible sources
FSC
www.fsc.org FSC® C018575   Printed and bound in Great Britain by MPG Printgroup

Contents

Figures

Contributors

Michal Bosworth is now retired after working for more than 30 years as an independent scholar. Her main interests lie in heritage, immigration and Australian food and diet.

Susan A. Crane is Associate Professor of Modern European History at the University of Arizona. She is the author of *Collecting and Historical Consciousness in Early Nineteenth Century Germany* (2000) and contributing editor of *Museums and Memory* (2000). Her recent publications have focused on photographs as historical evidence, particularly atrocity photographs from the Holocaust.

Jason Crouthamel earned his PhD in modern German history from Indiana University, and he is currently an associate professor at Grand Valley State University in Michigan. His recent publications include *The Great War and German Memory: Society, Politics and Psychological Trauma, 1914–45* (University of Exeter Press, 2009). He is completing another book, *An Intimate History of the Trenches*, which examines the effects of the First World War on ordinary German soldiers' conceptions of masculinity and sexuality.

Lindsey Dodd is a Lecturer in Modern History at the University of Huddersfield. She is interested in twentieth-century French history, specifically experiences of war, the history of childhood and the theory and practice of oral history.

Dr Hannah Ewence is Lecturer in Modern History at the University of Chester. Her primary area of research focuses upon the cultural and spatial representations of, and writings produced by, Jews and other minority communities in *fin de siècle* and twentieth-century Britain. She is currently completing her first monograph, *The Other in Our Midst: Jews, Gender and the British Imperial Imagination*.

Rosanne Kennedy is Associate Professor of Literature and Gender Studies at Australian National University. She writes about trauma, testimony and cultural memory in literature, law, memoir and film. Her articles have appeared in journals including *Comparative Literature Studies*, *Biography*,

Studies in the Novel, Women's Studies Quarterly, Life Writing and *Australian Feminist Studies.*

Tony Kushner is Director of the Parkes Institute and Professor of History at the University of Southampton. His most recent book is *The Battle of Britishness: Migrant Journeys, 1685 to the Present* (Manchester University Press, 2012).

Polly Low is Senior Lecturer in Ancient History at the University of Manchester. She has particular interests in interstate politics, imperialism and the history of burial and commemoration within and beyond Athens.

Franziska Seraphim is Associate Professor of Japanese History at Boston College. The author of *War Memory and Social Politics in Japan, 1945–2005* (2006), she is currently working on a comparative social history of convicted World War II criminals in Japan and Germany.

Susan M. Stabile is Associate Professor in English at Texas A&M University. Her interests in American Studies are interdisciplinary, combining gender theory, late eighteenth- and early nineteenth-century American women's literature and culture, material culture and museum studies, and contemporary women's memoir.

Joan Tumblety teaches History at the University of Southampton. She is author of *Remaking the Male Body: Masculinity and the Uses of Physical Culture in Interwar and Vichy France* (Oxford University Press, 2012) and is currently working on health cures in early to mid-twentieth-century France.

Acknowledgements

In some ways this book is the fruit of many years of scholarly engagement with historiography through teaching it to undergraduate and postgraduate students. I have relished the opportunity to communicate in print some of the discussions and arguments about both memory and the historical discipline that I have enjoyed with countless students and colleagues over the years. It is more directly the collective effort of a team of contributors whose original research on memory has made the volume possible. I would like to thank them for taking the task on board so receptively and for the imagination and rigour that has gone into their individual essays.

The volume is the result of discussions with series editor Eve Setch who first pitched the idea of a book about sources on memory to me. I would like to thank her for commissioning it and for her continuing engagement with the shape of the project. At Routledge I have also benefited from the helpful editorial support of Laura Mothersole.

I am grateful for the insightful and rigorous comments and suggestions for the volume offered by Jay Winter and W. Fitzhugh Brundage, in addition to the two anonymous readers sought by the press. The final text has been shaped by their ideas in many ways. I thank also the colleagues and peers who offered keen proofreading eyes and thoughtful feedback on parts of my own contribution to the volume – Susan A. Crane, Simon Kitson, Nicholas Kingwell, Tony Kushner and Matthew Brown.

Joan Tumblety
September 2012

Introduction

Working with memory as source and subject

Joan Tumblety

Memory is now as familiar a category for historians as politics, war or empire. Whether measured by the number of books, journals or doctoral dissertations poised to explore it, the array of scholarly conferences devoted to its dissection, or the number of university courses that engage with the concept, 'memory' has become over the past 20 or so years a familiar word in the vocabulary of academic history. And we ask a lot of this seemingly everyday term. We stretch it across cognitive and neural processes of remembering located in the human brain and the narrative expression of autobiographical memories found in memoirs; it serves for public acts of commemoration that mark significant events in the past, and for public apologies for past atrocities made by state authorities. We know it as public history, museum practice and 'heritage'; we spawn from it notions of social memory, collective memory and historical memory. And the so-called 'memory boom' – something that applies equally to the apparently renewed enthusiasm for the past in popular culture and to the scholarship that seeks to understand it – extends far beyond the disciplinary boundaries of history, to encompass not only other humanities and social science disciplines such as music and sociology, but cognitive psychology and neuroscience as well. As discussed below, historians are not always referring to the same thing when they speak of 'memory', and in their studies of this nebulous phenomenon there has been a tendency to slide – often in under-acknowledged ways – between approaching it as a source of raw material about the past, and as a subject for historical inquiry in its own right.

This book is devoted to the boom area of memory – as confronted by historians – in all its forms. It encourages historiographical reflection through a number of tangible, short case studies drawn from each contributor's own research made accessible to the non-specialist. What distinguishes it from the many other historiographical volumes about memory and history on the book shelves is its focus on sources. Here the authors offer up their original research through an explanation of what they are doing with their primary material, and a reflection on the difficulties of working with it. They identify both what is to be gained in the encounter, and what procedural, epistemological or perhaps ethical pitfalls await the historian who attempts to grasp something as elusive as memory in the process. Most strikingly, the recent turn to memory among historians has taken them far beyond an analysis of personal memories expressed in interviews and memoirs.

We must bear in mind, in fact, that historians do not approach memory just as source but as subject. That is, they seek evidence not only *of* memory (what is remembered), but evidence *about* memory (how and why the past is remembered in one way and not another). It is the question of how a certain view of the past is incorporated, sustained or alternatively eclipsed in the mediums of the present – at individual and social levels – that engages their interest. And it entails the investigation of multiple source bases: texts, objects and actions that serve as conduits for these selective processes of remembrance and memorialization. Across the chapters in this book you will encounter oral testimony generated through interviews conducted by historians; legal testimony given by witnesses in the court room; inscriptions on ancient monuments; works of art; photography in museum displays; legal polemic and journalism; letters written by war veterans; autobiographical fiction; the archive, conceived in the broadest sense; and material culture constituted by both everyday and exotic objects. There is a broad chronological and geographical sweep: the case studies encompass moments between the fifth century BCE and the twenty-first century; and they draw on examples from Europe, the United States, Japan and Australia. While there is no attempt at a comprehensive overview of approaches to memory among historians, I hope that the volume communicates something of the vastness and range of the enterprise.

To reflect this diversity of engagement with memory as source and subject across the discipline, the book is divided into three distinct parts. Part I offers a discussion of how oral and legal historians have approached the testimony of individual lived experience in their work – listening to it, recording it, understanding it, and turning it into written history. Part II is focused squarely on social acts of memorialization and commemoration, attempts on the part of groups or individuals who act as 'memory makers' in different times and places to articulate – via a range of mediums that bear the weight of the analysis offered – a certain view of the past, usually in the service of present-day objectives. Having set up this distinction between individual remembrance and social commemoration, Part III is poised to complicate it. In particular, the chapters in the final part of the book interrogate the interplay between these two types of 'memory at work'. They linger on the problem of 'collective memory' – what it might mean and how it sits in relation both to individual remembering and public acts of memorialization. Yet in keeping with the fluidity of approaches in the larger body of scholarship on memory, divisions between the parts of the book are not watertight. There is a common interest across the volume in how certain stories about the past become the dominant ones; and how those dominant stories may inform or be informed by individual action. Throughout the book careful attention is paid not only to political and social contexts, but also to the institutional contexts in which the chosen source material was generated and consumed – from the museum, court room or government department to the artist's studio and literary marketplace. The latter part of this introduction offers a reflection on the (sometimes unexpected) connections across the chapters, linking these shared themes and concerns to wider historiographical debates about the nature and mobilization of memory.

The 'history of memory'

Both scholarly and worldly trends help to explain the recent 'memory boom'. Undeniably, revised historiographical practice – in particular the 'cultural turn' of the 1970s and, in a distinct but related way, the development of 'new social history' in the previous decade – enabled a turn towards memory studies. What we now routinely describe as the cultural turn is a multi-stranded affair with its genesis arguably among historians of political thought who set about historicizing the ideas they studied in new ways. At the same time, ideas – or beliefs, sometimes 'mentalities' – loomed larger than ever before among an array of historians who set about uncovering the meaning that the social world held for men and women in the past by studying their representations of it. All of these historians recognized that their primary sources were rhetorical constructs rather than transparent windows onto past worlds. Indeed, these trends were nourished by the greater sensitivity to the ideological content of language, the new appreciation of the relationship between words and world, in short of the power of discourse, which was increasingly voiced by intellectual, social and political historians as well as feminist scholars from the beginning of the 1970s.[1] Historians increasingly accepted that the authors and subjects of their primary source material interpreted the world through a grid of thoughts and feelings – expressed in ideologically charged language – whose workings have to be grasped in order for the 'truth' of the past to be understood.

This presented a stark contrast to earlier professional models of historical enquiry. The empirical method (resting on positivist philosophy) that underpinned the new historical profession as it emerged in the nineteenth century was a self-consciously 'scientific' tool for uncovering the supposedly objective truth about the laws that produce social, political and economic structures in human societies, and it was to be wielded by ideologically neutral scholar-authors who had no impact on this process of discovery. Now the constructed-ness of the past that historians configure suddenly seemed rather self-evident.[2] In this vision, neither historians nor historical agents were 'value free' beings without subjectivity of their own. This new kind of self-awareness represented a profound shift in the methodological and epistemological bedrock of the history discipline. In putting the mind – and emotions – of the historical actor and the historian centre-stage, the memory boom, in the words of Jay Winter, 'moves in the opposite direction from positivism; it makes us all consider our own subject positions'.[3] And it allowed historians to see as a respectable subject in its own right the ways in which understandings of the past have come to be embedded in the present; how the past is invested with meaning among women and men who may never read history books.

But historians' interest in memory also emerged from the earlier development of new social history. Often overtly politically engaged, the approach is probably best exemplified by British Marxist and labour historian E.P. Thompson, whose magisterial study of the English working classes first published in the early 1960s promised to rescue the masses from 'the enormous condescension of posterity' by taking them seriously as historical actors and by paying attention to their conceptual universes.[4] To some extent Thompson's approach speaks to a quarrel with traditional Marxist scholars quick to dismiss both the consciousness and the agency of the working class; indeed to dismiss the importance of ideas and subjectivity in the past altogether. As like-minded historians started to explore in larger numbers the history of social groups – first workers, but also women and ethnic minorities – for whom the written record had left comparatively few traces, they in many cases turned to alternative sources of knowledge about such people, often by collecting their oral testimony. Thus oral history emerged, perhaps especially in the UK and United States, as a distinct sub-discipline. Social historian Paul Thompson was at its forefront, establishing the British Oral History Society in the early 1970s, which helped to turn oral history into an international movement.[5]

It would be wrong, however, to imply that oral historians and those taking the cultural turn have followed entirely separate trajectories. As the approach of E.P. Thompson itself suggests, there has been significant cross-fertilization between the two strands.[6] Oral historians have for some time been sensitive to the instabilities of language in their research. They have become attuned to the silences, conflations and omissions in oral testimony; and to the significance of body language in gauging the meaning of what they are told. They recognize that for cultural reasons women and men may encode their memories differently; and that the so-called inter-subjective element of the interview (the relationships between those present at it) can shape what is said. In short, they do not read oral testimony straightforwardly as a transparent window onto an individual's lived experience. Rather, oral historians usually approach this testimony as a narrative product that speaks not only to complex questions of selfhood but to the interplay between past experience and present recollection. Here they recognize that human memory (mainly what neuroscientists call episodic memory) is filtered as much as constructed. It is selective; it leaves things out, whether as a result of the kind of trauma that makes it harder for men and women to reconcile their past experience with a continuous sense of self, or because what is remembered is framed – perhaps in unconscious ways – by social and political needs in the present. In his well-received work of oral history about Australian First World War veterans, Alistair Thomson puts it this way: '[m]emories are "significant pasts" that we compose to make a more comfortable sense of our life over time, and in which past and current identities are brought more into line'.[7]

It is precisely these psychological and emotional dynamics of the recollection, as well as the social, cultural and political ones, that have engaged oral historians. The early work of Italian oral historian Luisa Passerini exemplifies some of these complexities. Drawing on revised Marxist perspectives, she used her oral sources to construct 'a history of working-class subjectivity' under fascist Italy. She approached oral testimony as a cultural anthropologist might, seeking to grasp how socially inherited 'symbolic structures' are filtered through individual reflection, and she found clues in the silences and jokes of her interviewees.[8] In these ways, oral historians see that testimony constitutes both a source *of* memory (autobiographical memory in this case) and a source *about* memory, both autobiographical and social. They have made a virtue of its famed unreliability, prompting questions about how and why testimony is simultaneously socially and psychologically framed.

But the 'memory boom' must be placed in historical as well as historiographical context. It is customary to draw attention to the powerful role played by the Holocaust in this regard. Many historians locate in the 1960s a new popular consciousness about the significance of the Holocaust, as a specifically Jewish tragedy. In 1961 the Israeli government tried Adolf Eichmann for wartime crimes against humanity, and the survivor testimony aired in the courtroom circulated much more widely. Conveying a 'duty to remember', these testimonies were received globally as authoritative documents about the history of the Holocaust in an unprecedented way. 'Bearing witness' in the quest not only for justice but for historical truth subsequently took on elevated status. Indeed, Annette Wieviorka has called the intervening period the 'era of the witness'.[9] More recent examples of this triangulation of justice, historical truth and the oral record can be found in the high-profile 'truth and reconciliation commission' set up in South Africa (after 1994), where perpetrators and victims of systemic violence have confronted one another. Although the commission did not have a specifically judicial purpose, it employed the rhetoric and spatial dynamic of the courtroom setting, where – as in the Eichmann trial – witness statements were valued for their 'testimonial' rather than 'documentary' value. Similar initiatives have resulted in oral history projects and the creation of archives of oral testimony.[10] The intention behind these important testimonial rituals has been to heal divided communities by remembering rather than forgetting the profound conflicts within them: they have provided a space (if not an entirely successful one) for 'memory work'.[11] These examples all involve the concept of traumatic memory, a category most systematically examined in relation to Holocaust survivors.[12] In fact scholars routinely suggest that it is the scale of destructive violence in the twentieth century that has generated the turn to memory of late: the need to work through trauma, to commemorate mass loss, to bring the perpetrators of genocide to justice, speaks to pervasive and deep-seated psychological and social needs. One might say, taking all of the aforementioned factors together, that the 'memory boom' of recent years has been over-determined.

If it is important to historicize the 'memory boom' in order to understand and explain it, we must also historicize the notion of memory itself.[13] As Geoffrey Cubitt points out, memory is a concept rather than an object, and as such its boundaries are malleable.[14] The meaning of the word and the embeddedness of the concept has probably shifted across time, shaped by profound changes in human society. Mnemonic and commemorative practices are bound to differ in societies where, as in Classical Greece, oral sources and orality as a medium of communication in general enjoyed a greater legitimacy than in those bound to the authority of the written word. Thus available technologies of communication constrain the available meaning of memory in a given time and place. Art historian Frances Yates showed some time ago that the 'art of memory' used to signify mental techniques for recalling information (i.e. mnemonic practices). Rooted in the oral culture of the Classical period, techniques for remembering nonetheless survived the invention of the printing press and were adapted by scholars in the Renaissance in ways that demonstrated an affinity with the organization of knowledge in seventeenth-century society.[15] One might say that autobiography and psychoanalysis – not to mention professional history – are among the 'modern arts of memory'.[16] If that is the case they reflect the shift to a 'conception of memory as something essentially personal and intrinsic to individual selfhood' that is most associated with the eighteenth-century Enlightenment.[17] The challenge for the historian is, as Patrick Hutton has put it, 'to decode the mnemonic schemes unwittingly employed' in each era.[18]

Most scholars see another key shift in the meaning of memory with the further entrenchment of print culture in the nineteenth century. Not only did mass literacy mean that more people than ever before were processing the world through the written text, but that the extended reach of state bureaucracy led to a proliferation of written records and information. As many scholars point out, the brain itself is fundamentally a 'technology of memory', operating differently depending on the cognitive functions required of it: 'a mind that was trained to remember telephone numbers is rather different from one that was not, or is not anymore; one that developed the capacity to perform long oral narratives is in important ways different from one that was trained to reproduce long written ones'.[19] It seems that there were also changes in the status of memory in the nineteenth century. One can chart a greater awareness of the past, and its contemporary uses, among European cultural, political and scientific elites in a period that coincided in many places with the ascendancy of the nation-state and mass education systems. It paid political elites to instil a sense of a specifically national past in citizens and subjects whose partially invented sense of belonging might make them easier to rule.[20] More elusively, scientific consideration of 'species memory', in which biologists argued that human instincts were preserved via remembrances passed genetically down the generations, seeped into social thinking: notions such as 'race' and the nation were widely conceived as memory-charged organisms.[21] It was an era in which the tendency to think of the social in organic terms structured many branches of knowledge and governance: it is not surprising that memory too was conceived in this way. To historicize memory, then, is not just a question of tracking changes and continuities in mnemonic and commemorative activities over time, but to ask – with much less chance of finding a clear answer – how forms of 'remembering' themselves may be time-bound cultural constructs. As Matt Matsuda puts it, '"memory" has too often become another analytic vocabulary to impose on the past; the point should be to rehistoricize memory and see how it is so inextricably *part* of that past'.[22]

Critical perspectives

One striking feature of scholars' turn to memory in recent years is how similar are their conclusions about the workings of the human mind. What emerges from research across quite divergent scholarly disciplines, including cognitive psychology and neuroscience, is that individual memory does not function like an archive of lived experiences deposited somewhere in the brain, but is rather constructed anew at each moment of recall.[23] Put another way, we do not have memory as much as remembrances, or even performances of remembering, where what is remembered is shaped fundamentally both by the meaning of the initial experience to the individual in question, and by the psychological – and inextricably social – circumstances of recall. Just as significant is the way that intervening presents shape what is recalled. Our 'memory system' becomes 'susceptible to distortion, as it sucks up other facts and convinces itself that they were part of the memory'.[24] This is the process of confabulation. As we have seen, even early oral historians such as Luisa Passerini, first writing in the 1970s, conceived of the functions of autobiographical memory in much the same way, if on the basis of different evidence.

It is clear that, despite the explosion in historical scholarship in this area and the broad convergence about the constructed nature of memory outlined above, there remain many contested and unresolved questions about how memory can meaningfully be interrogated by historians. Sociologists and historians alike have complained that there is not enough conceptual and theoretical reflection in the historical study of memory. This is especially the case where memory as subject (in particular collective memory) is concerned. First there is the problem of slippage. When historians move unannounced between different meanings of memory in their prose, when they refer alternately to cognitive processes of remembering, social acts of commemoration and to meta-entities such as 'collective memory' without qualification, their arguments lack precision. In the process memory becomes reified – treated in other words as a thing, an essence, cut adrift from the worldly networks in which its operations and their social purchase are enmeshed. It is often imbued with agency in its own right. This is the case even in the most systematic and influential writings on the subject. Take, for example, Pierre Nora, editor of the hugely successful multi-volume publishing project, *Les Lieux de mémoire* [Sites of Memory] (1984–92).[25] In the introduction to this series, which was also published as a foundational journal article in 1989, Nora writes that memory 'accommodates', 'nourishes', 'installs'; while history is 'suspicious of memory, and its true mission is to suppress and destroy it'.[26] Meanwhile, David Lowenthal, in a strident critique of the 'heritage' industry (encompassing museums and all public vehicles that communicate a mythic sense of the past), posits a similar set of agency-fuelled oppositions. For him, 'history seeks to convince by truth', while heritage 'exaggerates and omits', 'invents', 'forgets', 'thrives on ignorance'.[27] No doubt such formulations carry a weighty rhetorical punch, but they arguably lead to problems in how we think about what these terms mean. This kind of reification has been sternly and sarcastically criticized by Kerwin Lee Klein, whose spirited attack on the 'memory boom' *tout court* took in the 'elevation of memory to the status of a historical agent' and the impression given in much scholarship that 'we enter a new age in which archives remember and statues forget'.[28] To avoid these conceptual pitfalls it is important for historians always to grasp *whose* memory is in question, and to track authorship in the source material through which it is expressed.

Secondly, scholars complain that the question of reception is neglected. It is probably true that most historical studies about memory favour analysis of the textual, visual or oral representations of the past over the pursuit of evidence for responses to those cultural artefacts. Alon Confino puts it this way: 'the crucial issue in the history of memory is not how a past is represented but why it was received or rejected. … [I]t is not enough for a certain past to be selected. It must steer emotions, motivate people to act, be received; in short, it must become a socio-cultural mode of action.' Failure to address this question leads, in his words, only to 'memory from above'.[29] Wulf Kansteiner holds a similar position, urging historians to attempt the admittedly difficult task of tying such representations of the past to specific social groups.[30] In the chapters that follow the question of reception is perhaps posed more than it is answered. It is addressed by Jason Crouthamel (Chapter 8), who demonstrates how traumatized German war veterans rebelled in the interwar period against the interpretation of them as undeserving malingerers, unmanly and unpatriotic, falling outside the heroic version of the wartime past preferred by medical and political elites. It is there too in Susan A. Crane's essay (Chapter 7) on the use of photography in museums, when she shows how attempts by curators to frame photographic exhibits as narratives about the past were met at times by a public obstinate that their interpretation of history was the right one. And it is considered also in Polly Low's essay on Classical Athens (Chapter 4), when she acknowledges that inscribed monuments could be 'ignored, amended, destroyed (or just wilfully misinterpreted)'.

Bound up with the problem of reception is the elusive relationship between individual memory and the shared kind. Alon Confino's focus on reception in fact arose from his criticisms about how historians handled the notion of 'collective memory'. And one reason why Wulf Kansteiner wants historians to trace the impact of representations of the past on particular audiences is to try to grasp 'the specific social and cultural dynamics of collective remembrance'.[31] Although many sociologists and historians have deployed working distinctions between social memory, collective memory and historical memory, there is no strict consensus on what distinguishes them.[32] What is more widely agreed is that memory is always socially framed in one way or another. Here one must point to the impact of early twentieth-century French sociologist Maurice Halbwachs whose posthumously published work *On Collective Memory* has informed much recent scholarly thinking in this area. Halbwachs argued, initially in the 1920s, that '[n]o memory is possible outside frameworks used by people living in society to determine and retrieve their recollection'. He stressed that the need for group (especially family) bonds conditions the content of individual memories: social needs, for instance, can lead us to 'give them a prestige that reality did not possess'; conversely social bonds are strengthened by the sharing of individual memories.[33] The suggestion that autobiographical memory and different kinds of group memory interpenetrate has proven a nourishing insight for historians. Oral historian Alistair Thomson's work on Australian WWI veterans shows how the recollection of ostensibly personal experiences of war had itself been shaped by broader commemorative trends, incorporating the interpretive features of film, official histories and veterans' parades. Interviews he conducted in 1983 revealed that 'the memories of working-class diggers had become entangled with the legend of their lives'.[34] Without drawing overtly on the sociology of Maurice Halbwachs, it was precisely the dynamic between individual memory and group memory that Thomson explored: 'our remembering changes in relation to shifts in the particular publics in which we live, and as the general public field of representations alters.'[35]

But does this interplay between the individual and the collective mean that the distinction between them collapses? There is much division among scholars as to whether such a thing as 'collective memory' exists as a distinct and autonomous phenomenon, and sociologists – perhaps characteristically – are more likely to invest in the concept than historians. Noa Gedi and Yigal Elam are not alone in resisting the idea of collective memory as an entity in its own right, pointing to the failure even of Maurice Halbwachs to define how it works as a social mechanism. They admit only a metaphorical existence for the term, arguing – not unreasonably – that all memory must be rooted in individual minds.[36] Similarly, Geoffrey Cubitt sees collective memory fundamentally as an 'ideological fiction', albeit one that has purchase on the processes by which social memory (defined as the generalized 'knowledge or awareness of past events or conditions ... developed and sustained within human societies') takes root.[37] Others push harder at the potentiality of an independent phenomenon, while nonetheless pulling back from endorsing the existence of such a thing. In the inaugural issue of the journal *History & Memory*, Amos Funkenstein suggested that collective memory might function as a language – a system of signs and symbols comprising 'times of memory, names of places, monuments and victory arches, museums and texts, customs and manners'. But he refused its existence as a 'hypostatized' phenomenon, since in his view collective memory always depends on the acts of 'the speaking, acting, recognizing individual'.[38] The likening of collective memory to language is not uncommon. Alon Confino, Wulf Kansteiner and Jeffrey Olick (who describes language as the 'supra-individual phenomenon' *par excellence*) have all seen it in this way.[39] The challenge for these scholars is to locate the representation of the past in question within 'the full spectrum of symbolic representations available in a given culture'.[40] Susan A. Crane has suggested we look at the problem in a different way, and collapse the distinction between historical and collective memory. Arguing against the opposition between history and memory posed by Pierre Nora, she emphasizes the subjectivity of the 'historian' (conceived as the historically self-conscious modern human), who becomes the principal agent for the integration and transmission of collective memory. For Crane, then, collective memory is not a supra-individual phenomenon at all but lodged in the self.[41]

In a different interpretive move, Jeffrey Olick pointed to the mileage in what he calls 'collected memory' – 'the aggregated individual memories of members of a group' – not least because current scientific research on human memory suggests generalities that could help historians predict how memories are likely to be shaped in the wider group.[42] It is arguably what Alistair Thomson evokes in his work on the Anzacs – the multiply-authored anniversary ceremonies, speeches, television programmes and films that convey a view of the war experience. Conceiving of the problem in this way, however, does not resolve the fundamental conundrum of collective memory – what it is, how it functions and where it stands in relation to individual memory. In practice, historians tend to fall back either on a notion of 'collected memory' without articulating it as such, or use the term 'collective memory' to suggest a rather loose notion of popular knowledge about the past that exists 'out there'. While this approach betrays a lack of theoretical and methodological reflection on the part of historians, it contains one important virtue – refusal to let the problem of collective memory trump that of historical agency and thus to let essentialism in through the back door.

Connections across chapters

The chapters in this volume do not resolve these long-standing problems so much as animate and interrogate them. They do so partially and in different ways. The thorny notion of collective memory – the notion of a shared (and therefore social) sense of the past that is shaped, filtered and selected by actors in the present – haunts all three parts of the book. It becomes clear that, even for the oral historian whose source material derives almost exclusively from the testimony of individuals, an engagement with wider 'cultural scripts' about the meaning of the past is inevitable, especially in Lindsey

Dodd's essay (Chapter 2). It is precisely these 'cultural scripts' that furnish the source material in a good number of the chapters. Another common theme is that of the affective power of various mediums of memory: oral historians claim it for testimony in Part I, historians of art and photography for the visual in Part II, and a material culture specialist for touchable objects in Part III. What they agree on is the ability of memory mediums to convey the emotional rawness and humanity of lived experience in the past.

Two of the authors are particularly attuned to the power of visual culture where acts of memorialization are concerned. Franziska Seraphim, in her chapter on Japanese art (Chapter 5), suggests that 'we see with memory'; that visual representations of the past perhaps pack a greater emotional punch than written ones. It is not unusual for scholars of memory to make a special case for the power of the visual. Raphael Samuel, for example, reminds his readers of the key role played by sight in the mnemonic practices of the ancient, medieval and Renaissance worlds studied by Frances Yates, which in his words 'put the visual first' by linking ideas not to words but to images.[43] Susan A. Crane recognizes in her chapter (Chapter 7) the power of photographs in museums for 'staging a visual argument', not least through their supposed ability to represent past reality more authentically than any other medium of exhibition. If taste and smell have an acknowledged role to play in the formation of autobiographical memory, then so does sight. The part of the brain arguably most responsible for episodic memory, the hippocampus, has been described as a 'spatial framework for remembering' for the way that experiences are encoded there through a process of 'scene construction'. As Charles Fernyhough puts it, '[o]ur two eyes, stereoscopically aligned, allow us to see space; memory allows us to "see" time'.[44]

Another theme that cuts across the volume is materiality. One could say that there is a material element in all human memories, since the world is apprehended through the five senses, and lived experiences are at first encoded and then recalled in specific parts of the brain.[45] But in the social world, too, a range of sociologists and anthropologists have remarked that memory is often lodged in objects.[46] Thus one woman interviewed by Michal Bosworth in north-west Australia (Chapter 1) seemed to filter the deep sense of loss she felt when a cyclone destroyed her home through the destruction of her cherished cookery books. Earlier, Bosworth had found that food was crucial in opening up a route into the present and the pasts of the immigrant women she interviewed – because it had a direct connection to their particular sense of Italian identity, because it allowed her to learn about immigrant social networks that were closed to the wider community (in this case the delivery of foodstuffs to back doorsteps), and because sociability around meals provided a safe space for talking about a sometimes fraught past. It became an important vehicle for memory work, too, leading to a museum exhibition and books of recipes.

Susan M. Stabile (Chapter 11) lingers on the materiality not only of memory but of history. Indeed, for historian Michel-Rolph Trouillot, the presence of the past is irreducibly material: 'history begins with bodies and artifacts: living brains, fossils, texts, buildings ... A castle, a fort, a battlefield, a church, all these things bigger than we that we infuse with the reality of past lives, seem to speak of an immensity of which we know little except that we are part of it ... . They give us the power to touch it, but not that to hold it firmly in our hands – hence the mystery of their battered walls.'[47] In her chapter, Stabile attempts to communicate something of the haptic power that the past held for the nineteenth-century antiquarian whose efforts to preserve carefully selected objects from the American past and present provides the focus of her case study. He wanted the things in his relic box to evoke powerful sensory and hence emotional responses in future audiences, so that the meaning of the past would be communicated through the power of touch. It is true that museum curators today recognize the particular ability of the haptic to enhance visitors' engagement with exhibits, as opposed to those in the nineteenth century who privileged the visual.[48] Polly Low too (Chapter 4) considers the importance of the material when she examines the interactions between orality, the written record and materiality in the commemorative life of inscribed monuments in Classical Athens. In short, the reader is asked to think about how both individual remembrance and social acts of commemoration may involve encounters with things.

I have already noted how Michal Bosworth's interviewees (Chapter 1) invested their sense of family and cultural identity through food. In a sense, the foodstuffs in question – cardoons, artichokes, aubergine – were transported objects, serving to link their new lives in Australia symbolically with the specific patch of southern Italy they had left behind. It was just this powerful sense of place – and the intertwining of family identity with local industry there – that lay at the heart of the profound misremembering discussed by Lindsey Dodd (Chapter 2). And for Hannah Ewence (Chapter 9), minority authors of autobiographical fiction negotiate personal and national identity, as well as personal and national pasts, through the real and imagined place of suburbia. Another connection across chapters is the theme of marginality. The mentally ill, migrants and ethnic minorities appear as 'subalterns', whose individual memories mediate and are mediated by wider 'cultural scripts' about the past, as in the case studies by Jason Crouthamel (Chapter 8), Tony Kushner (Chapter 10), Michal Bosworth (Chapter 1), and Hannah Ewence (Chapter 9). In addition, the problem of trauma will be encountered in each part of the book, explored by Rosanne Kennedy (Chapter 3) in relation to witness testimony in the court room, by Franziska Seraphim (Chapter 5) in relation to artistic responses to the atrocities of war, and by Jason Crouthamel (Chapter 8) in relation to war veterans. The theme of law as a shaper of memory and counter-memory is there in Kennedy and Crouthamel's studies too, but also in Joan Tumblety's chapter (Chapter 6) on the centrality of purge trials as a vehicle for establishing memorial cultures in post-Liberation France.

One final connection worthy of comment is that which concerns public history and heritage, not least the importance of museums as generators of knowledge about the past. Susan A. Crane (Chapter 7) addresses head on the power of museal display to craft subtle narratives about the meaning of the past through images. The potential of curators to shape and reshape the meaning of artefacts in this way is also picked up by Susan M. Stabile (Chapter 11) when she suggests that an antiquarian understanding of the value of material objects for communicating cultural memory may be lost when a box of relics is passed to the modern museum, its constituent parts reclassified and rearranged. Both see that museums can influence the reception of historical artefacts in ways that have an impact on popular understanding of the past, for better or worse. Tony Kushner (Chapter 10) strikes a similarly critical note when he notes how museums sometimes unwittingly reproduce the double silence of the archive and contemporary political debate when presenting immigration in modern Britain. But – as Stabile's concluding evocation of her own experience of handling objects suggests – there are limits to the museum's power to fix the meaning of its displays. In relation to the use of photographs in museums, Susan A. Crane puts the subjective self at centre-stage by reminding us that 'each viewer will see the image through a personal lens pregnant with multiple memories, knowledge and experience'. If the implicit narrative about the past that the image conveys jars with what an individual holds to be true, it may well not be believed. Finally, readers will encounter heritage in a different guise in Michal Bosworth's chapter (Chapter 1). This is heritage without walls, located in the contested spaces of Western Australia where rival versions of the past held by state authorities and local communities come into conflict. Here the oral historian may be able to play a positive role in facilitating the memory work of communities whose grievances have not yet been heard.

Questions and practical guidance

The chapters in this volume certainly do not provide the last word on the study of memory as source or subject. Neither do they resolve the methodological problems highlighted by the scholars mentioned above, not least the mechanisms of collective memory and its status as a phenomenon apart from the collected remembrances or memory politics of a given number of individuals. One might venture that the notion of the 'cultural script' allows us to bypass the problem, since it conjures up the sense of known, discrete stories in general circulation, whether created and consumed among those who experienced the past in question or not. This casualness of terminology would not pass muster among serious theorists of collective memory, but it has the virtue of drawing attention to the artefactual base of those so-called scripts; in other words to the sources that comprise them and, ideally, to the intentions of their multiple authors. One must never lose sight of the questions of authorship and agency when approaching memory as source or subject. Taking this approach should prevent the sort of slippage, reification, essentialism and floating agency I criticize above, even if it will not satisfy those who yearn after the systematic study of the reception of these artefacts.

My advice to student readers is to pay singular attention to this question of agency when approaching sources of and about memory. Ask, to *whose* memory does the source attest? Is the source evidence of individual remembrance or social acts of commemoration? Who are the authors and how are they situated institutionally, socially, politically, culturally? Indeed, what do we know of the contexts of production of the source material? What purposes are served – either deliberately or inadvertently – by the particular configuration of the past in it? How, then, does the source *function* as evidence for the historian? In substantive terms, what rhetorical strategies (in short, attempts to persuade through language) exist in the source material? What might have been omitted? How might the source serve as a smokescreen, displacing one view of the past by imposing another? Consider too what we might know of its reception. Whatever the notional audience for this material, who – in as much as we can tell – formed its real audience? Has that real audience of readers, viewers, observers, changed over time? What is the impact of the memory-making in question, in as much as such a thing can be known? Is there any evidence to suggest that the reception of the source has helped to shape the shared stories about the past that historians often designate as social or collective memory? What kind of memory work – and for whom – is enacted through this process of creating, sharing and maybe revising this source material? Questions such as these motivated the studies in the following chapters, and illuminate the challenging, rewarding complexities of working with memory as source and subject.

Notes

1 See P. Burke, *What is Cultural History?* 2nd ed. (Cambridge: Polity Press, 2008); A. Arcangeli, *Cultural History: A Concise Introduction* (London & New York: Routledge, 2012); A. Green, *Cultural History* (Basingstoke: Palgrave, 2008). The so-called 'new cultural history' grew out of too many earlier approaches to mention here, not least the French Annales School pioneered by Marc Bloch and Lucien Febvre in the 1920s.

2 On the entrenchment of the empirical method in the history discipline and the positivist philosophy that underpinned it, see S. Davies, *Empiricism and History* (Basingstoke: Palgrave, 2003), pp. 25–42.

3 J. Winter, *Remembering War: The Great War Between Memory and History in the Twentieth Century* (New Haven, CT: Yale University Press, 2006), p. 289.

4 E.P. Thompson, *The Making of the English Working Class* (London: Penguin, 1991) [orig. Victor Gollancz, 1963], p. 12.

5 A. Thomson, 'Four paradigm transformations in oral history', *Oral History Review*, 34(1), 2006, pp. 51–52.

6 For a recent systematic account of oral history approaches see L. Abrams, *Oral History Theory* (London & New York: Routledge, 2010), esp. pp. 78–105.

7 A. Thomson, *Anzac Memories: Living with the Legend* (Oxford & Melbourne: Oxford University Press, 1994), p. 10. On the relationship between episodic memory (for events) and semantic memory (for facts), see C. Fernyhough, *Pieces of Light: The New Science of Memory* (London: Profile Books, 2012), p. 14.

8 L. Passerini, 'Work ideology and consensus under Italian Fascism', *History Workshop Journal*, 8(1), 1979, pp. 103, 104, 91, 84.

9 A. Wieviorka, *The Era of the Witness*, trans. Jared Start (Ithaca: Cornell University Press, 2006) [orig. French edition, Plon, 1998]. Peter Novick tracks the emergence of Holocaust memory in the USA over the same period in *The Holocaust and Collective Memory* (London: Bloomsbury, 2000).

10 See the 'Bringing Them Home' National Inquiry and associated oral history project in Australia, R. Kennedy, 'The affective work of Stolen Generations testimony: from the archives to the classroom', *Biography*, 27(1), 2004, pp. 48–77.

11 See Annie E. Coombes, 'The gender of memory in post-apartheid South Africa', in S. Radstone and B. Schwarz (eds) *Memory: History, Theories, Debates* (New York: Fordham University Press, 2010), pp. 442–57. See also A. Duffy, 'A truth commission for Northern Ireland?', *IJTJ*, 4(1), 2010, pp. 26–46, and for more on oral testimony in relation to attempts at conflict resolution, see Thomson, 'Four paradigm transformations in oral history', pp. 57–61.

12 See L.L. Langer's foundational and lucid treatment of survivor testimony in *Holocaust Testimonies: The Ruins of Memory* (New Haven & London: Yale University Press, 1991). It is worth noting that memory scientists dispute that there are distinct memory mechanisms for recalling (or repressing) traumatic incidents, thus 'traumatic memory' might be better understood as 'memory of trauma'. See Fernyhough, *Pieces of Light*, pp. 198–233.

13 This is the final appeal made by Alon Confino in his influential article, 'Collective memory and cultural history: problems of method', *American Historical Review*, 102(5), 1997, p. 1403.

14 G. Cubitt, *History and Memory* (Manchester: Manchester University Press, 2007), p. 6.

15 F.A. Yates, *The Art of Memory* (Chicago: University of Chicago Press, 1966). For an overview of her arguments, see P.H. Hutton, *History as an Art of Memory* (Hanover & London: University Press of New England, 1993), pp. 30–32.

16 Hutton, *History as an Art of Memory*, p. 10.

17 Cubitt, *History and Memory*, p. 12.

18 Hutton, *History as an Art of Memory*, p. 19. See also B.A. Misztal, *Theories of Social Remembering* (Berkshire: McGraw-Hill, 2003), pp. 27–49.

19 J.K. Olick, V. Vinitzky-Seroussi and D. Levy, 'Introduction', in J.K. Olick, V. Vinitzky-Seroussi and D. Levy (eds) *The Collective Memory Reader* (Oxford & New York: Oxford University Press, 2011), p. 6. But we must acknowledge that oral and print cultures existed side by side for centuries. See M.T. Clanchy, *From Memory to Written Record: England 1066–1307*, 2nd edn (Oxford: Blackwell, 1993), pp. 1–21.

20 This is the perspective developed in E.J. Hobsbawm and T.O. Ranger's immensely influential edited volume on the cultural aspects of nation-building, *The Invention of Tradition* (Cambridge: Cambridge University Press, 1983).

21 M.K. Matsuda, *The Memory of the Modern* (New York & Oxford: Oxford University Press, 1996), p. 9.

22 Ibid., p. 16.

23 S. Smith and J. Watson, *Reading Autobiography: A Guide for Interpreting Life Narratives* (Minneapolis: University of Minnesota Press, 2001), p. 16. See also the essays in Part 2.1 of Radstone and Schwarz, *Memory*.

24 Fernyhough, *Pieces of Light*, pp. 14, 114.

25 An abridged version has been published in English as *Realms of Memory: Rethinking the French Past*, 3 vols (New York: Columbia University Press, 1996–98).

26 P. Nora, 'Between memory and history: *les lieux de mémoire*', *Representations*, 26, spring 1989, pp. 8–9. For a lucid critique of Nora's position, see H.-T. Ho Tai, 'Remembered realms: Pierre Nora and French national memory', *American Historical Review*, 106(3), 2001, p. 920.

27 D. Lowenthal, 'Fabricating heritage', *History & Memory*, 10(1), 1998, 7.

28 K.L. Klein, 'On the emergence of memory in historical discourse', *Representations*, 69, 2000, p. 136.

29 A. Confino, 'Collective memory and cultural history: problems of method', *American Historical Review*, 102(5), 1997, pp. 1395, 1390.
30 W. Kansteiner, 'Finding meaning in memory: a methodological critique of collective memory studies', *History and Theory*, 41, May 2002, pp. 190, 192.
31 Ibid., p. 196; Confino, 'Collective memory and cultural history', p. 1391.
32 Cubitt, *History and Memory*, pp. 13–20, offers a lucid discussion of such terms.
33 M. Halbwachs, *On Collective Memory*, trans. and ed. L.A. Coser (Chicago: Chicago University Press, 1992), pp. 43, 51, 54–83.
34 Thomson, *Anzac Memories*, p. 7.
35 Ibid., p. 9.
36 N. Gedi and Y. Elam, 'Collective memory – what is it?', *History & Memory*, 8(1), 1996, pp. 30–50.
37 Cubitt, *History and Memory*, pp. 18, 14.
38 A. Funkenstein, 'Collective memory and historical consciousness', *History & Memory*, 1(1), 1989, pp. 7, 10.
39 J.K. Olick, 'Collective memory: the two cultures', *Sociological Theory*, 17(3), 1999, p. 343.
40 Confino, 'Collective memory and cultural history', p. 1391. See also Kansteiner, 'Finding meaning in memory', who argues that 'collective memories are based in a society and its inventory of signs and symbols', p. 188.
41 S.A. Crane, 'Writing the individual back into collective memory', *American Historical Review*, 102(5), 1997, pp. 1372–85.
42 Olick, 'Collective memory: the two cultures', p. 338.
43 R. Samuel, *Theatres of Memory*, vol. 1 (London & New York: Verso, 1994), p. viii, drawing on the work of medievalist Mary Carruthers.
44 Fernyhough, *Pieces of Light*, pp. 271, 150, 283.
45 Smith and Watson, *Reading Autobiography*, p. 21.
46 For example S. Turkle (ed.) *Evocative Objects: Things We Think With* (Cambridge, MA: MIT Press, 2011) [orig. 2007]; and D.J. Parkin, 'Mementoes as transitional objects in human displacement', *Journal of Material Culture*, 4(3), 1999, pp. 303–20.
47 M.-R. Trouillot, *Silencing the Past: Power and the Production of History* (Boston: Beacon Press, 1995), pp. 29–30.
48 F. Candlin, 'Museums, modernity and the class politics of touching objects', in H.J. Chatterjee (ed.) *Touch in Museums: Policy and Practice in Object Handling* (Oxford and New York: Berg, 2008), pp. 9–20.

Part I

Working with oral testimony

The chapters in the first part of the book all deal with oral testimony as source material, whether generated through interviews with the historian or in a judicial context. The first two of them – by Michal Bosworth and Lindsey Dodd – describe in practical detail the experience of interviewing people, especially women, about their past lives. Both authors put themselves in the frame, acknowledging how their presence and approach to questioning – whether they use a tape recorder, how familiar they are with the language of the respondents, the questions they choose to ask – might shape the auto-biographical stories they hear. Both also recognize the importance of using other sources to prepare for the interview and to contextualize the lives of their interviewees afterwards, even as they recognize the singularity of oral testimony for giving access to otherwise unrecoverable pasts. Dodd talks the reader through how she learned to listen differently to the testimony gener-ated in what she had at first written off as a failed interview: it spoke to autobiographical and historical truths that she had not initially expected to hear. In this, she develops the idea of 'cultural scripts', drawing on the work of oral historian Alessandro Portelli to push at the links between individual and social memory. Both she and Bosworth conceive of oral history, at least in part, as fostering 'memory work' among communities whose stories have not yet become part of the mainstream historical record – French children who experienced Allied bombing in the Second World War and immigrant women in Australia respectively. The interview tapes created through Dodd's wider doctoral research are lodged in municipal archives in France, and Bosworth her-self played an important role in facilitating the community cultural activities – museum exhibitions, a play and the publication of several memoirs and recipe books – undertaken by her immigrant interviewees. One might say that this oral history research has provided vehicles for the development of popular memory, in other words for incorporating into the collective record stories told by under-represented groups.

Rosanne Kennedy's chapter on the status of oral testimony in a judicial setting is at first glance concerned with entirely different issues, not least because she has not generated these oral sources herself. The witness statements examined in her chapter were produced under the exigencies of the courtroom, where evidence is subject to notions of proof and objectivity that tug in a different direction from the concerns of contemporary historians. For judges and lawyers the subjectivity of the witness is generally suspect; and these figures pursue judicial rather than historical truth, where there is little room for ambiguity. But despite the real differences in Kennedy's subject matter, questions about the subjectivity and reliability of testimony, and its affective power, remain central; as does the question of how witness testimony relates to the stories about the past in wider circulation. She explains how the trial of Nazi war criminal Adolf Eichmann in the early 1960s brought a new status to oral testimony in general – as autobiographical truth rather than as factual evidence. It also suggested that oral testimony has the power to influence wider 'cultural scripts' about the past however much it is also shaped by them. Although the 'testimonial' model established by the Eichmann trial (in which witnesses were given latitude to narrate their own stories) has become widespread in the quasi-legal context of truth commissions, the fundamental tensions between subjective and objective truth that it poses have not been overcome. Kennedy thus concludes on a rather pessimistic note – that the hurts of the past, this time in relation to the so-called 'Stolen Generations' trials in contemporary Australia, may be reproduced in the present when the aggrieved witness takes the stand in court.

1 'Let me tell you ... '

Memory and the practice of oral history

Michal Bosworth

Talking, listening, recalling and recording are pleasurable activities for the historian more usually constrained at a desk in front of a winking screen. But, as with all techniques for gathering information, these particular skills need to be refined. It may be easy to listen as someone else relates important moments in their life, but how do you, as a historian, use the information so gathered? Are you collecting a lot of undigested detail that requires considerable work to understand, or are you creating a primary document? Two things should be clear from the start. There is the question of technique – how you interview, what you do with the tapes you gather, how you find your subjects. These technical questions keep bobbing up because you must decide whether your funding will allow you to transcribe the tapes, whether you will always give copies of them to your interviewees, whether you will be able to deposit them in a library. Then there is the historian's eternal problem – how you think about the material, how you manage raising the questions you would like answered, how you approach the friendships you may make, how far empathy is necessary for successful interviews. Through a consideration of both sets of issues, I explore in this chapter how oral testimony can be used as a source for writing history.

I work in Australia. Most of the interviews I discuss here were recorded in Western Australia in the late 1980s and during the 1990s. They resulted from various projects in which I was employed so they range across a number of historical subjects. When working with individuals and their memories the historian comes face to face with the intractable nature of our discipline. We must remain alert to context and to other information, even when conflicts arise. As I heard one Holocaust survivor indignantly ask another historian, 'how can you possibly write about this when you were not there?' But that is what historians do: we write about things we did not directly experience. Oral history techniques are a part of our armoury, although the practice of oral history has changed over time. For one thing, technology is swifter, digitized, more efficient than it was 20 years ago and practitioners are realizing that they must understand how their recorders work before they begin. Once equipped most oral historians set out knowing where to put a microphone, if not always realizing the time it will take to collect the memories of a single person. But the approach is about more than recording techniques.

The development of oral history: problems and possibilities

Oral history has one great virtue over document-based research – its immediacy. Studs Terkel, the great American oral historian, produced a series of books from interviews which emerged from his work as a radio journalist. He began with an idea, for example, that Americans were forgetting the Great Depression,[1] or that they were far less mindful of the Second World War than he had thought,[2] or even more boldly, that workers had lost the possibility of hope.[3] He made lists of people he wanted to interview and others were found for him as each project gathered pace. As a 92-year-old, when interviewed about his aims as a historian, Terkel decried any larger purpose saying that he liked to listen; he was not a scholar.[4] His statement is a little disingenuous, as earlier in his career Terkel had been more forthright about his motives, the decisions he made when interviewing and the selection of words for publication. He edited interviews and changed the names of those who spoke to him. He organized his material so that various questions were raised and answered by more than one person, although he rarely included his questions in his publications. He was aware that some of his methods appeared a little unorthodox but he fielded questions about his techniques by claiming that they were the result of his 'respect' for his interviewees.[5] Terkel was an activist who was investigated by the Committee for Un-American Activities, although not called before it: he was not interviewing without purpose. He listened, recorded and fashioned his people's narratives, filling a gap in the historical record that other historians had found difficult to bridge. Along the way he sold a lot of books. Oral history, presented so ably, makes for compelling reading. *The Good War* won the Pulitzer Prize. For that work more than 120 interviews were recorded, and edited into four 'books', which in turn focused on issues such as 'Reflections on machismo', 'High rank', 'The bombers and the bombed', 'Crime and punishment' and 'Remembrance of things past'. Terkel may not have read the entire historiography of the Second World War, but he had some knowledge of it. We historians begin with what we think we know; our curiosity then pushes us to pose relevant questions.

Terkel's aims were less clearly articulated than E.P.Thompson's well-known statement of intent ('I am seeking to rescue the poor stockinger, the Luddite cropper, the "obsolete" hand-loom weaver, the "utopian" artisan, and even the deluded follower of Joanna Southcott, from the enormous condescension of posterity'), but both have inspired later social, labour and family historians to resort to the interview to rescue from historiographical oblivion the voiceless, the marginal, the less fortunate; those who do not appear in the state archives except as names in the births, deaths and marriage indexes.[6] Oral history has been growing in importance to Australian historians since the 1970s, part of an international trend.[7] There is now a professional organization that holds regular conferences. There are collections of tapes and transcripts held in most large public libraries. There are occasional short courses in technique delivered at universities, although, for most historians, it remains a subsidiary skill.[8] The exceptions are those researching within a particular community, and who find local memories a crucial element in their work. They may be employed by universities, but they also find local government or museums anxious for their skills. Family historians are among the most assiduous practitioners. Oral history is the art of talking with real people, but this does not mean that the empathy we require for such a task permits us to suspend our critical intelligence.

There are traps for young historians beginning this kind of work, traps I fell into during my first venture into oral history, which I can only describe as a disaster. In Sydney during the 1970s I interviewed a retired politician, Sir William McKell, a man who had been premier of New South Wales and later had become Governor General of Australia. At the time, I was employed by a historian who was writing a biography of Jack Lang, firebrand politician, leader of the Labor party in New South Wales before McKell succeeded him and, as I was to hear, a man thoroughly mistrusted by McKell.[9] My questions mostly related to the way the two men had worked together. I came away from a two-hour interview knowing that I had been given the official version of Labor history, one that was lacking detail about policy failures and concerned only to leave a good impression of the master at the helm, namely Sir William. I knew I had done badly. My interview technique lacked the necessary rigour, not only because politicians are difficult to interview.[10] I had not done enough research before broaching the topics I wanted to explore.

Approaching immigrant memories

When I returned to interviewing, some 15 years later, I took pains to read as much as I possibly could find about the group of people I had luckily happened upon. Among those who might have claimed until recently that their voices were rarely heard by historians are immigrant groups who have English as a second language. In this, my second venture, I consulted a number of elderly Italian women, who had no idea what a historian did, nor much interest in history, and who presented me with both a linguistic challenge and an urgent need for an entry point into their world. The project was to understand when and why they had migrated to a small port city on the western coast of Australia, Fremantle, as part of a larger study of the Italian immigrant community. Women's names rarely appeared in rate books, and not always on ships' passenger lists. They left no letters, they wrote no diaries. Their personal histories were a mystery. Some came between the wars, others arrived immediately after the Second World War as part of the great exodus from Italy; few undertook the journey after 1970. In Fremantle there were women who were proxy brides, girls who married young men from their village who had left years earlier. Such women may not have met their husbands to be, but their families were generally close in some way. There were young girls brought out with mothers to meet fathers whose faces had been forgotten, if ever known, and whose relationships with those newly introduced fathers presented some problems. Before I could talk with them at any length I needed to find a way to meet them, so it was fortunate that I was invited to join a newly formed social club designed to meet a need often commented on by outsiders, that women whose English was poor had few means available to integrate within the wider society. The Amicizia Club (Friendship Club) did not attract members outside the community, but I was permitted to join because of my expressed interest in the individual histories. Also, I spoke some Italian, which later proved of limited use because most of the women spoke dialect, so we generally conversed in English.

My reading included a number of books written by anthropologists about women's lives in southern Italy but my focus was on Fremantle, so I read local histories too. Accompanying my social conversations was my research into the bigger questions surrounding the history of the Italian community in this port city, a project funded by the local government authority. Elsewhere I was uncovering information about the lives of Italian men during the Second World War. Many had been interned as fascists. They were fishermen and had joined clubs that displayed fascist insignia and were endorsed by the local Vice-Consul, by definition a member of the Fascist Party. The discovery of a cache of information, much held in personal files, in the Australian archives about this period was a shock to the community when revealed in a paper delivered at a conference.[11] Fathers had not told their children about their wartime experiences; in some cases, the men had barely discussed them with their wives. Repercussions were immediate with family members, especially children and grandchildren rushing to read the relevant files, but the political side of life in those times was not easily discussed with the women. They claimed they either did not remember the period, having been children, or they had no interest in politics. That was men's business.

Women from families where men had been interned were unwilling to express anything about the political discussions they may have overheard, or taken part in, even when they themselves had suffered. Angela had returned from school to find both parents interned and she and her brothers and sisters left without an adult in the house. The parish priest had stepped in to find homes for the younger children. She spoke about her feelings of loss and abandonment; other women revealed their sense of confusion about their father's absence.[12] Yet others, who were small children when their father disappeared, were shocked at his reappearance. He had not been part of their lives. Some who did talk recalled the clubs merely as places where their parents went dancing. They tended to resent the fact that the family breadwinner was removed for some or all of the war years, and were happy to tell me of the ways they had survived, but political beliefs were not a subject on which most could be drawn. This absence of information in itself was of interest to me, suggesting a society divided by gender, where women knew their roles and men theirs. But communities are rarely a simple matter.

Women who had suffered in Italy during the war were not so reticent. One recalled her father being dosed with cod-liver oil by the local fascist thugs; another proudly showed me a lump on her buttock, which was a German bullet that had never been removed. A third lamented the loss of the farm animals, and the violent invasion of their village by German soldiers looking for partisans.[13] Indeed the ravages left by the war were largely responsible for their presence in Fremantle where they discovered a so-called 'Italian' community to whom they could not relate easily. 'They all spoke Sicilian,' said one woman recollecting her dismay.

So I looked for a way to talk about immigration without raising past animosities and fears. I found it in the meals they prepared for each meeting. Food, eating, recipes, nutrition, all have been globalized by television presentations, travel- and cook-books, but 20 years ago immigrant women still cooked in much the same way as their mothers had, and if they did not, they recalled their mothers' methods. Food then had an identifying quality. Women from small villages in southern Italy were proud cooks, aware that some of their food differed in small but important ways from the meals prepared by women from other villages.[14] Thus I came to understand that the word 'gnocchi' held different meanings for women from the south from those who came from the north.[15] I discovered that festivals – Christmas, Easter, births, marriages – demanded elaborate and specific recipes. I stumbled upon the idea that there were indeed pathways of supply in Fremantle that were closed to the wider community. Flour, fish, wine, cheese, were all delivered to the backdoor or were acquired from individual suppliers, often *compaesani*. Vegetables and some fruit were cultivated with generous abundance in backyards. Seeds were exchanged between gardeners. Tomatoes, in particular, were grown for specific purposes, to be bottled as sauce, to be dried, to be cut into pieces and preserved under oil; each family having its own specific recipes for this wide-ranging labour with both men and women involved.

Over a period of years, as I became friendly with some of the women, I visited their gardens and kitchens where I heard of the different migration routes they had taken. I listened to the desolation experienced by young brides who had never left home before but who travelled across the world to an unknown country without any English language skills. One woman spoke for many, recalling, 'I sat on the back stairs of the boarding house and cried and cried.' Others told of the unthinking racism that was often expressed when they stumbled over English words or phrases in shops. Yet others, especially those who arrived after the Second World War, or who grew up in the late 1940s, were not so negative about their first experiences of Australia and recalled kindnesses: 'My neighbour showed me how to roast a leg of lamb.' But the children who arrived to join a previously unknown father found that the most daunting experience. As Emma (whose experiences are described in greater depth in the following pages) recalled, 'I was so shy of my father. He was a complete stranger to me and I didn't know whether I liked him or not. I could not call him "Papa". It took me months to be able to do this and even then I was not easy about it. My brother told me he had been the same.'[16] Josephine had the same experience but interpreted it differently. She was left as a two-year-old to live with her mother and brother while her father emigrated supposedly for four or five years. It was to be 12 years before she saw him again and she did not recognize him. 'It was for this reason that we were a bit hesitant to go to him but when he saw Mary [who had been born after his departure] he just picked her up in his arms and I knew then that he would be a wonderful man to live with.'[17]

Every social group has its structure and the four women who had established the Amicizia Club differed among themselves over their personal priorities. All were interested in getting women to meet each other, but one was a fervent churchgoer, another was not. The third was a born administrator. A fourth was a member of the Italo-Australian Women's Association, to which the Amicizia Club was affiliated, and had connections with the political class, although was not apparently interested in party politics herself. They had come together because they were aware that many of the men in the community did not wish their wives to attend the Italian Club that had premises in the town. Patriarchy remained strong. Women seeing men in a club was frowned upon; women meeting with other women there was another matter. But the Amicizia membership encompassed many who had worked and who knew a lot more than they were given credit for. Widowhood came as a relief for some, for then they wanted to get out and about, to kick up their heels, and, for example, go to the Casino and gamble. The club began to organize bus trips to country towns, visits to Perth restaurants, and even proposed a holiday weekend in Melbourne.

As I joined these activities, the oral history project began to expand, taking new directions that had nothing to do with me but which I watched with interest. On the bus excursions I heard the women sing loudly and lustily. Their songs were memories, and were soon to be captured by another immigrant woman who was both musician and musicologist. She formed a choir, 'Le Gioie delle Donne', which she coached and for whose songs she wrote down the words. These words and melodies came from different regions and were thought to be largely forgotten back in Italy. She also composed new songs for them, illustrating some of their lives. They recorded an album.[18] My interest in food and things domestic led to suggestions for museum exhibitions, one displaying objects, mostly hand-woven embroidered linens and hand-made lace, brought from Italy as part of their dowries; another showing family kitchen and tableware that was accompanied by a bilingual recipe book, *Food Remembered: Ricette Ricordate*; and a third, which was much more ambitious, about the tomato and its place in cuisine and lives.[19]

One woman in particular grasped the opportunity that I, as the oral historian, offered when I told the group that I would like to talk to anyone who wished to tell me of their journey as an immigrant woman. In the case of Emma, who invited me into her house and then began to tell me about herself, I saw a vivacious, life-enhancing woman who became a good friend. I found that some of her memories fitted into the original plan to research the history of the Italian settlement in Fremantle, but while her particular story did illustrate a few of the issues explored in the bigger project, and Emma herself did provide a helpful introduction to other women, it was more relevant to a general understanding of women's history than we were attempting there. So a memoir was published three years before *Fremantle's Italy* was released. Five years later we brought out a second book, *Emma: A Recipe for Life*,[20] which included her autobiography but was enlarged by a discussion of food and the recipes she remembered. In sum, the oral history project begun in 1989 was completed six years later, having resulted in four books and three museum exhibitions, as well as a play written from *Emma: A Translated Life*, which utilized the choir and travelled around Australia. Wherever it stopped, a choir of local immigrant women was formed. None of my involvement could have taken place without the organization, participation and positive endorsement of the women who were moving from being a poorly recognized sub-culture into claiming an identity in the wider community.

What did I learn as a historian during these years when I was concentrating on understanding the various pasts of a particular group of women in Fremantle? In terms of oral history practice, I discovered that allowing myself extra time to pursue an idea or follow up suggestions made by individuals was immensely valuable. Technically, I found that a tape recorder inhibited a lot of the women, including Emma. They preferred to converse without a mechanical device recording their words; seeing me take notes did not dismay them nearly as much. Partly the distaste came from the old-fashioned tape recorders available then, partly it came from a fear that somehow their words would be used without their knowledge or control, and partly because we were mostly in a social situation where a quiet place to record was impossible to find. After I took notes I always gave each individual a copy of what they had said. Research was essential even when it came to recipes. Luckily I had access to some Italian language cook-books, including Pellegrino Artusi, *La Scienza in cucina e l'arte di mangier bene*, first published in the 1890s, which has an importance similar to Mrs Beeton's *Book of Household Management*. The women, once they learned to talk to me, were happy to discuss food and other domestic matters and were in effect able to endorse, expand or disagree with what others in the group had recalled. Their notions of good food and memories of it tended to elevate their home villages above all others. *Campanilismo* in this reading of history was alive and well.

Having given myself extra time, I learned a good deal about the hidden domestic histories of my respondents. Housework has suffered from the blindness of historians, but is a legitimate area of research for those interested in social history. It is notoriously difficult to document in any of the more usual sources but kitchens and gardens reflect individual histories in their physical aspects. Occasionally I saw a house with two kitchens, one for baking, which was often outside, or in the garage, and one in the house. I watched women produce particular recipes that were then included in the book that went with the museum display on food. I learned how to make tortellini by hand and was instructed on the technique of producing pastry with oil and wine, necessary for taralluc biscuits eaten on special occasions in the Abruzzi. I was directed to view suburban backyards that had been transformed into massively productive gardens where potatoes, lettuces, corn, beans and tomatoes jostled for space with grapes, peppers, garlic, basil and, on one occasion, bananas. I noted another family had terraced a small limestone rise and planted a hedge of prickly pear that bore huge amounts of fruit. Knowing that prickly pear is a declared pest in Queensland and New South Wales, I was astonished. I was also surprised to enjoy eating the fruit of this cactus. It is very refreshing on a hot day. These gardens were tangible evidence of personal memories and histories.

I also discovered plenty of unusual garden plants on my various visits – cardoons and artichokes, different kinds of aubergine and the range of tomatoes that were utilized for sauce, for drying and for cutting and preserving under oil. I heard of the disappointment that grown children were no longer interested in helping their parents in the garden or preparing the sauce. Nevertheless families shared out their bounty, sending bottles of home-made tomato sauce from Perth to Melbourne in one instance, to remind an absent child of the taste of home. Apart from food I discussed the significance of education for the children, and noted the religious observance of some of the women who held prayer meetings at home. A visiting Italian politician described this group of people as 'socially conservative' but I found their lives were layered and complex. Their memories of their departure from Italy, what they had seen and understood on return visits and their new status in Fremantle all contributed to a rich social history.

Oral history and heritage

During the 1990s, while still meeting the Italian women, I was engaged under contract as a heritage consultant on a number of occasions. Heritage work in modern Australia requires a team of experts. There is always an architect, sometimes a town planner, sometimes an archaeologist, and usually a historian. The technique was the same in all instances in that it focused on a building or a site rather than on the formation of a social group. Many of my more interesting jobs took place in the vast rural spaces of Western Australia where family and community histories are sometimes intertwined and where government policy papers, newspapers and contemporary maps or surveys provide useful background information. Occasionally the investigation of vernacular structures uncovered little documentary evidence of any substance and then oral history was pursued to fill the gap. Empirical evidence, including the date of the buildings, methods of construction and their use, can often be deduced to some extent from the building fabric or its remains, but historic and social values, two elements of a possible 'statement of significance' necessary when describing the heritage value of a building or site, are enriched by individual stories or memoir material. Memories are long in rural areas and history is a favourite topic of conversation. In small country towns, questions are rarely answered by one person alone; confirmation or disagreement over local history frequently depends on informal sources, even though there may be a recognized 'custodian' of local memory, the person to whom the researcher is always directed. He or she may even be writing a book, in which case they may not like a newcomer muscling in on their territory. These are the particular snares for the oral historian who, under contract, has little time to spare and must meet a deadline.

The Heritage Act WA 1990 may concentrate on the built environment, but practitioners are urged not to forget sites where indigenous and European peoples met: only too often these were sites of conflict. For the past two or three decades there has been a concerted effort to retrieve Aboriginal voices from the 'enormous condescension of posterity' and, one should add, in the context of Australian history and politics, the unthinking racism that seemed endemic, especially in country areas. Contested history can lead to silences of memory. Dowerin, a country town in the wheat belt, appeared to have no Aboriginal inhabitants, although it is perfectly possible that some lived in the area but did not come forward to identify themselves. The wheat farmers I met were knowledgeable about their land; they knew what could be grown, worried over rising salt (a problem in over-cleared pastures and the result of mistaken former agricultural practice), and directed me to odd structures in their surroundings, including the rabbit-proof fence which goes through this area, alleged camel tracks and camping sites of gold-seekers on their way to the fields. But they declared an ignorance of Aboriginal sites. 'There was never any trouble here,' said one woman firmly. Trouble there had been of course, but evidence of it was impossible to uncover in the time allowed for this particular project.[21]

Another site of contested memory, set in a country town not far from Perth, is that of the 'Battle of Pinjarra'. Here memory, oral testimony, archival information and material evidence all conflict. What is known beyond doubt is that a group of Aboriginal people was killed on the banks of the Murray River by soldiers led by James Stirling, governor of the colony in 1834. The event was recorded in governor's despatches and by the then Surveyor General, John Septimus Roe, one of the avenging party but allegedly not involved in the killing.[22] The local indigenous inhabitants of the town were eager to talk of the 'massacre', a word they have introduced to the discourse, as though it had happened yesterday. They knew where it had taken place, and they knew how many had been killed, although other, more conventional approaches to the past suggest that these facts remain uncertain. Their 'memories' might be described more as folk recall than history but, in the terms of the work we were pursuing in the town, no less important. Their voices had been unheard for a long time. They were incensed that there was no public recognition of the site however the 'massacre' was interpreted. At that time, in 1996, there was no marker, nothing to show that such an event had taken place, and the local government authority was unwilling to concede a memorial. The production of the report, which acknowledged these strongly held opinions as part of the heritage of the town, fed into the continuing debate about the history of contact between Aboriginals and white settlers.[23] Ultimately the Heritage Council of WA placed the agreed site on the State Register of Heritage Places, and a large rock with a plaque was erected to mark the approximate place of the killings. Written at a time when such matters were discussed with increasing acrimony, the oral history recorded as part of the larger report into the heritage of the town and its buildings was incidental compared to these outcomes.[24] The memorial may represent a political achievement, but it is not enough to assuage the pain still felt and expressed about the violent past.

Rather less contentious, but still troubled, was research into some shacks built in a remote part of the south-west coast of the state where the D'Entrecasteaux National Park is located. The park, more than 118,700 hectares, was gazetted in 1980. Before then, it had been crown land that was leased to various people, mostly graziers who drove their cattle along dusty tracks to the coast during summer months when pasture on their farms was particularly poor. The cattle could not remain long on the leases because the coastal soils are deficient in copper and cobalt and, after a certain length of time, the health of grazing animals begins to deteriorate. However, for around four months of each year some families had the right to live on their leaseholds and feed their animals. The shelters they built varied with time. The earliest, constructed in the 1890s, was a house with bedrooms and doors, an outdoor kitchen and rudimentary toilet facilities. In this home a governess was employed to teach the children. It was isolated, remote from the nearest town, and indeed from any neighbour. At that time the soil deficiencies were not known, but it was soon discovered that the animals sickened and died unless they were taken inland to better pasture. The house was then used only in summer. Other shacks had three rooms, built facing the ocean with an open middle room for air to circulate. Water was collected in a tank. Long drop toilets were constructed. Yet others were transported by dray from forestry settlements or were built bit by bit with the help of local townsmen who shared the facilities and stayed at weekends for the fishing. The state government had legislated to remove these structures, arguing that they were undemocratic and had no place in a national park which was meant to be used by everybody. Heritage legislation, however, demands an assessment process for government-owned buildings, which these were deemed to be, and thus the necessity for recording the history of these ephemeral structures.

The histories of the shacks turned out to be family history for many of the townspeople declared they were 'theirs'. These claims were often supported by names on the pastoral leases, but the assertions were more personal than that. Individuals, grandparents, parents and sons had expended time and energy in constructing and maintaining the shacks. Their occupations on the coastal strip were described, which were more than the old grazing lifestyle. A previously unknown fish-preserving factory had been established at one site, another had a complicated pulley and chain system for negotiating the cliffs and letting down a fishing boat. All locals appeared to know about the shacks and many who were not 'owners' or claimants had used them. They clearly played a part in the social life of the community. There was little difficulty in finding 'owners' to talk about their shacks. Each had a grievance about government policy and each was only too concerned to retain the right to use the shelter. Local officers of the government department, then called Conservation and Land Management (CALM), had some sympathy with these families, probably because they too had used the shelters, but they were more aware of the problems that shacks provoked in the management of a national park.

In this particular instance a number of interviews were recorded and written into the report with the knowledge and acceptance of the interviewees. That then went to CALM with heritage recommendations that some accommodation be reached with the families concerned.[25] These buildings were not only evidence of a long-gone way of life, but still played a part in the social organization of the local towns. The reality was that two pieces of legislation clashed. The oral histories and the heated feelings that were aroused by government intention to get rid of the shacks were enough to delay decisions, but not, in the long run, to alter the intention to demolish. Yet the local testimonies have added to the known history of the area. They included information about leisure activities, gender divisions (women used the huts less than men), and illustrated how these particular social groups interacted with each other and their surroundings, information which is very difficult to uncover in archival or other, more formal, sources.

Disasters

Australia is a land of climatic contrasts. Drought, flood or fire afflicts some part of the continent each year. The north-west coast of Western Australia is called the 'cyclone coast' and with good reason. Each year massive storms arise in the Indian Ocean and race down the coast. When they cross to land they deposit enormous amounts of water, always welcome in a parched country. In 1999, Tropical Cyclone Vance, which was category five, the most dangerous level, crossed the coast over a town called Exmouth more than 1,200 kilometres from Perth. It caused a great deal of damage and blocked access to the town for a couple of weeks as every creek bed between the airport and the town flooded. Two years later I visited Exmouth under the auspices of Country Arts WA to see if survivors of Cyclone Vance would be interested in relating their experiences.

Exmouth, although remote and relatively new – it was established in the 1960s – has a history that reflects Australian military ties with the US. During the Second World War it was the site of a radar station used by US air and marine forces. Its military importance was remembered, for without the imperatives of international treaties and the need for a surveillance site during the Cold War, there would have been no settlement on this remote part of the coast. A field of communication towers emitting a very low frequency (VLF) that reached the United States' large submarine fleet was engineered near the tip of the cape. A naval establishment, commemorating Harold Holt, the Australian Prime Minister who drowned in violent seas off Cheviot Beach in Victoria in 1967, was located a few kilometres away on the northern side of the peninsula. Here lay the nerve centre of the communications system, the operations rooms and some low-frequency equipment. East of the town, at Learmonth Airfield, another part of the communication network, a high-frequency receiver, was built. The technical splendour of the towers (the central one called 'tower zero' was the tallest structure in the southern hemisphere in the 1960s) and the triumph of the VLF technology becomes all the more impressive when seen in its environment. The builders and planners under-stood that cyclones had extraordinary power and constructed the towers and the town accordingly.

Two styles of houses were the result, one designed by American architects for the tough environment, built out of concrete blocks, air-conditioned, with flat roofs; the other, looking entirely more ephemeral, designed by Australian architects with experience in the north-west, built from timber, fibro and some brick. They all had iron roofs. When the 'big blow' arrived, it was the Australian houses that suffered the most damage. The American block homes and the American-built base provided sanctuaries for townspeople and stood up to the flying debris and the horizontal rain better than anything else, including modern homes that had been specially designed for cyclonic conditions. The American connection with Exmouth was the more poignant because my introductory visit took place only a couple of months before two planes crashed into the Twin Towers in New York City. For some time I wrestled with the idea of asking a complicated question about the ways individuals deal with disaster, but the differences between the two places and two events were extreme and my knowledge of the New York experience was too small.

The Exmouth story is full of voices, all different, all urgent in their way. Here I used a tape recorder as an aide-mémoire, transcribing the interviews as soon as I could and sending a copy to each respondent so they could be checked. Everyone signed a permission form allowing me to publish their memories. In the end, a book proved not to be possible, although the issues raised by the interviews showed themselves emblematic of those faced by later sufferers of this kind of natural disaster. The town itself is small. It has a population of around 2,000 swelling to 3,000 during the winter months when visitors arrive from colder parts of the state. Memories of the cyclone varied, although some themes were frequently mentioned. Most people remarked upon the noise the wind made and the driving force of the rain. They also praised members of the State Emergency Service, all volunteers, who helped them cope with the dangers the cyclone brought. Those dangers were real. Bernice's house collapsed around her. She was then in her eighties.[26] She watched as half another house was bowled up the road to hit hers and lift the roof. She was thrown to the floor, pinned to a wall and suffered a cracked rib. She was eventually found by her daughter and a neighbour, and although cold and wet, managed to survive. There were no deaths in the town, mainly because the storm passed overhead reasonably quickly.

Even when a house did not collapse there was a great amount of damage. Power lines and power poles were swept away, the water supply failed and although later, the inhabitants were assured that only 10 per cent of the town had been destroyed or badly damaged, June, who ran the childcare centre, remembered: 'You couldn't put a baby on the floor anywhere because of the glass, the debris and the water.' Many of the women and children went south while their menfolk cleared up the mess. Some families never returned. The interviews showed, more than the formal reports were able, how the townsfolk had coped, what social mechanisms a small remote settlement could find to deal with natural disasters and how much they were appreciated. When the water cleared from the long road into Exmouth, government employees arrived to repair the infrastructure and charitable organizations arranged for food, clothing and household goods to be flown in and distributed. In the meantime a local restaurant cooked for the town for more than a week and the Shire Council rose to the occasion by producing a management plan to prioritize the town's needs. They had to draw up schedules of work, remove debris from the roads, bury the rotting food stored in home freezers and collect the wet mattresses, carpets and other furnishings that owners had to throw out because they would not dry as rain continued to fall and the accompanying heat turned everything mouldy. Some losses sound minimal, but these remind us, just as the Amicizia women have, that it is in the small things around us that most of us find meaning. Photographs, favourite books, gifts from a husband or lover or child were washed away and mourned. Elizabeth recalled:

> … I lost all my cookery books. Not that I use them a lot. But I'd had them since I was married and you know you've got your favourites, things the kids like and stuff. They all grew fungus and they all had to be thrown out because they all got so wet. I didn't think I'd miss them that much but every now and then I think I'll make that, and then I realize that I haven't got the recipe any more. There are lots of new ones I know, it's really silly, but they were common recipes that I used all my married life and I haven't got them anymore … No great loss really, it's just funny how I miss them.

Conclusion

Oral history cannot do many things but it can bring a human dimension to historical questions. As a source, the oral record can tell the historian how individuals, at a specific moment, felt about things that mattered to them, whether it was food, housing or history. The immediacy of the interview, the

characteristics of personal expression, add depth and emotion to our understanding of events and of places and of what makes us the way we are. Talking
with others about their memories is no trifling business, all sorts of things can
go wrong, but when the interview works, it brings the historian closer to
understanding the ways individuals have dealt with significant moments in
their lives.

It is up to the historian to keep the questions on track, so that the initial
aim of the work is not lost in trivial detail. It goes without saying that
thinking about the language used and the issues that emerge becomes the next
step. Undigested source material, whether archival documents or interviews,
is not very interesting; it requires analysis and interpretation. The tools of the
historian who records other people's memories are not necessarily modern
technical marvels, although they help; more useful are sufficient funding,
plenty of time and empathy, and a suitable amount of research and critical
enquiry. With these caveats in mind, this historian believes that despite its
difficulties oral history adds to rather than detracts from the historical record,
and that collecting memories is a worthwhile activity for journeymen (and
women) in our discipline.

Notes

1 S. Terkel, *Hard Times: An Oral History of the Great Depression* (New York: Pantheon Books, 1970).

2 S. Terkel, *The Good War: An Oral History of World War Two* (New York: Pantheon Books, 1984).

3 S. Terkel, *Hope Dies Last: Keeping Faith in Difficult Times* (New York: The New Press, 2003).

4 S. Terkel with S. Lewis, *Touch and Go: A Memoir* (New York: The New Press, 2007), p. 171.

5 R.J. Grele, '"Riffs and improvisations": an interview with Studs Terkel, 10 April 1973', in Ronald J. Grele with S. Terkel, J. Vansina, D. Tedlock, S. Benison and A. Kessler Harris, *Envelopes of Sound: The Art of Oral History*, 2nd edn (Chicago: Precedent Publishing Inc., 1985), pp. 35–39.

6 E.P. Thompson, *The Making of the English Working Class* (Harmondsworth: Pelican, 1986) [orig. 1963], p. 12.

7 See P. Thompson, *The Voice of the Past: Oral History*, 2nd edn (Oxford: Oxford University Press, 1988) [orig. 1978] for some discussion of the history of this movement and its achievements.

8 See the *Oral History Association of Australia Journal*, published annually from 1978. The website of the NSW branch of the association www.ohaansw.org.au (visited 2 February 2011) gives detail of its aims and achievements.

9 See B. Nairn, *The Big Fella*, revised edn (Carlton, Victoria: Melbourne University Press, 1995).

10 See L. Niethammer, 'Oral History as a channel of communication between workers and historians', in P. Thompson (ed.) with N. Burchardt, *Our Common History: The Transformation of Europe* (London: Pluto Press, 1982), pp. 23–37.

11 M. Bosworth, 'Fremantle interned: the Italian experience', in R. Bosworth and R. Ugolini (eds) *War, Internment and Mass Migration: The Italo-Australian Experience 1940–1990* (Rome: Gruppo Internazionale Editoriale, 1992), pp.75–88.

12 See 'Angela Wayne, née Travia' in 'Oral histories of internment' edited by R. Bosworth in Bosworth and Ugolini, *War, Internment and Mass Migration*, pp. 112–14.

13 Interviews with women from the Amicizia Club held by the author.

14 More recent writers on food in Italy decry this kind of 'campanilismo', asserting that there are more similarities than differences between foods and cookery in Italy. See A. Capatti and M. Montanari, *Italian Cuisine: A Cultural History* (New York: Columbia University Press, 2003).

15 See M. Bosworth, 'Conversations of a culinary kind,' in R. Bosworth and M. Melia (eds) *Aspects of Ethnicity, Historical Studies of Western Australia*, XII (Nedlands: UWA Press, 1991).

16 E. Ciccotosto and M.Bosworth, *Emma: A Recipe for Life*, revised edn (Fremantle: Fremantle Arts Centre Press, 1998).

17 J. Cabassi, 'Oral histories of internment', in Bosworth and Ugolini, *War, Internment and Mass Migration*, p. 107.

18 K. Mazzella, 'Le Gioie delle donne', CD released 1991. The choir was formed in 1989 and is still performing in Perth as I write in 2011. See www.kavisha.com for other examples of her work.

19 G. Binetti and M. Bosworth (eds) *Ricette Ricordate, Food Remembered* (Perth: W.A. Museum, 1991). The Tomato Festival, 1995, was accompanied by a museum exhibition, a photographic display and a community demonstration of the art of making tomato sauce, accompanied by bilingual recipes for its use.

20 E. Ciccotosto and M. Bosworth, *Emma: A Translated Life* (Fremantle: Fremantle Arts Centre Press, 1990) and E. Ciccotosto and M. Bosworth, *Emma: A Recipe for Life* (Fremantle Arts Centre Press, 1995 [new edn, 1998]).

21 Research conducted for the Municipal Inventory of Dowerin, 1995, copy held in the library of the Heritage Council of WA.

22 Local historians, including Aboriginal historians, disagree with each other on this subject.

23 See the history section in *Pinjarra Precinct Planning Study*, S. Chaffer and Associates and Heritage and Conservation Professionals, Perth, 1996, copies held in the Shire of Pinjarra and in the library of the Heritage Council of WA.

24 Publication of *Bringing Them Home: Report of the National Inquiry into the Separation of Aboriginal and Torres Strait Islander Children from their Families* (Sydney: Human Rights and Equal Opportunity Commission, 1997) marked a turning point in the acceptance of Aboriginal points of view. The report is filled with poignant memories about the removal of children from their families and its effects. In February 2008, the Australian government under the leadership of Kevin Rudd apologized for this government policy, which had also affected individuals in Pinjarra.

25 The Department of Conservation and Land Management, having paid for the research and the report, now holds copyright of the interviews. *Huts in the D'Entrecasteaux National Park: Heritage Assessment and Conservation Recommendations*, 1999, prepared for the Department of Contract and Management Services on behalf of the Department of Conservation and Land Management, by Heritage and Conservation Professionals. Copies held in CALM and Heritage Council libraries.

26 Michal Bosworth, *Sirens ...* , 2002, unpublished manuscript, copies held in Exmouth public library, and by the author.

2 Small fish, big pond

Using a single oral history narrative to reveal broader social change

Lindsey Dodd

It was midday on 6 April 2009 and I was sitting on a bench in the Parisian suburb of Boulogne-Billancourt feeling discouraged. I reflected that, a day into my month-long field trip to France, my interviewing technique was poor. How else to account for the past few hours? I was there to collect material on the impact of the Allied bombing of France on children during World War II, beginning a tightly budgeted tour of three French towns for my PhD project. Boulogne-Billancourt was bombed heavily on 3 March 1942 – a Royal Air Force (RAF) air raid, the first of its size on a French industrial target, the Renault factories – again on 4 April 1943, and twice in September 1943, all by the United States Army Air Force (USAAF). A misunderstanding was at the root of the problem, it seemed: the woman I had just interviewed, Marguerite, was too old for my sample, and I had assumed I was interviewing her son. But on arrival, I found he had been born after the war. I reasoned, none-theless, that she could give a contrastive reflection from an adult's perspective, or some information on fears about air war during the interwar years. But, as I wrote in my field notes, 'She doesn't remember any talk of air war before the war!'

Yet I knew this interview was valuable. This chapter will consider how the interview has provided me with an insight into broad social processes beyond the scope of my doctoral research. From a methodological perspective, it sheds light on the nature of interviewing, and the problems of using memory as a historical source. From a substantive point of view, it allows us to see that historical memory acts as a gateway to understanding the relationship between the individual and the social.

In my notebook, I jotted further thoughts:

> most striking – she doesn't recall the bombing of 3 March 1942 – hardly any destruction – a few panes of glass – says few people died …

In the first part of this chapter, I show that Marguerite's misremembering of the events of 1942 provides an open door into meaning, rather than a missed opportunity to gather content. I will account for Marguerite's and my different understanding of events by looking at the divide between the relative impor-tance of our priorities, the lack of available cultural scripts for her to use when speaking of bombing, and the effect of my implied demand for her to slice a chunk out of a longer life story. Another section of my field notes comments upon Marguerite's 'good luck to get into shelter and so avoid the fate of those in the streets; bad luck that only [her family's] factory was destroyed': there is an oscillation between her own experiences and those of others. This dialogue between the one and the many will also be explored, showing how we can use one narrative to move between individual and group experience. The last part of the chapter focuses directly on the narrative itself, examining Marguerite's reflections on bombing, her family and the town of Boulogne-Billancourt. My field notes flag up this connection:

> [her family was] one of the biggest, most well-established of the *blanchisseurs* [laundry firms] – 4 April '43 raid destroyed the business … the end of an era in their family – and of an époque in the town.

The close connections between self, family, occupation and locality are examined in order to reveal the individual narrative as illuminating of broader social change. I conclude by considering the significance of a final note: '[t]he re-telling of … how [Marguerite's family] only just made it.' This recurrent anecdote further links the individual to the broader group: what did *not* happen to Marguerite happened to others, thus creating a sense of 'shared possibility' extending beyond personal experience.

My interview with Marguerite was the second in a series of 30 with elderly French people who had experienced the bombing of military, industrial and transportation targets in their country by the Allies between 1940 and 1945. Around 57,000 civilians were killed, and countless others made homeless, evacuated or affected physically or psychologically.[1] Neither the Allied bombing, nor the subjective experiences of French children in war, have received much scholarly attention, and my doctoral research addressed both.[2] Arriving at Marguerite's flat in Boulogne-Billancourt, the miscommunication became clear: she was 23 and recently married when war broke out in 1939.[3] Her husband was one of the 1.5 million Frenchmen taken as prisoners-of-war in 1940, not to return permanently until 1945.[4] While our discussion was interesting, and Marguerite remembered the raid of 4 April 1943, I gathered little material that seemed relevant to my study.

Boulogne-Billancourt[5] had long been a laundry town. From the late seventeenth century laundry services proliferated, using water from the River Seine to clean the linen of the growing French capital. By 1900 laundry was its main economic activity, employing 5,000 people in more than 500 businesses, many of which became industrialized washing factories. While the north-west part of the town was mostly laundries, the south-east side, Billancourt, was filled with factories – ceramics, enamels, chemicals, jam, candles and perfume. Louis Renault established his first automobile factory there in 1898. Other motor and aviation firms followed, and existed alongside the laundry industry. Boulogne-Billancourt became famous for the great Renault plants, and thus it became the RAF's first French industrial target in 1942. The German occupiers, as part of their systematic exploitation of French resources, were using Renault's factories to manufacture tanks and trucks. In the post-war era, the laundry industry declined because of the spread of domestic washing machines; however, as Marguerite's story illustrates, this industrial shift was given a helping hand by the inevitable inaccuracies of aerial bombardment.[6] While my interview did not produce material on children and bombing, it nonetheless was saturated with the 'meanings of the past in the present'.[7] In asking about a set of events from the early 1940s, I discovered broader changes at local, family and personal level over time.

Relative priorities

I will suggest three reasons that may account for the story I received. First, there was a disparity between my and Marguerite's relative priorities in speaking to each other, which highlights the inter-subjective nature of oral history interviewing. Second, given that the Allied bombing is rarely discussed in France at a public level, there are few standard ways of speaking about it, that is, no cultural script. This indicates the complex relationship between public-level discourse and the narration of local or personal experience. Finally, this was not a life history interview. I asked Marguerite to slice a chunk out of her life history. She could not help but use the bigger picture to make sense of events in her life over time.

The refocusing of oral history work around memory, identity and subjectivity from the late 1970s onwards[8] has led to an awareness of the interview as 'multi vocal'.[9] This point is crucial: you do not always 'get what you want'; in many cases, you 'get what *they* want', despite your best efforts to guide the interview. Yet as Alessandro Portelli noted, the story you think you do not want can be the key to understanding: 'I realized that there was more history in her personal love story than in her reminiscences about the anti-Fascist underground.'[10] The focus of my attention was a trigger for Marguerite to tell a different story. She continuously refocused the interview around her own priorities, which were centred on place and family. Gender affects the narration of the story; a woman is more likely to tie a narrative to the relationships of kin networks, while men tend to portray themselves as 'self-willed individuals'.[11] However, Portelli's experience of women's 'hospital stories' as a counterpart to men's 'war stories' indicated to him that while gender has determined what typically counts as history (events, public sphere) and what does not (undefined processes, private sphere), interviewees are not bound by such distinctions.[12] Through Marguerite's family-centred narrative, we see her engagement in public-world events.

Gender alone cannot explain the difference in the relative importance of our priorities. The relationship between the interviewer and interviewee, once at the root of criticism of oral history, is a rich source of analysis.[13] We tell the same story differently to different people, and while I did not know how often Marguerite has told this story – it was not the first time, as the nods and prompts of her son and daughter-in-law indicated – this situation was different. In the brief time we had together, she had to give me, a stranger, a coherent story. It had a beginning (the prosperous laundry), a middle (its destruction) and an end (her father's move from laundry proprietor to mechanic). My stated interest was really only the middle, but narrators will 'forcibly introduce' other elements, 'gathering together bundles of meaning, relationships and themes across the linear span of their lifetime'.[14] The historian's restricted interest is unlikely to chime with a narrator's understanding of the whole.

My priorities in asking questions were quite different to Marguerite's priorities in answering them, and part of my initial dissatisfaction came as a result of this disparity. I wanted to talk about bombs; she wanted to talk about her family's changing fortunes. This is one of the many reasons why oral history 'alters the epistemological base'[15] of historical enquiry: we find answers to questions we did not know existed.

Cultural scripts

The fact that my questions did not encourage the experiential descriptions of being bombed that I had hoped for had something to do with the nature of the topic, again, a result of my priorities. Alistair Thomson's work on *Anzac Memories* of World War I indicated the complexity of interaction between 'public' narratives and private experiences.[16] A gap can open between them if individuals' memories do not correspond with 'public' forms of remembering, and a feeling of alienation can develop. In more practical terms, remembering nationally recognized events often involves the use of 'shared cultural scripts' – recognizable, standardized reworkings of the past.[17] In this way the public version of events acts like a jelly mould, shaping personal memories to its contours. Publicly told – and heard – stories tend to conform to accepted versions, and feature components from fixed, or semi-fixed, cultural scripts.

What happens, then, when an interview touches upon subjects for which no cultural scripts are available? The Allied bombing of France has been described as a 'black hole in French collective memory of war'.[18] While my doctoral research found that it is remembered vividly at local, family and private level, it is rarely discussed at public or institutional levels.[19] The national preoccupation with resistance to the German occupation of France versus French institutional collaboration has obscured a number of lines of historical enquiry. Notably, this preoccupation accounts for the relative absence of children – generally neither resisters nor collaborators – from historical research, compared with other European countries, but also the Allied bombing, which occupies a strange position in relation to resistance and collaboration. It was both a sign of external resistance to Nazism and a symbol of French occupation and collaboration.

With little attention paid to bombing at a public level in France, no cultural script has developed that Marguerite could use to help structure her narrative.

There are no fixed components, no standard forms of telling this tale. The jelly is not yet set: collective memory at a national level has not yet standardized memories of bombing, and thus narrators have a great deal of storytelling space. For some I interviewed, this led to drifting off into more familiar territory of resistance and collaboration, or better known civilian problems concerning food.[20] Marguerite had had little outside input to shape her memories of bombing. Television, film, photographs and commemorations act as prompts and structuring devices. For example, when speaking of the civilian exodus of ten million refugees in advance of the invading German army in 1940 two interviewees, a couple, told me

LUCIEN: No, I don't have any memories of that. Or rather I do now because I've read so much –
SONIA: Yes, and we've watched so many television programmes![21]

They were aware that their 'memories' were reconstructed. But there has been little public discourse about the bombing of France, in stark contrast to, for example, the London Blitz.[22]

For Marguerite bombing is a backdrop to more pivotal changes: she spoke from a better known family script about the loss of the business, rather than a French cultural script about the Allied bombing. Her 'bombing story' mutated into a more recognizable family and local history: her family lost – in one air raid – its identity, just as her town lost its identity as a laundry town. Bombing was part of broader processes of social change, in the town and in her family. Marguerite told me what it was possible for her to talk about. The logic of her story was fixed, and no public narrative of the Allied bombing has challenged its integrity.

Sliced life histories

Finally, my interview with Marguerite may not have elicited the kind of material I desired because I was asking her to slice a chunk out of her life story. Portelli sees life stories as 'a wheel, with a circular rim, and spokes branching out in all directions from one central core of meaning'.[23] A sliced life history asks only about one of the spokes, but the central core of meaning remains the organizing principle. Even a chunk, or an anecdote, may contain the essence of that bigger story, its themes and motifs, its patterns and structure.[24] Every oral history interviewer needs time and patience, and new researchers, with limited resources, may not have enough of either. Portelli advises waiting for the whole to make sense;[25] but with another interview booked that afternoon, I had no time to ask for the whole life story. Yet Marguerite's narrative gives us a portion of the whole, and glimpses into its broader meaning.

In court, a witness is asked about a restricted set of events pertaining to the object of investigation. Testimony is interpreted solely according to external criteria, by lawyer or judge. And this is where oral history must be seen as something other than 'testimony', something other than a witness statement of 'truth'. A narrator performs a story where 'events and actions are drawn together into an organized whole by means of a plot'.[26] In conveying the relational significance of the events at the heart of my interest and the longer-term changes in her family and town, Marguerite told an emplotted story. Louis Renault and the USAAF airmen are minor characters whose acts contribute to the narrative development of the story of her life. The events of my enquiry were 'made meaningful by everyday storytelling':[27] Marguerite positioned them carefully inside the whole story, which itself is the construction of her identity over 95 years. 'We construct our identities by telling stories either to ourselves as inner stories or day-dreams, or to other people in social situations':[28] in the peculiar social situation of the interview, Marguerite naturally placed events into a story, and imbued them with broader meaning that touched the core of her personal identity as daughter and wife in a city torn between old and new industries.

It is not always practical for oral historians to gather entire life stories. But we must be aware that by asking questions about fixed chunks of time, we are asking narrators to do something quite difficult. The tendency of the storyteller is to shuttle back and forth in time, because the events inside and outside the pool of light our spotlight casts are, for them, bound together.[29] I was interested in the fixed event, but Marguerite narrated it as part of a dynamic process.

VIEWING HISTORY/EVENTS AS "BOUND TOGETHER" vs. "THE FIXED EVENT"

From individual to group

In trying to understand how one life story can provide insight into broader social change, we need to think about the relationship between the individual and the group: how can the individual represent the group, and how can we, as oral historians, negotiate the gap between the personal and the collective? As Lummis asked, how typical can a single account be, and can a few interviews provide the basis of a general social interpretation?[30] While oral history, like other types of qualitative research, is open to the criticism that it only offers a 'worm's eye view', we must not forget the worm's vital role in the ecosystem, like the individual's in the social system.

I will respond to the problem of the relationship between the individual and the group in three ways. First, the use of first-person narratives in general historical accounts not only has a long pedigree,[31] but within current historical practice using autobiographical materials such as letters, diaries and memoirs is well grounded. 'History from below' emancipated the voices and experiences of more ordinary men and women, and the 'biographical turn'[32] and the rise of memory studies towards the end of the twentieth century brought wide acceptance of the individual's role in illuminating the impact of historical change. Individuals can be used in two ways: first, as exceptional people who led exceptional lives. Such individuals are useful because of their specificity, because of what makes them unique. Second, they are useful as ordinary people who do not stand out because of illustrious or nefarious deeds, who are historical in their generality, not their particularity.[33] Without denying their individuality, such people make up the broad swathes of society whose aggregated decisions, motivations and actions 'influenced history' and were influenced by it.[34] Frisch describes them as invisible actors in historically visible forums. Ordinary people like Marguerite, while unique as individuals, participate in broader historical and social processes in which certain experiences will always be shared.

Oral historians often practise a kind of methodological 'bricolage', taking useful components from other disciplines. Ideas of representativity, sampling and case study research can offer useful insights. Pioneering oral historian and sociologist Daniel Bertaux brought from his original discipline a rigorous approach to sample size: his research into French artisanal bakeries was complete when repeated stories demonstrated 'saturation'. The large number of stories he gathered enabled him to discern specific patterns of transmission within the industry.[35] Yet this methodological stringency may be unsuited to certain goals of oral history. While gathering nearly 500 autobiographical accounts for the *Ten Pound Poms* project enabled patterns and generalizations, Alistair Thomson noticed that individual voices lost prominence; his next publication was 'a different type of book' comparing 'in more depth and detail' four of the original *Ten Pound Poms* interviewees' narratives, letters and family photographs. These women became the co-authors of the book.[36] He recognized that they were 'neither typical nor exceptional'; however, together their stories 'enrich and complicate our understanding of key illu-minated patterns of social and cultural change'.[37] While individual stories have value in themselves, they can also act as case studies. Indeed, one of the misunderstandings that Flyvbjerg corrects concerning case studies is that 'you cannot generalise from a single case study'.[38] You can, but only with full understanding of what your case study shows. It can be representative, it can typify, or it can be exemplary; it can be a critical case or a maximum variation case. As Grele remarks, we do not interview individuals because 'they present some abstract statistical norm, but because they typify historical processes'.[39] It is not necessary for oral historians to remain shackled to the idea of large, representative samples; it is possible to generalize from a few stories, and to learn a great deal from one.

A third way to think about individuals and groups is to understand that even though individuals may not be representative, their stories may be. While interviewing Valtèro Peppoloni, Portelli understood that one man's life story contained enough collective and shared elements to see it 'as a representative document of the local working-class culture'. Peppoloni's story contained *all* of the 'shared narrative patterns, structures and motifs' found less compre-hensively in others from the same social group; what is more, these motifs were more intense in Peppoloni's account than elsewhere. This story was not 'average', but it showed that he had absorbed all of the 'ingredients of shared possibility' appropriate to his situation, and retold them as his life story.[40] As we will see, parts of Marguerite's story are important because she is an 'ordinary' historical actor within a shared set of circumstances, and others help us understand industrial change in Boulogne-Billancourt; in the sections of her narrative that directly concern the bombing, the idea of 'shared possibility' brings insight from the single story into a shared social experience. As Samuel and Thompson pointed out, the individuality of each life is not 'an awkward impediment to generalisation',[41] but offers opportunities to understand the social groups in which those individuals are embedded. Not only do the stories we tell and hear form the 'cohesive glue' of the cultural and social groups to which we belong,[42] but their sticky nature links the storyteller to the broader historical process. As we will now see, Marguerite's narrative uses family and identity, as well as a sense of shared possibility to glue together her life and her times.[43]   *"SHARED POSSIBILITY"*

The narrative

The final section of this chapter will look closely at Marguerite's narrative to illustrate how a two-hour interview with one woman can go beyond a restricted 'worm's eye view'. It provides an illuminating perspective on the mechanisms of social life – of family responsibility, of employment, of industry. What struck me initially was Marguerite's response to my early questions about the first bombing of Boulogne-Billancourt on the night of 3 March 1942. She said:

> Oh, well, it wasn't very heavy. It was just, I would say, the windows which were broken, all the windows, but people could still keep working. The moment of the bombing was hard, but afterwards, well, it had happened, and we didn't think any more about it!

This appeared a significant departure from how this raid is and has been portrayed; the first of its kind on an urban target in France, it created a furious outcry in the French press because of the damage done. Over two hours, 235 aircraft dropped more than 500 bombs on Renault's factories, less than half of which fell in the target area. The raid caused more civilian casualties than any hitherto performed by Bomber Command – including raids on Germany – with 371 identified and around 100 unidentified dead in Boulogne-Billancourt and 317 injured. There were further dead and wounded in neighbouring suburbs.[44] The rest of her narrative revealed why Marguerite attached so little importance to this event: it was the next air raid, that of 4 April 1943, which altered her family's destiny. In the analysis that follows, which looks at Marguerite's family and local identities, their intertwined relationship, the mechanisms of family and local transmission and the nature of shared possibility, it will be clear that this story moves beyond the personal.

Marguerite was born in December 1915; she had an older brother born in 1912 and a younger sister born in 1920. On the biographical details form I had sent prior to the interview, her son had noted his grandfather's occupation as follows:

BEFORE THE WAR: laundry man
DURING: laundry man
AFTER: GARAGE OWNER[45]

The business had been in the family down the generations, and Marguerite showed pride in the photographs of her father's factory, which employed around 80 workers, and the quality of his machinery and clientele in its heyday prior to World War II:

> You can see, it's electric, it's very tidy, it was very clean … This is for washing, and this is for ironing, and folding. They did bath towels and towels for hairdressers … The workers delivered it across Paris. This van did such-and-such district, this one did another.

The photographs showed a smart stone building, and a fleet of liveried Renault vans, lined up to take neat piles of laundry across the city. The prosperous business was a result of a family's hard work across the generations, as Marguerite was keen to emphasize. Looking at another photo, she said:

> Oh, that's an old one, see how they're dressed … My father should be there, and my grandfather. And I had an aunt there. People in the family worked together … My mother looked after it during the [First World] War, to keep the business going as my father was away from 1914 … But it's a hard profession, laundry. You have to get up early in the morning, my father, at five o'clock, and you worked until evening. On Saturday he worked, and Sunday if there were no other workers.

This closeness of the family, and its intergenerational ties were not just manifested in the successful transmission of a business concern, but in the domestic environment too. After her grandmother was widowed:

> My father didn't want to leave her alone, so they moved in with her. And the whole family was reunited there in that house. We were nine people, every day, all around the dining table!

The centrality of the dining table to this happy, prosperous and large family would recur later in the story. The photographs she showed me, alongside others taken by a neighbour after the laundry factory was destroyed, would prove crucial in helping her father gain compensation for his losses; but for Marguerite the orderly buildings stand as evidence for her family's status, and the coherence of the occupational transmission. Her father's modern factory was simply the most recent, and most modern, iteration of several generations' hard work.

The transmission of the business is the first of three transmissions evident in the story. The next is a transmission of caring roles within the family. We have already seen that Marguerite's father took on the role of caring for his mother, moving his family in after his father's death. In Marguerite's depiction of the family around the table, we see her surrounded by care, her father dominant in the family group. Following her marriage in 1938, it might be expected that her focus would pass to her own household; but although the couple moved into an apartment nearby, they spent little time together over the next seven years, for her husband followed two years' military service *Family* beginning in 1938, with conscription and his immediate capture and intern- *Roles* ment in Germany. However, it is Marguerite's role *vis-à-vis* her parents that indicates a transmission of care brought about by the Allied bombing. A recurrent image in the interview is a recollection of her parents sitting on the pavement outside the ruined factory: 'my parents, they'd lost everything. They were sitting on the pavement, and there was nothing left'; later, 'you work all your life, and then, from one day to the next, nothing's left. And they were sitting there, both of them, on the pavement'; and again, 'I tell you, they were there on the edge of the pavement, they didn't know what to do with themselves.' This image is the low point of the family's fortunes, and the moment at which Marguerite took on a new role:

> Luckily I had a flat, with a dining room, a bedroom and a kitchen, and I said 'Come on, we'll manage, let's put a mattress on the floor', and so we put a mattress in the dining room, and they stayed with me until they found something else.

Marguerite's role as daughter now entered a stage where she was her parents' protector. This generational transmission of roles is typical, of course, but Marguerite's position was unusual, given that she was living alone, and her parents were not yet ready to retire.[46] Her parents received emergency furniture from the town hall, but the picture now was very different to the scenes around the table in years gone by:

> They got furniture, some chairs, the strict minimum, mind you, as there were so many that needed it. They had to accept what they were given as there was nothing else. If it was a plain wooden table, it was a plain wooden table. They couldn't choose.

The change from former prosperity to a dependence on state allocations was marked.

A further transmission evident in the narrative is the adjustment of the family's identity around a new profession, the profession of Marguerite's husband. As family leadership appeared to pass from her father to her husband, so the identity of the town passed forever away from laundry and, for the time being, to cars.[47] Her family had passed the baton of laundry down the generations, but now the chain was irreparably broken. Of her father, Marguerite said:

> He went a long time without work … And then he went to work for a fellow laundry man, to get a bit of money, because you can't live with nothing, and he'd put everything into the factory.

While she speaks only of the sympathy of his ex-rivals, she also noted that her father was growing too old for the hard labour of a laundry worker. He waited 12 years to receive his compensation. Marguerite said: 'He rebuilt. But not a laundry.' The compensation was delayed as he refused to leave the town, so strongly was his identity bound up in the locality:

> He said 'I'm from Boulogne, and I'll stay in Boulogne.' And when he saw that they wanted to give him a plot outside of Boulogne, he said 'No, no! I won't leave. I'm from here, I'm staying here. So you'll have to give me something else.'

He held out stubbornly until

> One day they said 'If you want to start up a garage, you can. You can open a garage.' My husband, who was a mechanic, he worked in the garage.

While the story perhaps represents the end of an era, and marks the swamping of tradition with modernity, it could also be seen, more optimistically, as a positive leap from a moribund industry – domestic washing machines would kill the mass laundry trade – to one better suited to the times. The explosion of car ownership during the '30 glorious years' of expansion and growth in post-war France meant that the forced shift started the family along a promising new path.

However, the issue is made more complex by the fact that the town's usurper industry was blamed for the assault, collateral or otherwise, on the traditional industry. During the air raid of 4 April 1943, Marguerite recounted that the people in the cellar-shelter she was in were saying 'Oh, they're bombing Renault!' But as they exited the shelter 'everything had collapsed. We said, "Well, it's not just Renault damaged. For all of us, it's the same. We've got nothing left."' Not only that, but the area did not get immediate emergency assistance. She said:

> [I]t was on fire, and the firemen couldn't come and put it out, because they were at Renault. We tried to put the fire out, but it wasn't easy.

Whether this was true or not is not the point; what matters to Marguerite is that Renault attracted the bombers, and then took priority over other districts damaged in the raid. She did not speak with bitterness, however; most interviewees in Boulogne-Billancourt seemed disinclined to berate Louis Renault for his accommodation of the Germans – who would have commandeered his factory had he refused to let them in;[48] neither did Marguerite criticize the Allies for their clumsy, devastating aim. She reasoned, as did others, that the USAAF pilots made reasonable errors:

> The neighbour's factory had two tall chimneys, and my parents had two, and they bombed in the middle of these four chimneys. It was the chimneys that guided them, and they must have done something so that the bombs fell in between.

Like other local people, Marguerite was not aware of the precision of Allied maps that showed precisely where Renault's factory and others committed to war work were located. By 1943, the US bombsights were also technically advanced. What is clear, however, is that Marguerite held no rancour towards the men who destroyed the family business:

> It's not really the fault of those who had to bomb us, you know ... They dropped their bombs as best they could, I've got to say.

Despite the havoc wreaked in that four-minute, high-altitude air raid in April 1943, Marguerite's lack of bitterness is not unusual of many of the people I interviewed across different French towns. What makes Marguerite's case interesting is the fact that the events of that day were bound up with the broader social changes that Boulogne-Billancourt, and France more broadly, was to experience in the post-war years. Bombing hastened the family's move towards the incomer industry, which itself was held responsible – if not angrily by Marguerite – for the demise of the traditional one through which her town and family identity were shaped. It also represented a generational shift, with Marguerite stepping into a caring role, and her husband, a family incomer, providing the occupational expertise for the family's new professional orientation.

It has been possible in the above discussion to discern some of the ways in which Marguerite's single story gives us insight into broader social and cultural changes. But I have said very little so far about the way in which Marguerite herself experienced the moment of bombing. The interview had initially seemed a little disappointing, and Marguerite's age prohibited much use of it in my doctoral analysis. However, as I transcribed it, I became aware of the important role that chance played in the narration; good and bad luck, and the idea of a near miss were very prominent. The rest of my interviews revealed these as generic motifs in bombing stories. In his analysis of shared possibilities at the heart of oral history narratives, Portelli notes that 'the subjective projection of imaginable experience' is key – not 'what materially happens to people' but 'what people imagine or know might happen'.[49]

What possibility am I speaking of here? A little fewer than around 57,000 French civilians were killed by the Allied bombs; far fewer than the number who were bombed, who cowered and shook, who were bombed out, ruined or hurt. The possibility of death or pain loomed so large for those not killed and not seriously injured that it shapes all of the bombing narratives I collected. What happened to 57,000 was the 'materialisation of everybody else's concerns'.[50] Thus one of the strongest ways in which a single story can provide evidence of broader historical change is as a narrative of shared possibility.

In Marguerite's case, her insistence on her narrow escape, and the fate that she later saw had befallen others, is evidence of her preoccupation with what might have been. When describing the moment the bombs began to fall, she said:

> We were going to the metro, and were stopped by the bombs. Dad said, 'we can't go any further, we can't go back, we have to get into a house to shelter.' But all the [cellar] doors were locked, because the Germans didn't want to keep them open. But then one was open, we went straight in. I can't recall going down the steps – the explosion of the bomb – we fell into the cellar. Do you understand? We'd have been killed under the bombs if we'd gone back to the house. An incredible stroke of luck!

Blasted into the cellar by the force of the explosion, Marguerite felt her family had a very lucky escape. At several points in the narrative she returned to the locked doors; the fact that so many were locked, but that in the nick of time one was open is crucial to enhancing the tightness of her escape. Likewise, she insists upon the fact that they were not at home, that they had left early to catch the metro: had they stayed at home, 'we would have been under the ruins; we would have been killed there'. The repeated refrain – almost a lamentation – of the interview, repeated over and over, was her relived anxiety of what might have been. She recounted the sight that greeted her family as they emerged from their shelter: 'they were there on the pavements, they were everywhere, the poor people'; and again, 'those poor people, poor people who were killed in the street. Like that, on the pavement', and later becoming more explicit: 'those people who were killed outside, it was because they weren't in a shelter. Those poor people, they were killed.' Finally, the image acquires its explanatory power, and threads the story of possibilities together. The lucky trip to the metro, the acumen of her ex-serviceman father who understood the noises he heard, the final door being unlocked, and the explosion which catapulted her into the cellar: 'I tell you, those people that were found on the pavement, that could have been us.' Marguerite's story gives us a clear insight into the shared experience of bombing; its dominant image is not death, nor loss of a loved one. The shared experience of bombing was fear: 'No matter where you were, you were afraid,' said Marguerite.

Conclusion

In conclusion, it should be clear that one woman's narration of a moment in time – the Allied bombing of her town in April 1943 – is tied concretely to a much wider set of experiences that touch the individual, but also provide insight beyond. Alessandro Portelli has written that oral history brings out the 'historicity of personal experience and of the individual's role in the history of society and in public events': these points are clearly articulated within Marguerite's short narrative.[51] Her personal experience is part of a broader set of historical experiences of war, but also of social and industrial change within her town. She, by way of her family, is implicated in public events, just like the many other small fish, the individual actors, who ran from the bombs, who trembled in shelters, who emerged into the dust, who sat on the kerb-stone, head in hands. This was a shared experience of hundreds of thousands of French people during World War II, but also of British, Italian, German and Dutch, and of countless others before and since. What is fascinating in Marguerite's case is that the destruction of her family's business was so clearly linked to the boom of its local rival in the post-war era – for the Allied bombs that fell on Renault's factories did very little structural, lasting damage.[52]

In oral history, memory becomes not simply a source for the investigation of the past, but an object of study in its own right. The way that memories are narrated, connected to each other and to other events, the way that they differ in the telling depending on who tells and to whom, the way that they struggle against and absorb parts or wholes of collective or public memories, the way that their notions of chronology are bulging with inherent meaning are integral to how historians use them; these slippery aspects of memory are what make it hard to work with, but enormously satisfying, for the insights it can bring to understanding the past are profound. Oral history is a 'powerful tool' for research and analysis,[53] but must always be approached with caution: without understanding of the interaction between individual and collective memory, of the inter-subjective nature of the interview process, of the (re) construction of memory and narrative, using this kind of source could be dangerous, not just in terms of misinterpreted data, but because of the impact it has on the lives of the interviewees. Yet when conducted and used skilfully and with sensitivity, oral history has the power to create new knowledge that brings into focus the ripples that these small fish make in the bigger pond of history.

Notes

1 The interviews conducted for this research formed part of my doctoral thesis, 'Children under the Allied bombs, France 1940–45' (unpublished PhD thesis, University of Reading, 2011), which was funded, with thanks, by the Arts and Humanities Research Council as part of the project 'Bombing, States and Peoples in Western Europe, 1940–45'. See also L. Dodd and A. Knapp, '"How many Frenchmen did you kill?" Allied bombing policy towards France (1940–45)', *French History*, 22(4), 2008, pp. 469–92 and C. Baldoli and A. Knapp, *Forgotten Blitzes: France and Italy Under Allied Air Attack, 1940–1945* (London: Continuum, 2012).
2 Neither French children as historical agents nor the Allied bombing of France fit very neatly into the well-entrenched historical paradigm of the opposition between resistance and collaboration during World War II, which shapes, in one way or another, most public and academic narratives on the subject.

3 Marguerite, interview with Lindsey Dodd, Boulogne-Billancourt, 6 April 2009. All interviews recorded for my PhD are archived in the municipal archives of my three case-study towns, Boulogne-Billancourt, Brest and Lille.

4 J. Jackson, *France: The Dark Years* (Oxford: Oxford University Press, 2001), p. 169. Marguerite's husband got permission for a visit home just after the family business was bombed in 1943.

5 The district Billancourt was formally joined to the prosperous town of Boulogne-sur-Seine in 1926. The town of Boulogne-Billancourt sits in a large meander of the River Seine to the west of Paris, abutting the 16th *arrondissement* of the French capital.

6 N. Ambourg, F. Bédoussac, S. Couëtoux and B. Foucart (eds) *Boulogne-Billancourt: Ville d'art et d'histoire* (Paris: Éditions de la Patrimoine, 2009), pp. 13–22; A. Bezançon (with A. Gaye and G. Caillet), *Histoire de Boulogne-Billancourt* (Boulogne-Billancourt: Ville de Boulogne-Billancourt and Éditions Joël Cuénot, 1984), p. 51.

7 A. Thomson, *Moving Stories: An Intimate History of Four Women Across Two Countries* (Manchester: Manchester University Press, 2011), p. 308.

8 See A. Thomson, 'Four paradigm transformations in oral history', *Oral History Review*, 34(1), 2007, pp. 49–70.

9 A. Portelli, 'There's always gonna be a line: history-telling as a multi-vocal art', in *The Battle of the Valle Giulia: Oral History and the Art of Dialogue* (Madison, WI: University of Wisconsin Press, 1997), pp. 24–39.

10 A. Portelli, 'Oral history as genre', in *The Battle of the Valle Giulia*, p. 6.

11 T. Lummis, *Listening to History: The Authenticity of Oral Evidence* (London: Hutchinson, 1987), p. 129; I. Bertaux-Wiame, 'The life history approach to the study of internal migration', *Oral History Journal*, 7(1), 1979, p. 29.

12 Portelli, 'Oral history as genre', pp. 7–8.

13 See Thomson, 'Four paradigm transformations in oral history' for a synopsis of the criticism and a concise analysis, with copious references, of the scholarship on inter-subjectivity in interviews.

14 A. Portelli, '"The time of my life": functions of time in oral history', in *The Death of Luigi Trastulli and Other Stories* (Albany, NY: SUNY Press, 1991), p. 63.

15 D. Bertaux and P. Thompson (eds) *Pathways to Social Class* (Oxford: Clarendon Press, 1997), p. 12.

16 See A. Thomson, *Anzac Memories: Living with the Legend* (Oxford: Oxford University Press, 1994).

17 See, for example, A. Portelli, 'The death of Luigi Trastulli: memory and the event', in, *The Death of Luigi Trastulli and Other Stories*, pp. 1–28.

18 J.-F. Muracciole, 'Le bombardement stratégique en France durant la seconde guerre mondiale: premier bilan et pistes de recherche', in M. Battesti and P. Facon (eds) *Les bombardements alliés sur la France durant la seconde guerre mondiale: stratégies, bilans matériels et humains* (Vincennes: Cahiers du CEHD no.37, 2007), p. 174.

19 For the concept of three levels of memory, see Portelli, 'There's always gonna be a line', p. 27.

20 France was starved of food by the German occupation. Sauvy notes that people struggled to supplement inadequate rations by other means. Food became a national obsession, and the tendency of my interviewees to turn to food, hunger, ingenuity and black marketing was marked. A. Sauvy, *La vie économique des Français de 1939 à 1945* (Paris: Flammarion, 1978), pp. 110–32.

21 Sonia and Lucien, interview with Lindsey Dodd, 29 April 2009, Villeneuve-d'Ascq, France.

22 For example, the challenging conclusions of Angus Calder's important work *The Myth of the Blitz* (London: Pimlico, 1992) have not been universally embraced, so much do they damage the broadly and popularly held understanding of united, stoic, cheerful London in 1940–41.

23 Portelli, '"The time of my life"', p. 65.

24 D. James, *Doña Maria's Story: Life History, Memory and Political Identity* (London & Durham, NC: Duke University Press, 2000), p. 185.
25 A. Portelli, 'What makes oral history different', in R. Perks and A. Thomson (eds) *The Oral History Reader* (London & New York: Routledge, 1998), p. 70.
26 D. Polkinghorne, 'Narrative configuration in qualitative analysis', in J. A. Hatch and R. Wiesniewski (eds) *Life History and Narrative* (London: The Falmer Press, 1995), p. 7.
27 Thomson, *Moving Stories*, p. 300.
28 Thomson, *Anzac Memories*, pp. 9–10.
29 A. Portelli, 'Form and meaning of historical representation: the Battle of Evarts and the Battle of Crummies (Kentucky: 1931, 1941)', *The Battle of the Valle Giulia*, p. 101.
30 Lummis, *Listening to History*, p. 12.
31 See, for example, P. Thompson, *The Voice of the Past* (Oxford: Oxford University Press, 1978), ch. 1, for the genesis of oral history.
32 P. Chamberlayne, J. Bornat and T. Wengraf, *The Turn to Biographical Methods in Social Science: Comparative Issues and Examples* (London: Routledge, 2000).
33 M. Frisch, 'Oral history and *Hard Times*: a review essay', in Perks and Thomson, *The Oral History Reader*, p. 34.
34 V.R. Yow, *Recording Oral History* (Thousand Oaks, CA: Sage, 1994), p. 11.
35 D. Bertaux and I. Bertaux-Wiame, 'Life stories in the bakers' trade', in D. Bertaux (ed.) *Biography and Society: The Life History Approach in the Social Sciences* (Beverly Hills, CA: Sage, 1981), pp. 187–88.
36 Written accounts were used alongside interviews with 181 people, J. A. Hammerton and A. Thomson, *Ten Pound Poms* (Manchester: Manchester University Press, 2005), pp. 15–16, 359; Thomson, *Moving Stories*, p. 4.
37 Thomson, *Moving Stories*, p. 14.
38 B. Flyvbjerg, 'Five misunderstandings about case-study research', *Qualitative Inquiry*, 12(2), 2006, p. 219.
39 R.J. Grele, 'Movement without aim: methodological and theoretical problems in oral history' in Perks and Thomson, *The Oral History Reader*, p. 41.
40 A. Portelli, 'The best garbage man in town: life and times of Valtèro Peppoloni, worker', in Portelli, *The Death of Luigi Trastulli and Other Stories*, p. 137.
41 R. Samuel and P. Thompson (eds) *The Myths We Live By* (London: Routledge, 1990), p. 2.
42 K. Nelson, 'Self and social functions: individual autobiographical memory and collective narrative', *Memory*, 11(2), 2003, p. 125.
43 Portelli, 'Oral history as genre', p. 6.
44 Dodd, 'Children under the Allied bombs, France 1940–45', pp. 61–64.
45 I have retained his original capitalization as the emphasis is important.
46 Marguerite did not mention that she did any paid work; it is unclear where her income came from. Wives of prisoners of war received a small pension, and were sometimes assisted through charitable contributions. This lack of contextual information illustrates some of the shortcomings of the interview.
47 Renault's headquarters remain in Boulogne-Billancourt, although the main manufacturing plant closed in 1992.
48 On Renault's reasons for collaboration see, for example, A. Rhodes, *Louis Renault: A Biography* (London: Cassell, 1969), pp. 182–84.
49 A. Portelli, 'Philosophy and the facts: subjectivity and narrative form in autobiography and oral history', *The Battle of the Valle Giulia*, pp. 86–87.
50 Ibid., p. 88.
51 Portelli, 'Oral history as genre', p. 6.
52 Rhodes, *Louis Renault*, pp. 182–83; G. Hatry, 'Billancourt sous les bombes', *Bulletin de la section d'histoire des usines Renault*, 30(5), 1985, p. 249.
53 M. Frisch, *A Shared Authority: Essays on the Craft and Meaning of Oral and Public History* (Albany: SUNY Press, 1990), p. 188.

3 Memory, history and the law

Testimony and collective memory in Holocaust and Stolen Generations trials

Rosanne Kennedy

> Testimony is a crucial source for history. And it is more than a source. It poses special challenges to history.
>
> Dominick LaCapra[1]

Legal trials – including case materials, evidence, courtroom transcripts, and judicial opinions – have for decades provided rich source materials for historians, particularly cultural and legal historians. For instance, important contributions to the rise of the 'new history' in the 1980s – such as Natalie Zemon Davis' *The Return of Martin Guerre*[2] and Carlo Ginzburg's *Ecstasies*[3] – used ecclesiastical and law court records, either directly or indirectly, to reconstruct the lives of women, the working class and the rural poor, who were traditionally excluded from histories. Historical inquiry and judicial inquiry, however, are two very different things, and historians and judges approach questions of evidence and proof in very different ways.[4] The judge regards uncertainty negatively, whereas the historian sees it as an invitation 'to link the specific case to the context'.[5]

Scholars of memory have, in any case, only recently begun to analyse the law as a 'site of memory', whether in relation to personal memory (and how it is judged when it enters the courtroom as legal testimony), or for its role in the construction of collective memory.[6] A good deal of this work is concerned with analysing how legal and quasi-legal institutions – trials, international military tribunals and criminal courts, and truth and reconciliation commissions – have responded to and adjudicated the mass atrocities and genocides of the twentieth century. Events that involve extreme violence are often characterized by a 'crisis of truth'.[7] Testimony is called for when 'the facts upon which justice must pronounce its verdict are not clear, when historical accuracy is in doubt and when both the truth and its supporting elements of evidence are called into question'.[8] Yet, in many cases, testimony – particularly survivor testimony – does not resolve disputed facts but instead reveals the complex legacies of violent events on memory in the present. As a public forum, legal trials throw into relief the conceptual and ethical issues surrounding survivor testimony, which is simultaneously subjected to the juridical demands of proof, the ethical demands of bearing witness, and the vicissitudes of personal and collective memory. Identifying some of the methodological, conceptual and ethical issues that emerge in the fields of history, law and memory in relation to survivor testimony – the memory of trauma – is my focus in this chapter.

Historian Dominick LaCapra speculates that the surge of interest in memory stems in part from the belated effects of traumatic experiences, and their implications for memory and identity, especially for the survivor.[9] As a form of witnessing grounded in personal memory of atrocities and violence, survivor testimony 'has emerged as a privileged mode of access to the past and its traumatic occurrences'.[10] Traumatic and violent experiences are often characterized by denial, forgetting, and psychic and social blocking, which manifests in a delay in the emergence of personal and collective memory of events.[11] This delay has meant, in practice, that trials and truth commissions often take place decades after the events in question, as in the cases of the Holocaust, apartheid, and historical injustices arising from colonialism. Consequently, many survivors give testimony about their experiences long after they occurred, which casts doubt on the reliability of memory as a source of historical truth. Moreover, traumatic events may produce memories that are fragmented and non-linear, subverting the expectation that the witness should be able to give a coherent account of events. Or testimonies may be laden with pathos and produce affective and embodied responses in the audience – sobbing, shock, anxiety.

While judges and many historians may be troubled by these features of traumatic memory, literary and cultural critics, as well as some historians, value survivor testimony for its affective power, its subjective insight into events, and its ability to transmit memory to the public and to later generations. In the early 1990s, psychoanalytic literary critic Shoshana Felman and the late psychoanalyst Dori Laub pioneered a new understanding of testimony, which has found particular purchase in Holocaust studies. Reflecting on the effects of trauma on testimony, they rejected the common legal assumption that testimony should be evaluated in terms of its accuracy as a description of reality or narrative account of a past event. Instead, they proposed that 'one does not have to possess or own the truth, in order to effectively bear witness to it … the speaking subject constantly bears witness to a truth that nonetheless continues to escape him, a truth that is, essentially, not available to its own speaker'.[12] In this view, testimony is not a *re-presentation* of knowledge; it is a *process* through which knowledge – often not consciously known to its own speaker – is discovered. This understanding of testimony has extended the range of speech acts, bodily gestures and texts that are now read as instances of testimony and witnessing, but it has also revealed that the relationship between testimony and historical event is neither direct nor transparent.

To illuminate the ways in which scholars have used and analysed testimony inside and outside of the courtroom, as a source for studying history and collective memory, I take a comparative approach. Specifically, I compare survivor testimony, as it is framed and evaluated in selected Holocaust trials, with the framing of Stolen Generations testimonies in both a human rights inquiry and a legal trial. The rich body of scholarship on Holocaust trials offers an excellent case study for examining how historians and memory scholars have used legal trials and testimony as source materials. While Holocaust trials have received considerable attention from scholars of cosmopolitan memory, legal responses to contested histories and injustices resulting from colonialism have received less attention beyond national borders. In the final part, I aim to contribute to this emerging field through analysis of Stolen Generations testimony in the Human Rights and Equal Opportunity Commission report, *Bringing Them Home*,[13] and in a legal case, *Cubillo v Commonwealth* (2000).

The Nuremberg and Eichmann trials: between history and memory

The crimes of the Holocaust presented an enormous challenge to the law. Neither normative criminal law, grounded in principles of national sovereignty, nor existing humanitarian law, which was developed in the late 1800s to regulate the treatment of civilians in war, was equipped to respond to the magnitude and brutality of the crimes perpetrated by the Nazis, especially against European Jewry. Adjudicating crimes of the Holocaust required a good deal of imagination and innovation on the part of the prosecutors and the court.[14] As Lawrence Douglas observes, 'the law has struggled to locate an idiom adequate to the task of representing and judging traumatic history – events so disruptive to structures of collective cultural and social meaning that they resist being assimilated into conventional vernaculars of memory and understanding'.[15] The court faced problems of representation, belief and proof: what evidence could be adduced as proof of crimes that defied ordinary understandings of criminality and were widely disbelieved, without shocking or repulsing the audience?[16] Two war crimes trials are today iconic for their contributions to law, history and memory – the Nuremberg trials, held in Germany in 1945–46, and the Eichmann trial, held in Israel in 1961. Both are regarded as 'show trials', which were undertaken not only to render justice, but also for didactic historical and pedagogic purposes. For my examination of the use of legal sources, it is significant that the lead prosecutors in these trials deployed contrasting evidential and representational paradigms – documentary versus testimonial – with differing implications for history and memory.[17]

The Nuremberg trials, conducted by the four victorious Allied nations, are sometimes considered an exercise in 'victor's justice'.[18] In the first trial, which did not focus on Jews as a targeted group, 13 of the top leaders in the Nazi party were charged on 13 counts, including war crimes and waging an aggressive war. Robert Jackson, the US prosecutor at Nuremberg, chose to base the case against the defendants 'on documents of their own making'[19] and avoided witnesses because they 'would always be chargeable with bias, faulty recollection and even perjury'.[20] As a result of Jackson's documentary approach, the team working for the Allied prosecutors collected and organized a mass of documentary and oral evidence, which provided 'a paramount historical source'[21] for later historians of the Holocaust. Although the Nuremberg trials were groundbreaking in their contributions to international human rights law, particularly in using the novel concepts of 'genocide' and 'crimes against humanity', they were not successful in conveying a memory of the atrocities to the public, and therefore did not contribute significantly to collective memory.[22]

The Eichmann trial is widely regarded as a landmark event in the collective memory of the Holocaust, which has shaped understandings of it both in Israel and globally. Eichmann, a bureaucrat in the Nazi administration before and during WWII, was responsible for implementing Nazi policy towards Jewish people in Germany and in 16 occupied territories. He oversaw the mass deportation, murder and brutal treatment of tens of thousands of European Jews. The Prime Minister of Israel, David Ben-Gurion, regarded the trial as an opportunity to publicize the atrocities the Nazis had inflicted on the Jewish people in a 'specific and unparalleled act',[23] which aimed for 'the complete extermination of the Jewish people'.[24] He regarded it as 'the duty of the State of Israel, the only sovereign authority in Jewry, to see that the whole of this story, in all its horror, is fully exposed'.[25] In focusing on crimes against the Jewish people, this trial would differ from the Nuremberg trials, which foregrounded Germany's aggressive acts of war. Acting on Ben-Gurion's vision, the attorney general and lead prosecutor, Gideon Hausner, approached the Eichmann trial as a 'history lesson' – an opportunity to explain to young Israelis, who had grown up in a militarized culture, and to the world, why European Jews did not anticipate and resist the Nazi regime more forcefully. Recognizing that the Nuremberg trials 'had failed to transmit, or to impress on human memory ... the knowledge and the shock of what had happened',[26] he decided to showcase survivor testimony. Hausner's important innovation, which Douglas refers to as his 'radical theory of the trial',[27] was to reverse standard legal priorities: 'instead of the testimony serving as a means of proving the state's case, Hausner asks one to imagine the trial itself as a means of offering public testimonial ... '.[28] To bypass the problem of unreliability, Hausner chose witnesses who had documented their testimonies earlier, on the belief that 'their memories could more easily be refreshed by their writings'.[29]

The Eichmann trial has been both a touchstone and a subject of controversy for decades. Most famously, Hannah Arendt, in her report on the trial, *Eichmann in Jerusalem*, objected to the place granted to survivor testimony, much of which did not relate directly to charges against Eichmann, and in any case, exceeded what was needed to convict him. She regarded the Eichmann trial as a struggle between two competing forces – justice, which should be impartial and apolitical; and the state of Israel, which used the trial for nation-building.[30] Some critics have sided with Arendt's formalist approach, which views the sole purpose of the criminal trial as rendering justice to the defendant; others have argued that it is legitimate for a trial, especially one involving mass atrocity, to have multiple aims, including shaping collective memory and educating the public.[31] Their analyses illuminate how scholars from different fields use legal materials as a source for history and memory, and why the court-room may be considered to be 'the quintessential lieu de mémoire today'.[32] But their analyses support differing and often competing conclusions about the place of law, and the value of testimony, in history and memory.[33]

Legitimating the witness: survivor testimony in the Eichmann trial

Lawrence Douglas studied several Holocaust trials, including the Eichmann trial, to examine the challenges law faced in adjudicating unprecedented crimes of extreme violence and horror.[34] His nuanced analysis of the presentation of testimony, and the legal and ethical tensions that emerged between the pro-secutor, the defence and the court over managing it, provides an exemplary case study. The Eichmann trial, he argues, was characterized by a struggle over the purpose and presentation of survivor testimony. This struggle went to the heart of competing versions of the trial: the prosecutor viewed the trial as a forum for bearing witness, while the court was concerned with preserving its legitimacy. Rather than following the conventional, tightly structured ques-tion-and-answer format of legal examination, Hausner allowed witnesses to deliver their testimony in narrative form. The testimony of Ada Lichtman, the first survivor called to the stand, revealed the affective power of narrative testimony. Two features of her presentation had striking effects on the audi-ence: firstly, she gave her testimony in Yiddish rather than Hebrew, and 'suddenly, the language of the exterminated Jewish population of Europe filled the courtroom'.[35] The acoustic impact of her testimony reached far beyond the courtroom, since the trial was broadcast live on radio in Israel, and on television in other countries. Secondly, she wore sunglasses while testifying, which created the impression that she was blind, contrasting sharply with her words: 'I saw everything.'[36] The unintended irony produced by the juxtaposition of 'having seen everything' and the refusal to see clearly, or to be seen, reveals 'a truth that is, essentially, not available to its own speaker'[37] – that the horror of what she had seen had led her to choose blindness.

Scholars who use survivor testimony as a source must be sensitive both to its figurative and rhetorical shaping, and its affective dimensions.[38] Significantly, Douglas analyses the presentation of the testimonies not simply in terms of their content, but for their impact on the audience – how did this 'history lesson' affect the citizens of the new state of Israel, and what impact did it have in shaping national identity and national memory? Many in the audience were survivors, and are captured in photographs 'overcome with emotion: sob-bing in anguish, staring in wide-eyed horror, collapsing altogether'.[39] 'The value of testimony [was] not simply as evidence of crimes,'[40] argues Douglas. Rather, 'the expressions of horror etched in the faces of spectators in photo-graphs of the trial must be understood in terms of a more complex shock of recognition ... The faces of the spectators ... express the horror and release one feels when one's deepest and most traumatic memories find public expression. A horrific and silenced past had intruded upon the present.'[41] Through the legal process of giving and listening to testimony, the traumatic past was reactivated in the present space of the courtroom, and the witness and spectators relived, with intense affect, past experiences, thereby collapsing the distance between past and present. This 'shock of recognition' was significant in bringing Holocaust survivors, who had been marginalized in Israeli society, into the forefront of national consciousness, and making the Holocaust central to national identity and remembrance in Israel.[42]

Hausner gave survivors ample scope to transmit their memories to the public, but his approach caused tensions both with the defence counsel and the court. These tensions emerged early in the trial, in response to the testimony of Leon Wells, a respected engineer who had published a book on his experiences during the Holocaust. His narrative, delivered in terse, unadorned language, exposed the tension he felt between wishing for his own death and the imperative to survive to bear witness to the suffering of others.[43] Indeed, much of the testimony that was presented at the Eichmann trial demonstrated the physical and emotional affect generated by the memory of horrific events on the survivors, who by their own embodied reactions verified the 'truth' of the testimonies. The defence counsel, Robert Servatius, acknowledged that testimony is useful in a historical process, but he argued that 'a courtroom is … probably the least appropriate place for the research of historical truth'.[44] He sought to focus the court narrowly on the issue of the responsibility of the defendant rather than on the crimes perpetrated by the Nazi regime, and argued that testimony had to relate to the accused's conduct.[45] In contrast, Hausner's approach relied on the conventional principle of complicity, in which every Nazi participant was deemed to have contributed to the outcome. This broad approach allowed him to include testimony such as Wells', and achieve his objectives in recovering a silenced history and in communicating a collective memory of the Holocaust.[46]

The court, like Servatius, became impatient with Hausner's approach: it was time-consuming, and the testimonies were not sufficiently linked to the charges against the defendant, which risked the court's legitimacy.[47] The competition between two understandings of the trial – as a forum for survivors to bear witness to their suffering, and as a process of proof directly linked to arriving at a just verdict – put the court in an awkward position.[48] Perhaps the most spectacular, and, for the court, challenging, moment in the presentation of testimony was the incident in which one of the witnesses, Yehiel Dinoor, a writer who had gone by the pseudonym K-Zetnik – a slang term for concentration camp inmates – collapsed in court. Douglas argues that his collapse, and the repeated screening of the scene on television, 'serves as a noteworthy example of the power of trials not simply to shape collective memory but to serve as sites of memory, placeholders invested with fraught and liminal traces of the past'.[49] The meaning of Dinoor's collapse, however, is ambiguous, which enables critics to project different meanings onto it.[50] Despite these tensions, Hausner used the legal process of proof and the theatrical space of the courtroom to transform survivor testimony into 'heroic memory',[51] which in turn contributed to nation-building and national identity. It is the policing of the conceptual limit – between the legal understanding of testimony as evidence and the moral understanding of bearing witness – that preoccupied the Eichmann court. In many ways, then, the Eichmann trial was successful in creating a legacy in collective memory precisely because it exceeded the limits of legal formalism.[52]

In its final judgment, however, the court implicitly rejected Hausner's use of the trial as a forum for survivors to bear witness publicly, insisting that testimony was 'to be regarded as by-products of the trial'[53] and not a justification for it. The court suggested that literary forms are more able to represent and comprehend the Holocaust.[54] Indeed, the Eichmann trial would appear to have its most enduring legacy in art rather than law. Many critics regard Claude Lanzmann's nine-hour film, *Shoah*,[55] composed entirely of interviews with survivors, bystanders and perpetrators, as the artistic sequel to the Eichmann trial: indeed, some of the witnesses who testified in the trial were also interviewed by Lanzmann. Felman contends that both Arendt's trial report and *Shoah* 'added *a new idiom*'[56] to the discourse of the Holocaust – witness testimony.[57] This idiom, she argues, provided a 'collective framework of perception' and a 'vocabulary of collective memory',[58] which 'modif[ies] our *vocabularies of remembrance*'.[59] In privileging survivor testimony, the Eichmann trial anticipated the testimonial idiom of *Shoah*, which abandons the representational logic of most documentaries by avoiding the use of archival footage.

'But does one learn history?': testimony between history and memory

Traditionally, like the judge, the historian has been sceptical of oral testimony: it relies on personal memory, which is considered too subjective and vulnerable to the passages of time and the influences of culture, and it is laden with emotion, threatening law's critical distance. Annette Wieviorka, a French historian, succinctly presents the case against writing history based on an uncritical acceptance of the 'truth' of survivor testimony; rather, she wants us to historicize testimony, to study how the figure of the witness has become authoritative in contemporary society.[60] The Eichmann trial, she argues, played a pivotal role in legitimating testimony as a form of 'truth telling' about the past. Victim testimony acquired an 'extraordinary force' due to the judicial setting, which 'lent it all the weight of the state's legitimacy and institutions and symbolic power'.[61] The trial created a new socially recognized identity for survivors, and gave them a ' … new function: to be the bearer of history'.[62] This development, she argues, has had a negative impact on the writing of history: as a result of the demand for survivor testimony, 'the genocide came to be defined as a succession of individual experiences with which the public was supposed to identify'.[63] Identification does not, however, provide a strong foundation for writing history, as demonstrated in Daniel Goldhagen's controversial book, *Hitler's Willing Executioners*.[64] With its foregrounding of 'horror stories',[65] this work uncannily reproduces the methods used by Hausner. For both Hausner and Goldhagen, feeling is a substitute for analysis and explanation. Moreover, Goldhagen blurs the line between history and law, by adopting the tone of prosecutor and judging the past, rather than explaining it.[66]

Wieviorka contends that testimony is valuable for telling us about psychological responses but not for writing history because it focuses on the present not the past. Discussing testimonies by Jewish children who were hidden during the war and have only recently begun to tell their stories, she questions their historical value:

> Reading or hearing the voices of these 'hidden children', one learns much about childhood and about humanity, about the violence inflicted by certain traumas in their irreparable character. But does one learn history? The repercussions of an event inform us about the power of that event but do not account for what the event was.[67]

These reflections resonate with Peter Novick's discussion of the differences between collective memory and history. He argues that collective memory works selectively; it is a form of myth-making that is shaped by the needs of groups, and the formation of group identity, in the present.[68] By contrast, historical consciousness is concerned with 'the *historicity* of events' and recognizes 'that they took place then and not now'.[69] A historical approach recognizes the complexity of past events and the moral ambiguity of the intentions and actions of protagonists, whereas memory simplifies, and reduces complexity to overarching archetypes. The decision either to privilege the past by reconstructing 'what the event was' for the society in which it occurred, or to examine the effects of past events in the present, is one of the fault lines between historians and memory scholars today. The line between history and memory is not always distinct, however, and some historians advocate that it is crucial not only to study the history of collective memory, but to bring memory and witness testimony into the writing of history, to challenge the engrained protocols of the disciplines.

In contrast to historians who are wary of testimony, Felman, regards the Eichmann trial as a landmark in the collective memory of the Holocaust because it enabled the transmission of traumatic memory from the private realm of the survivor to the public sphere of national and global memory; the trial granted 'authority to trauma' through 'a legal process of translation of thousands of private, secret traumas into one collective, public, and communally acknowledged one'.[70] It brought into the public sphere the unspeakable dimensions of memory, and the intense effect of the memory of horror, conveyed through bodily gestures, silences and gaps in speech. Furthermore, drawing on the work of Friedrich Nietzsche, she argues that the 'monumental significance'[71] of the trial was to recover the victim as an agent of history. Observing that Jewish victims were 'subhuman' in the language of the Nazis, she argues that the process of testifying in court enacted a 'revolutionary transformation of the victim' from 'mute bearers of a traumatizing history' to 'speaking subjects' in 'a legal act of authorship'.[72] In her view, this was 'the trial's major contribution not only to Jews but to history, to law, to culture – to humanity at large'.[73] It is precisely this survivor-centred vision of history that Wieviorka criticized. Felman writes not as a professional historian however, but as a psychoanalytic literary critic: her concerns thus differ from those of the historian. She is more interested in the transmission of memory, and in the relationship between law and art – represented by the Eichmann trial and *Shoah* – than in a historical reconstruction of the events.

The split between historians and memory scholars is not, however, as totalizing as the positions of Wieviorka and Felman would suggest. While some historians believe that 'feeling' leads to the abandonment of critical thinking, others argue that an affective entanglement can enhance critical reflection. James Young, for instance, is troubled by the near-blanket exclusion of the survivor's voice from normative histories of the Holocaust.[74] This exclusion, he suggests, results from 'the somewhat forced distinction historians have maintained between memory and history: history as that which happened, memory as that which is remembered of what happened'.[75] Like Wieviorka, he acknowledges that the processes involved in writing history and moulding memory are perceived to be incompatible; the former requires distance and dispassion, whereas the latter stems from personal involvement and incites emotional intensity. He contends that the 'deep memory' of survivors – the embodied, sensory memory and its incompatibility with historical narrative – constitutes one of the central challenges to Holocaust historiography. Although deep memory can be conveyed indirectly, through the kinds of testimonial performances we see, for instance, in the Eichmann trial and in *Shoah*, Young contends that it is 'essentially unrepresentable'.[76] He regards the work of Saul Friedlander, a child survivor and historian, as a productive attempt to bridge the gap between history and memory by inserting the survivor's voice into Holocaust historiography. Dominick LaCapra argues that survivor testimony can challenge the historian to become aware of his or her own position in historiography. He has developed the widely used concept of 'empathic unsettlement'[77] to suggest how the historian may be open to the unsettling dimensions of survivor testimony, while being wary of the lures of identification, and continuing to recognize the difference between one's own position and that of the survivor.

Stolen Generations: the testimonial paradigm in human rights and law

The latitude given to survivors in the Eichmann trial to testify at length, outside the usual interrogative format, was something of a legal aberration. Typically, testimony in legal trials is subjected to harsh cross-examination, and skilful lawyers can undermine the authority of even the most experienced witness.[78] But as Wieviorka observes, 'the functions assigned to testimony at the Eichmann trial ... persist to this day',[79] even if today the functions of testimony – including bearing witness to violence or injustice in a public forum – are more likely to be carried out in truth and reconciliation commissions, transitional justice forums, and human rights investigations, designed to hear testimony about injustice and violence in a non-adversarial context.[80]

In Australia, the late 1990s was marked by a long overdue reckoning with the post-colonial legacy of what has become known as the 'Stolen Generations'.[81] In 1996, the Human Rights and Equal Opportunity Commission conducted a landmark national inquiry into the policies, practices and effects of removing children of mixed Aboriginal and Torres Strait Islander and Caucasian descent from their families and communities. In 1997, the Commission published its powerful report, *Bringing Them Home*. It asked Australians to listen to the testimonies with 'open hearts and minds'.[82] In addressing Australians in moral and affective terms, the report drew on a discourse of ethical witnessing, thereby positioning members of the 'Stolen Generations' as victims who deserve our empathy. These intimate testimonies of family destruction are widely believed to have generated an empathic response from non-indigenous Australians, who could readily identify with the grief of having their children taken.

The national inquiry brought together two paradigms – legal and testimonial – that emerged in the wake of WWII and the Holocaust. Despite using legal concepts such as 'genocide' and 'crimes against humanity', the inquiry was neither a truth commission nor a legal trial. Consequently, none of the evidence presented was subjected to a legal standard of proof. Thus, the issue of the fallibility of personal memory, which in a legal trial would be particularly significant since many survivors were recalling events that occurred decades earlier, was sidelined. Yet the inquiry shared with the Eichmann trial the aim of enabling victims – in this case of child removal – to tell their stories and to bring into the public sphere the suffering and grief that resulted from policies formulated by state and federal governments, and carried out both by government and church officials. These testimonies would also contribute to creating a new collective memory of the effects of European settlement on indigenous peoples in Australia, with the additional aim of contributing to the healing of individuals and the healing of the nation by enabling people to tell their stories publicly. Human rights commissioners listened with 'open hearts and minds'[83] – exemplifying Dori Laub's psychoanalytic insight that listening attentively can aid healing.[84]

The memory work around the Stolen Generations issue also pervaded the courtroom. In 1996, two plaintiffs from the Northern Territory, Lorna Cubillo and Peter Gunner, brought a test case for the Stolen Generations against the Commonwealth of Australia in the Federal Court. A high-profile trial, *Cubillo v. Commonwealth of Australia* presented the court with the opportunity to pass judgment on the historic policy of child removal and compulsory assimilation.[85] The community saw the case as determining whether members of the Stolen Generations could expect justice from the Australian legal system. Counsel for the applicants summarized the charge:

> By the actions of the Commonwealth, Lorna Cubillo and Peter Gunner were removed as young children from their families and communities. They were taken hundreds of kilometres from the countries of their birth ... They were made to live among strangers, in a strange place, in institutions which bore no resemblance to a home. They lost ... the chance to grow among the warmth of their own people, speaking their people's languages and learning about their country. They suffered lasting psychiatric injury ... Decades later, the Commonwealth of Australia says in this case that it did them no wrong at all.[86]

Cubillo, Gunner, and their legal team faced the challenge of translating their pain, suffering and loss into recognizable legal claims. As Justice O'Laughlin noted, 'a matter of social conscience' does not necessarily translate into 'a legal course of action'.[87] Identifying an actionable legal claim was particularly difficult because, in the so-called 'first Stolen Generations case' – *Krueger & Ors v. Commonwealth of Australia ('Krueger')*[88] – the High Court of Australia upheld the constitutionality of the Northern Territory's Aboriginal Ordinance (1918) ('the Ordinance'),[89] which authorized the removals of Cubillo and Gunner. The Ordinance appointed the Director of Native Affairs the legal guardian of all Aboriginal children, including children of mixed descent, regardless of whether they had a living parent. The Ordinance also granted the Director, or those acting on his behalf, the discretionary power to remove a child from its mother, where he deemed removal to be 'in the best interest of the child'; the mother's consent was not required. In *Krueger*, the High Court rejected the applicants' claim that the Ordinance authorized genocide by permitting the transfer of children of a racial group to another group with the intent of destroying the culture. All justices concurred that the Ordinance lacked genocidal intent; it was not 'punitive legislation' but was designed to benefit the children. Thus, *Krueger* blocked further cases on the grounds that removals of mixed descent children were either unconstitutional or genocidal.

Cubillo and Gunner did not challenge the legality of their removals. Instead, they claimed that the Director of Native Affairs, or those acting on his behalf, did not exercise the powers of guardianship in their best interests. They sued the Commonwealth for wrongful imprisonment; and for breaches of statutory duty, fiduciary duty and a duty of care. They sought damages arising from mental and emotional distress and post-traumatic stress, loss of cultural, spiritual and social life, and loss of entitlements under the Aboriginal Land Rights (Northern Territory) Act 1976 (Cth). Cubillo sought exemplary and aggravated damages for the Commonwealth's 'wanton, cruel and reckless indifference to her welfare and rights' and for causing 'substantial humiliation, distress and injury to her feelings'.[90] The cases were tried together before Justice O'Laughlin over three months in 1998. By then, the issue of the Stolen Generations had achieved significant visibility, and the findings of the national inquiry were fresh in the minds of the public. In an opinion of several hundred pages, Justice O'Laughlin found in favour of the Commonwealth.[91]

One of the achievements of *Bringing Them Home* was to bring into visibility the systemic nature of child removal and to recognize it as a collective injury. O'Laughlin mentioned the report specifically to let the public know the court was aware of these matters.[92] He resolutely refused, however, any notion of the case as representative of the Stolen Generations. 'The trial', he stated, 'is ... limited to the personal histories of Lorna Cubillo and Peter Gunner'.[93] By narrowing the focus to the two cases, he rejected the framing of child removal as a collective injury. Citing the judgment in *Nulyarimma v. Thompson*,[94] another case involving indigenous litigants, O'Laughlin sought to dampen expectations that the trial would make reparations for the past: 'It is not within the Court's power, nor is it its function or role, to set right all of the wrongs of the past ... '[95] He rejected the claim that child removal was systemic, finding no evidence of a 'blanket policy' of removal in the cases of Cubillo and Gunner. The absence of 'crucial witnesses' and 'documentary records' made it impossible for him to determine precisely why Cubillo had been removed.[96] Nonetheless, he found that her removal broadly accorded with the policy operating at the time, which was to remove illegitimate children of white fathers. He speculated that since her biological mother had died, Lorna might have appeared to outsiders unfamiliar with Aboriginal kinship networks to be an orphan.

O'Laughlin's approach to testimony was, in many ways, diametrically opposed to that of the national inquiry. He distinguished the forensic process of the court from an empathic approach. 'The task of the Court,' he asserted, 'is to examine the evidence – both oral and documentary – in a clinical manner, devoid of emotion.'[97] 'Where evidence has a logical probative value, a judge will rely on it; where it contains discrepancies, displays inadequacies, is tainted or otherwise lacks probative force, the judge will, in all probability, reject it ... '[98] The belated nature of the case raised concerns about the fallibility of memory, particularly regarding memory of events from early childhood. O'Laughlin repeatedly questioned and rejected sections of Cubillo's testimony, which did not always conform to the court's expectations of consistency and rationality. While he did not believe she was 'deliberately untruthful' he expressed concern about her 'ability to recall, accurately, events that occurred so many years ago', when she was a small child.[99] One example that particularly troubled him was her testimony about an alleged experience dating from her early childhood at Banka Banka, a station some 25 miles from Philip Creek. She testified that she was with her grandmother when two patrol officers stopped her, and washed her leg. One then identified her to the other as a 'half-caste'. She claims that the officers, whom she named, took her from her grandmother to another depot. This testimony was not material to the case, since the trial concerned her removal from Philip Creek four years later. O'Laughlin, however, doubted its veracity, and questioned how she – a four-year-old who spoke little English – could understand or remember the word 'half-caste'.[100] The opposing counsel questioned Cubillo's psychiatrist about what a four-year-old would remember; he agreed she would be unlikely to remember the details of such an incident. O'Laughlin described this testimony as 'subconscious reconstruction'.[101] Cubillo and Gunner, he speculated, had on numerous occasions 'unconsciously engaged in exercises of reconstruction, based, not on what they knew at the time, but on what they have convinced themselves must have happened or what others may have told them'.[102] Ironically, although Cubillo and Gunner had been removed and institutionalized, and suffered as a result, the judicial methods for assessing their testimony effectively put them, rather than the Commonwealth, on trial.

Cubillo reveals a clash between two conflicting approaches to testimony. In advocacy contexts such as the national inquiry, oral history and testimonial archives projects, testimony is valued for the subjective insights its reveals into a person's experience of an event, regardless of whether the testimony is factually correct in every detail. In the courtroom, however, testimony is judged and valued in terms of factual veracity. In the courtroom, Cubillo's testimony was questioned under cross-examination. She may have felt that the constant questioning of her interpretation of events silenced her before the law. For instance, she testified that at Retta Dixon she was 'flogged' for speaking her native language. In response to cross-examination, Cubillo reiterated testily: 'I was flogged, I was flogged, I know what happened to me … people like you removed me.'[103] In this exchange, Cubillo testifies that she was punished for speaking her language: in other words, she was silenced unless she conformed to Western cultural norms by speaking English. In the courtroom, when she asserts 'I know what happened to me',[104] she is attempting to force the court to hear her on her own terms. This is the crux of the matter – that her experience is being questioned and judged by the same colonialist regime that deemed it acceptable to remove her in the first place. To be heard, she has to conform to the expectations of the court, just as when she was a child. When she and the other children were removed from Philip Creek, the wailing of the children, their mothers and the community was not 'heard' by authorities. Felman argues that when a court confronts trauma, 'it is often inflicted with a particular judicial blindness that unwittingly reflects and duplicates the constitutional blindness of culture and of consciousness toward the trauma. A pattern emerges in which the trial, which tries to put an end to trauma, inadvertently performs an acting out of it.'[105] When O'Laughlin interprets Cubillo's testimony as 'subconscious reconstruction', and claims that she is prone to 'magnifying' events and allowing her unhappy memories to distort her testimony, he rejects her accounts of her experience for failing to conform with legal expectations.[106] For Cubillo, the legal methods of questioning, cross-examining and rejecting parts of her testimony may have constituted a repetition rather than a resolution of the original trauma of removal. This interpretation is suggested by her own words in court: 'I feel defeated'.[107] And to the extent that this case has entered collective memory, it is remembered as a rejection of the Stolen Generations narrative. In refusing to acknowledge the collective dimension of the case, the court refused to acknowledge and hear the historic issues of injustice and trauma that the case raised.

Conclusion

Partly as a result of its prominence in Holocaust memory, testimony has today become a transnational cultural form, which is used widely in truth and reconciliation commissions, in human rights campaigns, in documentary film, in museums, and in online digital testimony projects, as well as in the courtroom. As such, the study of testimony provides a vast array of sources for the scholar of history and memory. As the trials I have discussed above indicate, testimony does not necessarily help to resolve the crisis of truth, because memory is not particularly reliable as evidence for empirical facts. But testimony has an affective charge, both on the witness and on the audience, and is valuable for revealing the way that past events live on in the memories of individuals in the present. Testimony provides insights into the psychological or emotional state of the witness, and may bring out aspects of events that escape the medium of the written document. Given the place of individual testimony in producing historical truths and collective memories, Wieviorka urges scholars to examine 'the conditions under which testimonies have been produced and how these conditions have changed over time' and 'the role of testimonies in the construction of history and collective memory'.[108] She proposes, for instance, that one could study the ways in which the testimonies of witnesses in the Eichmann trial 'have migrated from their first forms, in books or in depositions preserved in various archives to their current forms'.[109] Studying the historicity of testimony – the ways in which it is legitimated or not, in differing national contexts, genres, institutional sites and the like – is crucial for assessing the contribution of testimony to the construction of collective memory, especially about contested or unfinished events. In an era of the witness, in which testimony is used widely in human rights campaigns not only by victims of abuses, but by their advocates, a history of the witness will provide crucial insight into the construction of memory and the legitimation of 'truths'. It would also enable scholars to track how testimony is used in national contexts, how it is reframed as it travels from embedded geographical locations to cosmopolitan spaces, and how it is mobilized in differing contexts, ranging from truth commissions, to documentary films to activist campaigns. A powerful legacy of the Holocaust has been to legitimate and give voice to the survivor, but it is crucial that we also remember the difficult lessons the Holocaust has had to teach about the moral complexities of witnessing and the opacity of testimony.

Notes

1 D. LaCapra, *History and Memory after Auschwitz* (Ithaca, New York: Cornell University Press, 1998), p. 11.
2 N. Zemon Davis, *The Return of Martin Guerre* (Cambridge, MA: Harvard University Press, 1983).
3 C. Ginzburg, *Ecstasies: Deciphering the Witches' Sabbath*, trans. R. Rosenthal, ed. G. Elliot (London: Hutchinson Radius, 1990).
4 C. Ginzburg, *Threads and Traces: True, False, Fictive*, trans. A.C. Tedeschi and J. Tedeschi (Berkeley, CA: University of California Press, 2012), p. 52.
5 Ibid., p. 57.
6 For a recent survey of work on law and memory, see A. Gross, 'The constitution of history and memory' in A. Sarat, M. Anderson and C.O. Frank (eds) *Law and the Humanities: An Introduction* (Cambridge & New York: Cambridge University Press, 2010). See also A. Sarat and T. Kearns (eds) *History, Memory and the Law* (Ann Arbor: University of Michigan Press, 2002).
7 S. Felman and D. Laub, *Testimony: Crises of Witnessing in Literature, Psychoanalysis, and History* (New York: Routledge, 1992), p. 6.
8 Ibid.
9 LaCapra, *History and Memory after Auschwitz*, pp. 10–11.
10 Ibid., p. 11.
11 C. Caruth, 'Introduction', *American Imago*, 48(1), 1991, p. 3.
12 Felman and Laub, *Testimony*, p. 15.
13 *Bringing Them Home: Report of the National Inquiry into the Separation of Aboriginal and Torres Strait Islander Children from their Families* (Sydney: Human Rights and Equal Opportunity Commission, 1997).
14 See G. Simpson, *Law, War and Crime: War Crimes Trials and the Reinvention of International Law* (Cambridge: Polity Press, 2007); I. Buruma, *The Wages of Guilt: Memories of War in Germany and Japan* (New York: Meridian, 1994); D. Hirsch, *Law Against Genocide: Cosmopolitan Trials* (London: GlassHouse, 2003).
15 L. Douglas, *The Memory of Judgment – Making Law and History in the Trials of the Holocaust* (New Haven: Yale University Press, 2001), p. 5.
16 Ibid., p. 257.
17 In both the Nuremberg and the Eichmann trials, the rule prohibiting hearsay evidence was relaxed so that survivors could testify. Douglas, *The Memory of Judgment*.
18 For an overview, see M.R. Marrus, *The Nuremberg War Crimes Trial, 1945–46: A Documentary History* (Boston: Bedford Books, 1997).
19 Robert Jackson as cited in S. Felman, *The Juridical Unconscious: Trials and Traumas in the Twentieth Century* (Cambridge, MA: Harvard University Press, 2002), p. 133.
20 Robert Jackson as cited in Felman, *The Juridical Unconscious*, p. 132.
21 D. Bloxham, *Genocide on Trial: War Crimes Trials and the Formation of Holocaust History and Memory* (New York: Oxford University Press, 2001), pp. 4–5.
22 Ibid., p. 5.
23 Cited in Felman, *The Juridical Unconscious*, p. 113.
24 Ibid.
25 Ibid.
26 Ibid., p. 133.
27 Douglas, *The Memory of Judgment*, p. 106.
28 Ibid.
29 A. Wieviorka, *The Era of the Witness*, trans. J. Stark (Ithaca, NY: Cornell University Press, 2006), p. 74.
30 Arendt covered the trial at the time for the *New Yorker*, and later published the essays as a controversial book, *Eichmann in Jerusalem: A Report on the Banality of Evil* (London: Faber & Faber, 1963).

31 Douglas, *The Memory of Judgment*; A. Gross, 'The constitution of history and memory'.
32 A. Gross, 'The constitution of history and memory', p. 416. See also Pierre Nora, 'Between memory and history: les lieux de mémoire', *Representations*, 26, 1989.
33 See O. Bartov, *Germany's War and the Holocaust: Disputed Histories* (Ithaca: Cornell University Press, 2003); M. Marrus, *Holocaust in History* (London: Weidenfeld & Nicolson, 1988).
34 Douglas, *The Memory of Judgment*. See also Buruma, *The Wages of Guilt* and Felman, *The Juridical Unconscious*.
35 Douglas, *The Memory of Judgment*, p. 103; also Wieviorka, *The Era of the Witness*.
36 My account here draws on Douglas, *The Memory of Judgment*, pp. 97–122.
37 Felman and Laub, *Testimony*, p. 15.
38 On the figurative dimension of testimony, see H. White, 'Figural realism in witness literature', *Parallax*, 10(1), 2004, pp. 113–24. For analysis of evidence, truth and proof in Holocaust historiography, see R. Braun, 'The Holocaust and problems of historical representation', *History and Theory*, 33(2), 1994, pp. 172–97.
39 Douglas, *The Memory of Judgment*, p. 107.
40 Ibid., pp. 108–9.
41 Ibid., p. 109.
42 Today it is widely recognized that testimony is used in humanitarian campaigns because its affective impact has an ability to solicit the empathy of the public. See D. Fassin, 'The humanitarian politics of testimony: subjectification through trauma in the Israeli-Palestinian conflict', *Cultural Anthropology*, 23(3), 2008, pp. 531–58.
43 Douglas, *The Memory of Judgement*, pp. 125–6.
44 Ibid., p. 129.
45 Ibid.
46 Ibid., p. 134.
47 Ibid., pp. 135–37.
48 Ibid., p. 138.
49 Ibid, p. 148.
50 M. Hirsch and L. Spitzer, 'The witness and the archive' in S. Radstone and B. Schwarz (eds) *Memory: History, Theories, Debates* (New York: Fordham University Press, 2010), p. 397.
51 Douglas, *The Memory of Judgment*, pp. 154–73 passim.
52 Ibid., pp. 6, 182.
53 Ibid., p. 149.
54 Ibid., p. 148.
55 C. Lanzman, dir. *Shoah* (New Yorker Films, 1985).
56 Felman, *The Juridical Unconscious*, p. 106.
57 See Hirsch and Spitzer, 'The witness and the archive'.
58 Felman, *The Juridical Unconscious*, p. 106.
59 Ibid., p. 107.
60 Wieviorka, *The Era of the Witness*.
61 Ibid, p. 84.
62 Ibid, p. 88.
63 Ibid.
64 D. Goldhagen, *Hitler's Willing Executioners: Ordinary Germans and the Holocaust* (New York: Knopf, 1996).
65 Wieviorka, *The Era of the Witness*, p. 92.
66 Ibid., pp. 90–95.
67 Ibid., p. 149.
68 P. Novick, *The Holocaust and Collective Memory* (London: Bloomsbury Publishing, 2001), p. 4.
69 Ibid.

70 Felman, *The Juridical Unconscious*, p. 124.

71 Ibid., p. 112.

72 Ibid., p. 126.

73 Ibid.

74 J. Young, 'Between history and memory: the voice of the eyewitness' in A. Douglass and T. Vogler (eds) *Witness and Memory: The Discourse of Trauma* (New York: Routledge, 2003), p. 276.

75 Ibid.

76 Ibid., p. 277.

77 D. LaCapra, *Writing History, Writing Trauma* (Baltimore: Johns Hopkins University Press, 2001), p. 78.

78 Survivor testimony can easily be discredited through the adversarial methods of the Anglo-American legal trial. See, for instance, Douglas' discussion in *The Memory of Judgment*, p. 226, of the *Zundel* trial in Canada in which the testimony of a seasoned survivor witness was undermined by a defence counsel who did not feel compunction to respect survivor testimony.

79 Wieviorka, *The Era of the Witness*, pp. 88–89.

80 See A. Orford, 'Commissioning the truth', *Columbia Journal of Gender and Law*, 15, 2006, pp. 851–83.

81 The following section draws on material published in R. Kennedy, 'Australian trials of trauma: the Stolen Generations in human rights, law, and literature', *Comparative Literature Studies*, 48(3), 2011, pp. 333–55.

82 *Bringing Them Home*, p. 3.

83 Ibid.

84 See Felman and Laub, *Testimony*, pp. 71–72.

85 (2000) Federal Court of Australia (FCA) 1084, [174]. Hereafter referred to as *Cubillo*.

86 *Cubillo*, [2].

87 *Cubillo*, [79].

88 (1997) 190 Commonwealth Law Reports (CLR) 1.

89 This legislation has been repealed.

90 *Cubillo*, [28].

91 For an excellent overview and analysis of the *Cubillo* case, especially in relation to the interpretation of the past and the role of historians in the case, see A. Curthoys, A. Genovese and A. Reilly, *Rights and Redemption: History, Law, and Indigenous People* (Sydney: University of New South Wales Press, 2008).

92 *Cubillo*, [80]. O'Laughlin mentioned *Bringing Them Home*, and the apologies offered by some state and territory parliaments, 'so that members of the general public may appreciate that the Court has, at all times, been aware of these matters'.

93 *Cubillo*, [69].

94 (1999) FCA 1192.

95 *Cubillo*, [79].

96 *Cubillo*, [442].

97 *Cubillo*, [79].

98 *Cubillo*, [118].

99 *Cubillo*, [125].

100 *Cubillo*, [402]. For further analysis of this testimony, see T. Luker, '"Postcolonising" amnesia in the discourse of reconciliation: the void in the law's response to the Stolen Generations', *Australian Feminist Law Journal*, 22(1), 2005, pp. 67–68.

101 *Cubillo*, [405, 446, 593].

102 *Cubillo*, [125].

103 *Cubillo*, [588].

104 *Cubillo*, [393].

105 Felman, *The Juridical Unconscious*, p. 5.
106 *Cubillo*, [446, 593].
107 *Cubillo*, [650].
108 Wieviorka, *The Era of the Witness*, p. xiv.
109 Ibid., p. 81.

Part II

Memorialization and commemoration

The chapters in this part of the book turn to questions of memorialization and commemoration, and they focus on sources other than oral testimony. They move beyond the remembrances of individuals to consider how the actions of certain 'memory makers' were poised to influence the meaning of the past shared among wider social groups, often on a national scale. The authors are less concerned than those in Part I with the psychological dynamics of remembering, focusing instead on political dimensions. They chart how – whether in Classical Athens or modern Europe and the United States – individuals acted socially to promote certain stories about the past (or certain interpretations of the present) that might forge a new 'collective memory' about the meaning of that past. In other words, they describe a process of instrumentalization – how 'useable pasts' are shaped in somebody's interest in the present. The authors approach 'collective memory' in different ways, however. If Franziska Seraphim and Joan Tumblety see it as the supposedly dominant, or perhaps officially sanctioned, representations of the past in public circulation at a given place and time, Susan A. Crane – resisting oppositions between personal, historical and collective memory – locates it instead in each historically conscious individual mind. And Polly Low asks questions about the interactions of material, oral and written sources in determining the (ultimately unknowable) forms it might have taken in the distant past.

Low writes about some of the material traces left behind by political elites in fifth-century BCE Athens, specifically the political decisions inscribed on surviving monuments. While acknowledging the difficulties involved in interpreting such things, she explains how these inscriptions may be read as evidence of elite power strategies – as inherently commemorative acts, which directed the observer to remember an interpretation of recent events that cast the rulers in a flattering light. Seraphim suggests that art collections in modern Japan and the United States have also been inherently commemorative, designed by the artists who created them and the curators who exhibited them as interventions that would take a view of the past to a wider audience, whether to 'sell' a certain idea of Japan in the outside world or to correct – for contemporary political reasons – the dominant 'cultural script' about Japan's wartime record that suppressed some of the most brutal aspects of it. In particular, she shows how the medium of artistic representation was used to confront official silences over the massacre of Chinese forced labourers in 1945. Tumblety similarly considers the political stakes of commemoration in her chapter on post-Liberation France, showing how those aggrieved by the defeat of the Vichy regime used legal polemic and journalism to counter the dominant memorialization of the war in the service of ideological goals. Museums have played an important role in facilitating the presence of the past. Susan Crane's chapter treats the evolving role that photographs have played in museal display, tracking changes in curatorial preferences over the nineteenth and twentieth centuries. She argues for the power of photographs as visual documents that serve not only as 'authentic' artefacts but as a medium for communicating implicit memorializing narratives to the public.

Despite this focus on strategic and instrumental manipulations of the past, questions of subjective experience are never far away, especially in the chapters that deal with the twentieth century, whose traumatic events have left so many traces in living memory. Low, who writes about a period definitively beyond living memory, admits that the thoughts and feelings of Classical Athenians are beyond the historians' reach – doubly so since the orality of the culture compounds the difficulties of its temporal remoteness where the search for surviving documentation is concerned. The theme of subjectivity is treated especially by Seraphim, who turns at the end of her chapter to artists who have used the affective power of the visual to shock the viewer into reconsidering received historical memory; and by Crane, who reminds us that whatever the power of the museum, there are limits to its reach. The public may be challenged by the memorial narratives at work in museum photographs, but viewer response is ultimately outside curatorial control, especially where exhibits conflict with deeply held beliefs about the past.

4 Remembering and forgetting

The creation and destruction of inscribed monuments in Classical Athens

Polly Low

The city-state of Athens in the Classical period was among the most prolific producers of inscribed monuments in the ancient world. From the early fifth century BCE, and increasingly frequently over the next 200 years, the city carved onto stone and put on public display thousands of texts, recording a whole spectrum of civic activities. These texts are an exceptionally rich resource for the historian of Classical Athens: in the absence of any other substantial source of archival material for this period they provide our most important 'primary' records of the city's political, diplomatic and economic activities. But these inscribed monuments are also significant pieces of evidence in their own right: they reveal not just what the Athenians did, but also how they chose to commemorate those actions. Studying the reasons why inscriptions were created and the ways in which they were used after their creation can offer extremely valuable insights into the processes by which the Athenians, as individuals and as a collective, shaped and reshaped the memories of their community.

This chapter explores the uses of inscriptions from various perspectives, although it focuses on a single type of inscribed text: the decrees of the Athenian popular assembly. It starts with an apparently simple question: why did the Athenians set up inscriptions? It is tempting to assume that a monument on stone must have a commemorative function: this is, after all, true of the inscribed monuments with which we are most familiar today (gravestones, statue bases, war memorials). The situation in Classical Athens is more complex: commemoration is certainly one function of inscriptions, but it is not the only one; indeed, scholarly opinion remains divided as to both the nature and the importance of the commemorative function of inscribed monuments. Complexity of a different sort is added when we turn to look at the uses of inscriptions: the evidence reveals a constantly shifting relationship between the actions recorded in inscribed monuments and those preserved through other forms of collective memory.

Explaining the Athenian 'epigraphic habit'

Writing must have been widespread in Classical Athens, although much of what was written is now lost to us.[1] Most private writing (letters, account books, wills) used perishable materials that have not survived; some public records were set up on wooden boards or whitewashed panels and these too have been lost.[2] The fact that we have a drastically incomplete and unrepresentative sample of Athenian written texts cannot be ignored, but nor can we dismiss the prominence of inscribed stone material as simply an accident of preservation. The Athenians were well aware that some forms of writing were more durable than others, and so their decision to inscribe a text on stone (rather than use some other medium) deserves attention: why was this form of commemoration thought appropriate for some actions, and not for others?

Classical Athenian inscriptions take many forms. Some of these are found throughout the Greek world (epitaphs and religious dedications, for example), but others are more specific to this time and place – above all the inscriptions that record the city's political activities: decrees of the popular assembly; lists of magistrates, traitors, casualties of war; accounts of sacred treasuries and imperial revenues. It is this political manifestation of the 'epigraphic habit' that has attracted most attention, partly because of its volume, partly for its distinctiveness: it has been estimated that about 20 per cent of all ancient Greek inscriptions come from this one state,[3] and it seems that Athens was also the first Greek city regularly to commit a substantial proportion of its collective decisions to stone.[4]

Attempts to explain the Athenian epigraphic habit have often focused on political factors. This is not illogical, for two reasons. First, the really unusual aspect of Athens' epigraphic record is the use of inscriptions to record political actions. Second, this epigraphic explosion is roughly contemporaneous with two major political developments of the mid-fifth century: Athens' acquisition of an empire, and the increasing radicalization of the city's democratic form of government. Those who emphasize external political developments note that Athens' imperial expansion brought with it a new flurry of regulations that had to be promulgated both among the Athenian officials who were required to enforce them and the imperial subjects who were required to obey them. Publication on stone was the best way to achieve these objectives.[5] Those who highlight the importance of Athens' domestic politics tend to see inscribed monuments not as symbols of control, but as emblems of transparent government. The idea that written texts can act as a safeguard of popular rights does appear in contemporary sources, such as (for example) Euripides' *Suppliant Women*:

> when the laws are written down, rich and weak alike have equal justice, and it is open to the weaker to use the same language to the prosperous when he is reviled by him, and the weaker prevails over the stronger if he has justice on his side.

(Eur. *Suppl.* 433–37)

The inscriptions themselves seem to echo this view of their function. Athenian inscribed decrees usually include a 'motivation clause', which gives a reason for setting up the inscription, and it has been noted that these clauses often seem to chime with a democratic ideology of open and accountable governance: inscriptions are set up 'so that everyone can see' what has been decided, or 'so that all may know' how the Athenians have acted.[6]

All these explanations of the function of inscribed texts share a basic assumption: inscriptions are intended to serve an essentially practical purpose (albeit a practical purpose that might have wider ideological implications). That is, the primary role of inscribed texts is to convey information. From a modern perspective, this assumption might seem unproblematic. The texts can be very detailed, preserving names, dates, financial data, as well as sometimes complex regulations or agreements. As was noted above, modern ancient historians often see inscribed texts as their richest (and most reliable) source of factual information, and it can take some effort to shake off the belief that the same would have been true for the original users of the texts. Nevertheless, the effort is worth making, and can be channelled in two directions: more careful analysis of exactly what is – and what is not – recorded on the stone can be extremely revealing of exactly what the Athenians were attempting to communicate or commemorate in these monuments; and examination of the evidence for the uses of inscriptions after their creation can help us establish whether those attempts were successful.

Creating inscriptions: the commemoration of a process

A productive strand of recent scholarship has argued that ancient historians should move away from their traditional habit of mining inscribed texts for the detailed facts that they record, and should focus instead on the way in which these facts are presented.[7] This work has emphasized that the form in which decrees were written up highlights certain aspects of Athenian political practice and obscures, or even completely omits, others. When read in this way, inscribed decrees can be seen almost as a form of selective history-writing. The inscription serves as a record of the past actions of the Athenian assembly but, unlike other forms of historiography, this record is one that has been collectively agreed by the Athenian people (the *demos*). A decree cannot be inscribed on stone until it has been approved by the Athenian *demos*; an inscribed decree is therefore necessarily a record of past events that claims the endorsement of the whole community.

Athenian decrees are quite formulaic, so one example can serve as a good illustration of the general picture. I quote here the complete text of an inscribed decree, passed towards the end of the fifth century BCE, in which the Athenian assembly voted special status (*proxenia*: roughly equivalent to honorary consulship) to a loyal non-Athenian, Oiniades.

> Gods. The Council and People decided; in the prytany of Antiochis; when Eucleides was secretary and Hierocles was president; in the archonship of Euctemon; Dietrephes made the proposal (lit. 'said'): since Oiniades of

Palaiskiathos is a man good to the city of the Athenians and keen to do all the good he can, and does good to any Athenian who arrives at Skiathos, he should be praised and recorded as *proxenos* and benefactor of the Athenians, together with his offspring. Whatever Council is in office and the Generals and the *archon* in office on Skiathos are to protect him against harm. The Secretary of the Council is to write up this decree on a stone *stele* and set it up on the Acropolis. He is to be invited to hospitality at the Prytaneion tomorrow.

Antichares proposed (lit. 'said'): otherwise as proposed by the Council, but to change the resolution so that instead of 'of Skiathos' is written 'Oiniades of Palai[skiathos]'.

(ML 90)

What we see in this text is a reconstruction (of sorts) of the process by which the decree was created, a process which begins with the words of individual Athenian citizens (Dietrephes in lines 6ff; Antichares in lines 26ff). But these individual speech-acts are set in a distinctively civic frame. The words belong to Dietrephes and Antichares, but they are recorded only because they received the approval of the council and the assembly: it is this approval that opens the text, and underpins everything that follows. The civic context is reinforced by the list of magistrates and officials that precedes the body of the decree. What the text records, and what it arguably encourages its reader to recreate, is precisely the point at which individual initiative receives the endorsement of the collective, at which the words of a single citizen become accepted as the views of the whole *polis*. In that respect, therefore, these texts not only commemorate a democratic 'moment', but also insist that this moment is recalled in a specifically democratic form: Athenian democracy allows and requires freedom of speech, but it also insists on the sovereignty of the collective; both of those essential principles are incorporated into this form of commemoration.

The argument can be taken further. As we have seen, the decrees are presented as a record of the words spoken in the assembly, and the inscription must reflect, to some extent, the shape of the assembly debate (this is visible most clearly in the reporting of Antichares' amendment to the original proposal). However, it is clear that a huge amount must have been omitted from this record. Above all, what is missing is any sense of dispute or disagreement, or even any material that might allow us to reconstruct what disagreement might have looked like.[8] The honours given to Oiniades are not trivial. In order to justify the award, Dietrephes would surely have had to provide more details of Oiniades' status and services than those recorded here: the bland assertion that Oiniades is a 'good man' is hardly particularly persuasive. Skiathos, in northern Greece, was a strategically sensitive area for Athens; this almost certainly motivates the award of this honour, but would also have made it very likely that the details of Athens' policy in this region would have been subject to intense discussion in the assembly. None of this is visible in this text, and it has been suggested that this omission is deliberate: it removes the possibility that the restaging of the debate which this mode of commemoration entails could also allow for the *reopening* of the debate, and, with it, the unravelling of the decisions of the Athenian people. This mode of recording the decisions of the people is not, therefore, as artless as it might appear. Rather, it is deliberately aimed at creating a version of the past that privileges certain aspects of the behaviour of the *demos* – the productive co-operation of individual and group, the collective agreement of a shared course of action – while occluding other, potentially problematic, elements of the Athenian democratic process.

This approach to reading inscribed monuments is very helpful in allowing us to reach a more nuanced assessment of their intended commemorative function. Where it is less successful is in demonstrating whether monuments were actually used in this way. Studies of commemorative monuments from other periods have clearly demonstrated that their meanings are often very fluid: memorials of the First World War, for example, have functioned at different times and for different people as sites of celebration, of mourning, and of remembrance.[9] Our evidence for the afterlife of ancient Athenian monuments is inevitably less complete, but it is still potentially illuminating. Athenian reactions to their inscribed monuments are recorded both in literary texts and in the inscribed stones themselves; it is the second of those areas to which we now turn.

Reshaping monuments, revising memory?

That the Athenians sometimes thought it necessary to emend or even completely destroy inscriptions is in itself a good indication of the importance of these monuments. But the evidence for the alteration of inscriptions also reinforces the view that their function was more than simply practical. Although there is some evidence of attempts to ensure that inscriptions accurately reflect current political realities, it is clear that Athenian treatment of their inscribed monuments was shaped by much more than a straightforward desire to maintain accurate records. Inscribed monuments could continue to play an important commemorative function even once their immediate political purpose had faded.

The basic principle that guided the treatment of inscribed material seems clear enough: when a monument became outdated, it should be added to, deleted from or destroyed entirely. An example of the last option appears in an alliance between Athens and Thessaly of 361/0 BCE (RO 44). One of the conditions of the agreement is the stipulation that a previous treaty between Athens and Alexander of Pherae (an enemy of Thessaly) should be removed (lines 39–40). The treaty is no longer valid; therefore the stone that records it should be destroyed. This makes intuitive sense: if an inscribed monument functions as the physical embodiment of the collective decision of the Athenians, then a reversal of that decision should, logically, entail the removal of the monument. It might even be argued that we should put the process of cause and effect the other way around: that is, it is not revoking an agreement that requires the removal of a monument, but the removal of the monument that formalizes the annulment of an agreement.[10]

But this same example reveals that things were not always so straightforward. By 361/0, Athens had already been fighting Alexander of Pherae for some time: the alliance between Alexander and Athens was made in 368; but in 364 Alexander shifted his allegiance to Thebes; by 362 and 361 he was attacking Athenian allies and Athenian ships, and even staged a raid on Athens' harbour at Piraeus.[11] It was not, however, until the treaty with Thessaly was made in 361/0 that the Athenians got round to removing the treaty with Alexander, even though that treaty cannot have had any formal force for several years.

Why were the Athenians content to let this misleading monument remain standing? Simple inefficiency cannot be ruled out, but a more satisfying answer might lie in the relationship between inscribed text and other, unwritten, forms of collective knowledge. What this example suggests is the possibility for productive exploitation of the gap between the written record of the past and other versions of the past. We find in the speeches of the fourth-century politician Demosthenes the suggestion that Athens ran the risk of serious embarrassment if their inscribed monuments said one thing while their actions suggested something else (*Against Leptines* 36–37). But a desire to focus exactly that embarrassment on one of their enemies might underpin the Athenian failure to take down their treaty with Alexander of Pherae. The physical record of the broken treaty continued to serve an important symbolic function in acting as testament to the promises that had been broken by Alexander, even after its practical function – to record the current state of Athens' diplomatic obligations – had faded.

A different manifestation of the same basic principle is recorded by the historian Thucydides. In 421 BCE, Athens and Sparta made peace; the agreement quickly crumbled, but (according to the Athenians at least) the Spartans were the first to definitively violate its terms:

> The next winter the Spartans managed to elude the vigilance of the Athenians, and sent in a garrison of three hundred men to Epidaurus, under the command of Agesippidas. Upon this the Argives went to the Athenians and complained of their having allowed an enemy to pass by sea, in spite of the clause in the treaty by which the allies were not to allow an enemy to pass through their country ... The Athenians were persuaded by Alcibiades to inscribe at the bottom of the Spartan inscription that the Spartans had not kept their oaths, and to send the Helots at Cranii to Pylos to plunder the land.
>
> (5.56.1–3)

Two points are worth noting here. First, that the violation of the treaty was, on this occasion, explicitly recorded on the inscribed copy of the monument.

Second, that the Athenians, having noted that the Spartans had broken their word, then went on to do exactly the same themselves: assisting the Helots (Sparta's enslaved class) to fight against their masters was explicitly prohibited under the terms of the peace agreement.[12] In this case, then, the original purpose of the inscribed monument – to record a peace treaty between the two states – had completely disappeared. However, the monument could still perform a commemorative function, in recording not just Athens' attempt to make peace with its great rival, but also Sparta's responsibility for undermining that attempt. (Athens' own contribution to the failure of the peace treaty was, unsurprisingly, omitted.) What had been a record of interstate co-operation was transformed into a monument to Spartan betrayal.

These two examples suggest the existence of two different approaches to the role of the written word in creating, and reshaping, the record of Athens' interstate activities: Sparta's (alleged) betrayal is recorded in writing; that of Alexander of Pherae is left unacknowledged, at least in monumental form. It might be tempting to try to map these differences onto a changing attitude to the importance of maintaining accurate written records, but this would probably be misguided: the evidence as a whole suggests that the Athenians were consistent only in their inconsistency – sometimes even in their treatment of a single monument. The most striking example of this is the 'Prospectus of the Second Athenian League', a decree of 378 BCE that set out the terms under which the Athenians hoped to establish a new multilateral alliance of Greek city-states. The decree includes a clause specifying that 'on this *stele* shall be inscribed the names of the cities which are allies and any other which becomes an ally' (RO 22, lines 69–72), and the stone reveals that the Athenians did follow this instruction: about 58 names are listed at the bottom and on one side of the inscription; the fact that these names have been carved by multiple different hands indicates that the Athenians did attempt to keep the monument up to date for some time. However, other sources reveal that the list is not complete; it follows, therefore, that at some point (before they ran out of space on the stone) the Athenians no longer thought it necessary to maintain a complete list of league membership in this public, inscribed form.[13]

The same inconsistency applies to deletions from the stone. The original decree specified that the new alliance would not interfere with an existing peace settlement brokered by the Persian king, the major imperial power of this period (lines 12–15). This clause was erased from the stone, and it is generally assumed that this erasure should be connected with a shift in Athenian policy towards Persia (a shift which can be dated from other sources to about 367 BCE).[14] Here we see a parallel to (and a reversal of) Athens' behaviour in the case of the peace with Sparta: in that example, a Spartan shift in policy was marked by an addition to the original monument; in this case, evidence which would reveal an Athenian u-turn is concealed from view. The policy of deletion was not, however, systematically applied. The opening clauses of the decree (lines 9–12) singled out Sparta as the chief enemy of the new alliance, and depicted the Spartans as threats to Greek freedom and autonomy. In 369 BCE, Athens entered into an alliance with the Spartans,[15] yet this part of the inscription, and with it the public declaration of Athenian hostility to Sparta, remained untouched.

We can only speculate about the reasons for the uneven treatment of this monument, but it is worth considering the practical factors that might have shaped these patterns of addition and deletion. It was noted above that the process of creating a monument began with individual initiative: an Athenian had to stand up in the assembly and make a proposal. It seems very likely that the same applied to the destruction or emendation of monuments. As the Thessalian decree reveals, the removal of a *stele* required the approval of the *demos*, and that approval had to be actively sought by an Athenian citizen. Another example (a pair of decrees, inscribed on the same stone, honouring the city of Neapolis: ML 89) shows that the same principle applied to the emendation of inscribed monuments: the later decree requests that the hon-orands not be described as colonists of the city of Thasos (lines 58–59), and this label has duly been erased from the text of the earlier decree (line 7). It seems reasonable to assume that the erasure from RO 22 of the reference to the Persian alliance came about by the same process: an individual Athenian thought it important to remove this piece of text; the Athenians as a whole were persuaded to agree. The same was not true of the reference to the Spartans. Frustratingly, it is impossible to know where the process came unstuck: was the proposal to delete this part of the text never made, or was the Athenian assembly unwilling, for some reason, to agree to amend this section of the inscription? What initially appears to be simply a haphazard approach to commemoration might, therefore, have had some logic to it, based on a combination of political and practical factors; but the logic is no longer visible to us. What we can see, however, is that in the alteration of documents as well as in their creation the views of the city as a whole are privileged: just as the *demos* has ultimate authority in deciding which of its actions are commemorated on stone, so it also controls how the stones are treated after their creation. This is collective commemoration, both in its origins and in its afterlife.

Inscriptions in their context: commemoration and memory

The discussion so far has emphasized the textual content of these monuments, and focused on the importance of the precise words carved onto the stone. This emphasis can seem natural: modern users of ancient inscriptions find their texts presented, precisely, as texts, often with little or no reference to their physical form.[16] But a moment's thought makes it obvious that ancient audiences encountered inscribed texts in a very different way: they would find inscriptions scattered around their city, sometimes in prominent locations but sometimes also in less easily accessible contexts. A fourth-century law court speech even boasts about the inaccessibility of an inscribed regulation – a striking contrast to the presumed ideology of transparency discussed above:

the Athenians wrote this law on a stone pillar, and set it up in the sanctuary of Dionysus by the altar in Limnae (and this pillar even now stands, showing the inscription in Attic letters, nearly effaced) ... They set it up in the most ancient and most sacred sanctuary of Dionysus in Limnae, in order that only few might have knowledge of the inscription; for the sanctuary is opened only once in each year.

([Demosthenes] 59.76)

The speaker's observation about the legibility of this text is also worth noting, and would almost certainly have been an issue for other inscriptions too. Not only did letters fade and erode over time, some inscriptions might not have been particularly legible to begin with. The 'Athenian Tribute Lists' for example (records of sums of money given to the goddess Athena), although located on the relatively accessible Athenian Acropolis, stood over three and a half metres high and contained row after row of closely-packed figures. It is hard to imagine that many, if any, Athenians could ever have used these inscriptions as a practical guide to the finances of the sacred treasury.[17]

To modern eyes, then, Athenian behaviour can start to seem slightly bizarre: why invest so much effort (and money) in creating records that so few would be able to read? But modern eyes are probably unhelpful here; more particularly, modern assumptions of a strict division between written and oral communication provide too rigid a framework for understanding the role of these monuments. Written communication and commemoration were still relative novelties in this period: although the technology of writing was known in Greece from the eighth century, the spoken word retained a privileged position in many spheres.[18] Several contemporary texts exemplify or explore this point. The *Histories* of Herodotus, for example, although composed in writing, reveal throughout the enduring power of oral tradition: Herodotus' sources are not, for the most part, documentary, but rather the oral testimony (or testimonies) of the communities whose histories he reports.[19] Plato's *Phaedrus* includes an extensive discussion of the relationship between written and spoken communication. Socrates' suspicion of the written word in this dialogue is unsurprising (given his own refusal to commit his own beliefs to writing), but the form which it takes is illuminating:

And every word, once it has been written, is bandied about, both among those who understand and those who have no interest in it, and it does not know who to speak to and who not to speak to; when ill-treated or unfairly reviled it always needs its father to help it, for it has no power to protect or help itself.

(275e)

One of Socrates' reservations about writing is that it is *less* fixed than oral communication: the spoken word remains under the control of the speaker, and the speaker can ensure that his audience takes the intended meaning from it;

but written words, because they have an existence separate from that of their creator, are more susceptible to reinterpretation, and misinterpretation, by their readers.

Socrates presents an extreme view, but his emphasis on the instability of the meaning of written texts can helpfully be applied to our inscribed material. On this model, inscribed texts should not be seen as uncomplicated bearers of information, but rather as 'mnemonic aids'.[20] That is, the value of an inscribed monument need not be that it provides a single, authorized version of past events, but rather that it provides a framework around which members of the community could shape their own version of the past.

This view of the function of inscriptions has various advantages. It provides a way of sidestepping the worries about legibility and accessibility that were just discussed: if inscriptions are simply a prompt to collective memory rather than the absolute source of that memory, it becomes less problematic that not every member of the community can actually read them. More importantly, this interpretation of the role of inscriptions is consistent with the ways in which they were used by contemporary writers and speakers. For example: when Demosthenes wanted to persuade the Athenians that they had a responsibility to act as the political and moral leaders of the Greek world, he based part of his argument on the actions of their ancestors. Athenians of today (according to Demosthenes) have been distracted by selfish interests, and misled by corrupt politicians:

> That this is so, you surely see for yourselves with regard to the present, and you need no evidence from me, but that it was the opposite in the days of old I will prove, not in my own words, but by the written record of your ancestors, which they engraved on a bronze *stele* and set up in the Acropolis. 'Arthmius of Zelea', it says, 'son of Pythonax, outlaw and enemy of the people of Athens and of their allies, himself and his family.' Then is recorded the reason for this punishment: 'because he conveyed Persian gold to the Peloponnese.' This is what the inscription says. I earnestly beg you to consider: what was the intention of the Athenians who did this thing?
>
> (*Third Philippic* 41–43)

It is worth noting the symbiotic relationship between written record and wider narrative. The inscribed decree forms an essential part of Demosthenes' argument: his claim about the past is made stronger because he can assert that it rests not just on his own impressions, but on the 'written record of your ancestors'. (The second person plural is important: this record was created by *your* – that is, every Athenian's – ancestors.) But the content of the decree cannot stand alone. The words quoted by Demosthenes record only the actions of the people involved: the treachery of Arthmius; the response of the Athenians. The reasons for that response – the 'intention' of the Athenians – are preserved, not in the written text, but in the shared memory of the audience. Admittedly, this is a memory that requires some excavation (and, almost certainly, re-shaping) by Demosthenes before it re-emerges at the surface of Athenian collective consciousness. Nevertheless, it is significant that Demosthenes can plausibly assert the existence of this shared memory of an event that had taken place long before the lifetime of any member of the audience. The inscribed record helped to preserve the memory of the event, but the Athenians remembered, or could be claimed to remember, much more than the inscription reported.[21]

A second example shows how this approach could also be applied to groups of monuments. The episode again revolves around an attempt to use inscribed records as proof of the actions and beliefs of earlier generations of Athenians, and, by extension, as a guide for the behaviour of contemporary citizens. The orator (Aeschines) is attempting to prove to the Athenians that they have never been willing to grant excessive honours to their politicians, even those who have performed exceptional services to the city. In order to do this, he takes his audience on a kind of virtual 'guided tour' around a series of inscribed texts in the Athenian *agora*, describing some and quoting (or purporting to quote) others verbatim (*Against Ctesiphon* 181–91). These monuments were set up over several decades: the earliest (the 'Painted Stoa') is a memorial to the Battle of Marathon of 490 BCE (although it also depicts earlier, mythical, battles), the most recent dates to the turn of the century (some 70 years before this speech). The monuments are equally varied in their form (a stoa; an inscribed *stele*; a series of religious statues). They could not have been conceived of by their creators as part of a single commemorative entity. But Aeschines is able to use these disconnected monuments as the foundation for his construction of a much richer, coherent version of the ideology of the Athenians' ancestors. The inscribed monuments are a necessary part of his attempt to persuade his audience of his version of their shared past and shared ideals, but they are not in themselves sufficient: the message of the monuments becomes clear only under the guidance of Aeschines. And this message, of course, is one that is shaped precisely to fit Aeschines' agenda at this point; different viewers of the monuments in this part of the city, we must assume, would have combined them in different ways, and constructed different versions of the past from them.[22]

It is, therefore, essential to be wary of ascribing fixed meanings to commemorative monuments: they may well have been set up with specific intentions, but it does not follow that they were always or only used for those purposes. On the other hand, these examples also demonstrate that users of these monuments do not have completely free rein: the content of the inscription does matter; at times even the precise words of the inscription seem to be central to the argument that is being constructed. While it would be a mistake, therefore, to assume that the existence of the written word made unwritten memories irrelevant, it would be equally misguided to think that either the existence or the content of these written monuments could be completely ignored.

Destruction and reconstruction

So far, I have talked rather simplistically of 'Athenian' attitudes to commemoration and responses to monuments, but not every viewer of an Athenian
monument was interested in (or even supportive of) the commemorative
agenda set by the Athenian *polis*. The ways in which specific individuals
responded to collective commemorative monuments remain elusive, but it is
possible to say something about the ways in which non-*polis* groups interacted with the commemorative strategies of the city as a whole. A particularly
instructive episode is the oligarchic coup of 404/3 BCE, and the democratic
reaction to it. Here, too, it is the treatment of monuments after their creation
that is especially illuminating.

The oligarchic regime (known as 'the Thirty') is depicted in various sources
as destroying monuments that in its view symbolized (or legitimized) the old
democratic government. According to the Aristoteleian *Constitution of the
Athenians*, the Thirty

> removed from the Areopagus the laws of Ephialtes and Archestratus
> about the Areopagites, and also such of the ordinances of Solon as
> were of doubtful purport, and abolished the sovereignty vested in the
> popular courts, claiming to be rectifying the constitution and removing
> its uncertainties.
>
> (35.2)

The basic practice is familiar: repealing laws (here, laws passed by famous
democratic reformers such as Solon and Ephialtes) entails or is perhaps even
effected by the removal of the monuments on which those laws are inscribed.
The act of removal surely had a symbolic as well as a purely legalistic intention:
by removing these monuments that celebrated a particular, and particularly
democratic, version of the Athenian past, the Thirty cleared the way for the
development of a different version of that past. Immediately before this episode, the author notes that the Thirty attempted to represent themselves not
as innovative revolutionaries but as traditionalists, who were simply reviving
Athens' original form of government ('they pretended to be administering the
ancestral form of constitution'). This act of monumental reshaping therefore
goes hand in hand with a policy of historical revisionism.[23]

The Thirty's destructive tendencies extended beyond purely constitutional
documents. A small group of decrees honouring various foreign diplomats
were destroyed by the oligarchs at the end of the fifth century and re-erected
when the democracy was restored.[24] One well-preserved example (Tod 98)
records the destruction and recreation of the decree awarding *proxenia* to five
Thasian citizens. Thasian–Athenian relations were closely linked to internal
political developments: in Thasos, support for Athens was regularly aligned
with support for democracy,[25] so it is not terribly surprising to find that
Athenian oligarchs saw no need to maintain a connection with democratic

Thasian *proxenoi*. For the Thirty, destroying the *stele* marked both the formal annulment of the privileged status of these men, and a more general repudiation of the democratic past that such agreements recorded.

This much is relatively unsurprising: the oligarchic attitude to inscriptions and their meaning seems, in fact, very similar to the democratic approaches already discussed. More unexpected, however, is the democratic response to this oligarchic destruction. The restored monument reports a decree of the Athenian Council (not the Assembly, the normal decree-passing body) which noted the Thirty's destruction of the earlier monument and authorized the creation of a new *stele*. What is not recorded is the original fifth-century decree that had actually awarded the Thasians their favoured status; the decree inscribed on this stone simply gives permission for the Thasians to set up (and pay for) a monument recording the destructive actions of the Thirty.

Why did the Athenians not think it necessary to reinscribe the original decree? And why were the Thasians, who as funders of the new monument might expect to have some say over its appearance, happy to go along with this? The absence of the original decree implies a departure from the conventional assumption that destroying a monument also annulled the agreement inscribed on it. But that departure could be logically justified. As we have seen, the destruction or emendation of a monument required the formal approval of the Athenian state; the Thirty were not (in the eyes of the restored democracy) a legitimate governing body, and therefore did not have the authority to remove or repeal the democracy's decisions; it follows, therefore, that their destruction of inscribed decrees could have no formal significance. To put it more simply: the Thirty had destroyed the monument but not the act that the monument commemorated; to put things right, the democracy needed only to replace a monument, not reactivate a decree.

As a record of the current status of these Thasians this monument might therefore seem uncontroversial. But as a monument to recent events in Athenian history it is perhaps rather more unusual, both in what it says and in what it leaves unrecorded. One significant absence has already been noted. The original honorific decree, presumably passed by the Athenian *demos* sometime in the fifth century, operates as a sort of absent presence in this monument: it is not explicitly recorded, but the monument would have made sense only if the decree existed, and, more importantly, only if its validity was recognized by those who saw this inscription. Once more, therefore, we have to allow for a society in which public commemoration and other, perhaps unwritten, forms of memorialization worked alongside each other.

A second important absence concerns the identity of those commemorated in this text. As we have seen, Athenian inscribed decrees were typically framed as actions of the Athenian people as a collective, unanimous group. But because this text does not record the decree of the *demos*, it allows the focus of attention to be shifted away from the views of the collective, and towards the actions of two sets of individuals: the Thirty (who destroyed the original record), and the five Thasians (on whose initiative the new monument was created). The monument creates a direct link between the Thirty and the Thasians and allows these five men to insert themselves directly into the story of the oligarchic coup in a way which (I suspect) bears little relation to their actual role in the events of that period. The Athenian *demos*, meanwhile, is pushed towards the commemorative margins. Perhaps their interests were simply sidelined by the Thasians (we should remember, again, that behind each of these monuments lies a complex series of political negotiations); or perhaps the *demos'* absence from the monument provides further proof that physical commemoration was not always the most important way of preserving the memory of an event. On this occasion, was the unwritten collective memory of the people's role in creating the original decree thought to be sufficient?

Conclusion

Athenian inscribed monuments perform an important commemorative function, which can transcend their role as carriers of practical political information. This commemorative role is visible in the content of the inscribed texts: the choice of what to record, and what to leave out, allows the Athenian *demos* to pre-serve a particular version of its own past. The importance of inscriptions as sites of commemoration is also visible in the ways in which they are used after their creation: the changes which are made to inscribed texts must indicate the existence of a desire to ensure that the monuments accurately reflect the views not just of their original creators but also of their contemporary users. Something that is conspicuously absent from Athenian attitudes to their inscribed texts is any impetus to preserve these records for purely historical or archival purposes: once a monument, or a part of a monument, was deemed no longer to be serving a useful purpose it could simply be obliterated. The Athenian view of the past, as mediated through these monuments, must therefore have constantly been shifting in accordance with the requirements of the present. (Indeed, studies on other aspects of ancient Greek memory have shown that this approach to the past is not restricted to Athens nor to this specific form of commemoration.)[26]

Collectively endorsed commemoration is not, however, identical to collective memory. Inscribed monuments could certainly contribute to the shaping of Athenian collective memory, but they did not completely dictate it. We should remember, first of all, that reactions to monuments were not fixed: monuments could be ignored, amended, destroyed (or just wilfully misinterpreted). We have to allow for changing uses of monuments and changing constructions of memory over time, and we also need to assume (even though it is not always easy to prove) that individuals or groups of individuals might have employed these collectively-endorsed records as a means of shaping or validating their own versions of the past. Finally, we must remember that these texts formed part of a larger set of ways of engaging with and representing the past, many of which, because they were unwritten, are no longer accessible to us. Glimpses are occasionally visible, as when, for example, inscriptions are combined with other sources of collective memory in assembly and law court speeches, but it is important to be aware that we are seeing only a very small fragment of the total picture. We have to be careful not to suppose that these inscribed monuments that are so prominent in our view of the memory culture of Classical Athens would have dominated the collective memories of the Athenians themselves to quite the same extent.

Abbreviations

ML: R. Meiggs and D.M. Lewis, *A Selection of Greek Historical Inscriptions to the End of the Fifth Century BC*, revised edn (Oxford: Oxford University Press, 1988).

RO: P.J. Rhodes and R.G. Osborne, *Greek Historical Inscriptions 404–323 BC* (Oxford: Oxford University Press, 2003).

Tod: M. N. Tod, *A Selection of Greek Historical Inscriptions, Vol. 2: From 404 to 323 BC* (Oxford: Oxford University Press, 1948).

Notes

1 The most recent discussion of Athenian writing and literacy is A. Missiou, *Literacy and Democracy in Fifth-Century Athens* (Cambridge: Cambridge University Press, 2011); see also W.V. Harris, *Ancient Literacy* (Cambridge, MA: Harvard University Press, 1989), ch. 4.

2 Briefly discussed by P.J. Rhodes, 'Public documents in the Greek states: archives and inscriptions, part I', *Greece and Rome*, 48, 2001, pp. 33–36.

3 C.W. Hedrick, 'Democracy and the Athenian epigraphical habit', *Hesperia*, 68, 1999, p. 391.

4 For decree-passing (and inscribing) practice outside Athens, see P.J. Rhodes with D.M. Lewis, *The Decrees of the Greek States* (Oxford: Oxford University Press, 1997); D.M. Lewis, 'Democratic institutions and their diffusion', in *Collected Papers in Greek and Near-Eastern History*, ed. P.J. Rhodes (Cambridge: Cambridge University Press, 1997), pp. 51–59.

5 On imperialism and epigraphy, see P.P. Liddel, 'Epigraphy, legislation and power within the Athenian Empire', *Bulletin of the Institute of Classical Studies*, 53, 2010, pp. 99–128.

6 Hedrick, 'Democracy and the Athenian epigraphical habit', pp. 408–25.

7 For this approach, see especially R.G. Osborne, 'Inscribing performance', in S.D. Goldhill and R.G. Osborne (eds) *Performance Culture and Athenian Democracy* (Cambridge: Cambridge University Press, 1999), pp. 341–58; N. Luraghi, 'The *demos* as narrator: public honours and the construction of future and past', in N. Luraghi, L. Foxhall and H.-J. Gehrke (eds) *Intentional History: Spinning Time in Ancient Greece* (Stuttgart: Steiner, 2010), pp. 247–63. The discussion here is heavily indebted to their analysis.

8 Osborne, 'Inscribing performance', p. 344.

9 J. Winter, *Sites of Memory, Sites of Mourning: The Great War in European Cultural History* (Cambridge: Cambridge University Press, 1995), ch. 4.

10 See further P.J. Rhodes, 'Public documents in the Greek states: archives and inscriptions, part II', *Greece and Rome*, 48, 2001, pp. 136–39; cf. S. Bolmarcich, 'The afterlife of a treaty', *Classical Quarterly*, 57, 2007, pp. 477–89.

11 Theban alliance: Diodorus Siculus 15.80.6; attacks on Athens and her allies: Xenophon *Hellenica* 6.4.35, [Demosthenes] 50.4, Diodorus Siculus 15.95.

12 Thucydides 5.23.4.

13 Aeschines 2.70 reports that the League had 75 members; Diodorus Siculus 15.30.2 mentions 70. For a full discussion of this inscription and its problems, see P.J. Rhodes and R.G. Osborne, *Greek Historical Inscriptions 404–323 BC* (Oxford: Oxford University Press, 2003), pp. 92–105.

14 RO 31 and 33 show Athens still supporting the peace with Persia in 369/8 BCE; Xenophon *Hellenica* 7.1.33–40 reveals a shift in attitude by 367.

15 Xenophon *Hellenica* 7.1.1–14.

16 A brief discussion of the history of the publication of Greek inscriptions can be found in A.G. Woodhead, *The Study of Greek Inscriptions* (Cambridge: Cambridge University Press, 1981), ch. 9.

17 Assessments of levels of literacy among the Athenian population vary widely: for a pessimistic estimate, see Harris, *Ancient Literacy*, p. 328 (literacy rate of 5–10 per cent); for an optimistic picture, Missiou, *Literacy and Democracy* (arguing for 'mass literacy', p. 133).

18 R. Thomas, *Literacy and Orality in Ancient Greece* (Cambridge: Cambridge University Press, 1992); R. Thomas, *Oral Tradition and Written Record in Classical Athens* (Cambridge: Cambridge University Press, 1989).

19 O. Murray, 'Herodotus and oral history', in N. Luraghi (ed.) *The Historian's Craft in the Age of Herodotus* (Oxford: Oxford University Press, 2001), pp. 16–44. On Herodotus' use of inscriptions, see S. West, 'Herodotus' epigraphical interests', *Classical Quarterly*, 35, 1985, pp. 278–305.

20 Thomas, *Literacy and Orality*, esp. pp. 65–73, 87.

21 The story of Arthmius' treachery seems to have gained particular resonance in the fourth century: it is also appealed to by Aeschines (3.258) and Dinarchus (2.24–25). The episode itself (probably to be dated around 477) is discussed in R. Meiggs, *The Athenian Empire* (Oxford: Oxford University Press, 1972), pp. 508–12.

22 The symbolic and commemorative significance of the monuments of the Athenian *agora* is discussed in detail by J. Shear, 'Cultural change, space, and the politics of commemoration in Athens', in R.G. Osborne (ed.) *Debating the Athenian Cultural Revolution: Art, Literature, Philosophy, and Politics 430–380 BC* (Cambridge: Cambridge University Press, 2007), pp. 91–115. See also P.C. Millett, 'Encounters in the Agora', in P.A. Cartledge, P.C. Millett and S. von Reden (eds) *Kosmos: Essays in Order, Conflict and Community in Classical Athens* (Cambridge: Cambridge University Press, 1998), pp. 203–28

23 J. Shear, *Polis and Revolution: Responding to Oligarchy in Classical Athens* (Cambridge: Cambridge University Press, 2011), ch. 6.

24 Other examples are listed in M. Walbank, *Athenian Proxenies of the Fifth Century BC* (Toronto: Stevens, 1978), p. 8 and nos. 26, 61, 63, 72, 79.

25 *IG* XII.8.263.6 (of 411 BCE) reveals that one of the men named in this decree (Apeimantos) was punished for his pro-Athenian sympathies by an oligarchic regime in Thasos.

26 Studies of collective memory among Greek historians developed initially out of work on oral tradition (an important example is Thomas' *Oral Tradition and Written Record*). More recent work has engaged more directly with theoretical studies of collective and cultural memory (J. Assman, *Cultural Memory and Early Civilization* (Cambridge: Cambridge University Press, 2011) [originally published in German in 2007] has been very influential), and has been particularly concerned with exploring the political significance of the manipulation of collective memory: e.g. N. Loraux, *The Divided City: Remembering and Forgetting in Ancient Athens* (New York: Zone, 2002); A. Wolpert, *Remembering Defeat: Civil*

War and Civic Memory in Ancient Athens (Baltimore: Johns Hopkins, 2002); Shear, *Polis and Revolution*. Another important field has been the study of the creation and significance of the collective memory of battle and war: e.g. A. Chaniotis, *War in the Hellenistic World* (Malden: Blackwell, 2005); E. Bridges, E. Hall and P.J. Rhodes (eds) *Cultural Responses to the Persian Wars* (Oxford: Oxford University Press, 2007).

5 Visual cultures of memory in modern Japan

The historical uses of Japanese art collections

Franziska Seraphim

Art is a product of past history combined with present conditions.
It develops from this fusion of past and present.[1]

Okakura Kakuzo, 1884

Guiding a group of New England art collectors on a trip to old temples in Japan in the mid-1880s, art dealer and historian Okakura Kakuzo spoke about art the way we now speak about historical memory. Memory, like art, is contextual. In fact, all cultural products are products of their time, informed, in different ways, by longer-standing practices, experiences or habits of mind. All historians are interested in contexts, that of the historical event or product they are studying as well as the context in which they work. But the historian of memory is specifically interested in the processes by which these different contexts interact or fuse. Art historians look primarily to the artistic composition of a work of art, in which they recognize old and new themes and techniques as part of the contemporary art world. Cultural historians tend to use visual materials as a contemporary commentary on the social and cultural milieu in which they were produced. Those attentive to the processes of memory find in art a particularly potent medium of remembering, whether through the collecting and exhibiting of selected artworks, the creation of commemorative art specific to an event or experience, or the engagement with visual language to draw connections between otherwise separate moments in time with implications for the future.

One might also think of this as layers of memory, which the historian peels back to understand the composite dynamic of remembering. In the case of Japan, and Asia in general, there is an added layer every Euro-American scholar has to contend with, and nowhere is this more apparent than in dealing with visuals. This is the history of looking at Japan *as memory*. Our inquiry into Japan's visual culture of memory is already bounded by a century and a half of visualizing 'Japan' by certain motifs and in a certain style, so much so that Japanese artists who paint in Western style are often regarded as not authentically 'Japanese'. Edward Said termed the creation and recreation of such essentialism 'Orientalism'.[2] As a habit of mind, it remains with us even today. Consider, for example, the authoritative six-volume *Cambridge*

History of Japan, published around 1990 and covering Japan from prehistory to the twentieth century. Each of the six volumes features the same dust jacket, no matter what time period it covers – a reproduction of an eighteenth-century painting of Ryōgoku Bridge in Edo (today Tokyo). It is as if Japan was frozen in late-feudal society, peopled by women and men in elegant kimono and umbrellas enjoying a leisurely outing against the background of an exotic temple-dotted landscape.[3] The uniqueness of Japan is a memory of a bygone era, in essence timeless, unchanging. Of course this image is itself historically constituted and thereby adds a layer of memory with which a historian using Japanese art as source material has to contend.

To demonstrate how historians might use visual sources to understand the place of memory in public culture, I focus on art collections rather than individual works of art. By that I mean art exhibitions at museums and fairs, photo albums that were once commercially available or have now been preserved for public consumption, series of postcards or woodblock prints that were designed as collections and form certain narratives, but also an artist's body of work insofar as it addresses a particular concern. A collection offers an immediate *context* for a piece of art. At the same time, it demands a certain space in public culture, where cultural products compete for visibility. Moreover, collections are almost always *commemorative*, whether a curator puts together an art show as a retrospective, a print-maker retells a series of events to witness and mourn, or a painter pushes against the limits of received memories to prompt new ways of imagining the future. Most importantly, collections remind us that memory is *selective*, even reductionist, and committed to a particular meaning or purpose to the exclusion of others. A collection hides as much as it reveals in ways more easily recognizable than with a single work of art.

These, then, are the three areas of memory work I discuss in this chapter: first, *Japan as memory and myth* focuses on the making of memory as national identity by both Americans and Japanese through collecting and exhibiting 'old Japan' at three historical moments – world fairs and commercial photo albums in the late nineteenth century, Japanese art exhibits in America and Meiji centennial celebrations in Japan in the 1950s and 1960s, and the web-based project on image-driven scholarship 'Visualizing Cultures' of the 2000s. Second, *Visualizing counter-memory* walks the reader through a book of 53 original Japanese woodcuts published in 1951 that retells the wartime massacre of Chinese forced labourers at a mine in Hanaoka, Japan, as an example of how local custodians of traumatic memory staked out a place of their own on the contemporary political map. Third, *Layers of memory* uses the life work of the artists Iri and Toshi Maruki, who painted murals of the Hiroshima atomic bombings and other mid-twentieth-century mass atrocities, to reflect on the potential of witness art 'to push at the limits' of knowing the past, to prompt an inquiry into what is not remembered, so that it may inspire fresh, ethically responsible action in the future. This is about what it means to let art move the viewer (an outsider to the original event, a belated witness) to come to new conclusions rather than replicate established memories. In this sense, 'art does not reflect memory, it anticipates it'.[4]

Japan as memory and myth: collecting the past

Art exhibition catalogues are wonderful resources, not only for their beautiful reproductions of artwork, but also for their essays, which tend to frame the collections in easily discernible ways. *Splendors of Meiji: Treasures of Imperial Japan – Masterpieces of the Khalili Collection*[5] documented an exhibition of nineteenth-century art-craft held in 1999 at the First USA Riverfront Arts Center in Wilmington, Delaware. The more than 400 pieces of exquisite metalwork, lacquer, enamel and porcelain exhibited here had been produced in the second half of the nineteenth century by the Meiji state's most renowned artists specifically for international display and consumption. Europeans, but especially Americans, became enthralled with the exuberance of Japanese arts and crafts at the international fairs then in vogue, which shaped in large part the public sense of a uniquely 'Japanese' – or broadly 'Oriental' – aesthetic. For much of the twentieth century, however, these arts of the Meiji era were all but ignored by Western art historians and collectors, who concentrated on the post-World War II era Japan's older and more austere Zen-inspired art or were drawn to the simplicity of twentieth-century folk art. All the while, the Iran-born scholar, collector, and philanthropist Nasser D. Khalili assembled Meiji decorative art objects in the United Kingdom and at the end of the 1990s was ready to reacquaint the American public with the origins of its sense of Japanese taste.[6]

In many ways, the 'Splendors of Meiji' exhibit was about Americans remembering their own discovery of Japan from the 1860s on, after Commodore Perry had forced the establishment of relations with the US, and the new Meiji regime promoted Japan's international visibility. One might argue that Japan in the 1870s was more accurately represented by the ubiquitous popular woodblock prints of Western-style accoutrements, captured most vividly in the series 'Famous places in Tokyo' – featuring telegraph wires, the brick buildings along Ginza, and most of all the first steam train between Tokyo and Yokohama – but those did not capture the American imagination at the time.[7] The focus on lacquer boxes, folded screens, vases, cabinetry and sword cases was a deliberate decision by the Meiji state following the recommendation of a German advisor, who sought to appeal to foreign tastes for exotic goods (in place of bridges and railroads) in light of Japan's low level of industrial development. And it worked. Japan first formally participated at the Vienna World Exhibition in 1873, but it was the Philadelphia Centennial Exposition in 1876 that put Japan firmly on the visual map. Tens of thousands of visitors were charmed by its 'antiquities' [...] grace and elegance of design and fabulous perfection of workmanship', as one critic commented. The fine bronze cranes, translucent enamel demon-quellers, samurai battle gear, and intricate rice-harvesting-scene engravings were, of course, not ancient but new, yet the motifs reached back into Japan's past and contrasted enormously with the American and European displays, such as Alexander Graham Bell's telephone, the John Bull steam locomotive, or the latest Krupp steel cannon.[8]

The Japanese, for their part, held their own industrial expositions, at which their latest textile loom, modern bridge and railway were on display. On the international stage, however, money was to be made by producing 'exotic goods for globetrotters', as a chapter in the *Splendors of Meiji* catalogue detailed, and thereby feeding the 'world-wide craze' for Japanese art wares concentrated on the treaty ports. The bestsellers were Shibayama ware, a hybrid of lacquer, metalwork, ivory and other materials that appropriated 'motifs and techniques from any and every nook and cranny of both Japanese and Chinese decorative traditions ... that would encapsulate the whole of "Oriental" culture' for the busy traveller.[9] In similar ways, foreign photographers such as Felice A. Beato (c. 1832–1909) created commercial photo albums of Japan's historic sites, landscapes, and people that were at their most successful when they offered a coherent narrative that captured the essence of Japanese culture in just the way their foreign clientele wanted it.[10] Such narratives visually equated Japan's exotic otherness with backwardness in historical time – Japan as memory and myth.

The commercialization of 'old Japan' in the 1860s and 1870s found its highbrow counterpart in the following decades thanks to close collaborations between American and Japanese intellectuals turned art collectors. Ernest Fenollosa, a Harvard man who taught philosophy in Japan, was on a mission to rescue Japanese art from decay and wanted it preserved in the West, much in the tradition of British archaeologists in Egypt and elsewhere at that time. His friend Okakura Kakuzo, the author of the quote with which this essay began, on the other hand, developed an 'aesthetic nationalism' through which he glimpsed, for example in a seventh-century Buddhist *kannon* statue, a cultural essence that was clearly Asian (owing to China) and at the same time distinctly Japanese.[11] Together, they collected the authentic 'old Japan' – mainly religious art – and donated these treasures to the Museum of Fine Arts in Boston, where Okakura served as the first curator of the largest collection of Japanese art outside Japan, then as today.[12] Whether in museums or in ordinary folks' living rooms, Japan established a visual presence in America (and to a lesser degree in Europe) at the end of the nineteenth century by way of a national identification with the art-crafts of its pre-modern past, whether newly created or indeed old.

A second significant phase of 'collecting Japan' occurred in the 1950s and 1960s in the course of rehabilitating Japan from former enemy to ally and friend. John D. Rockefeller III and his wife Blanchette, both Asian art enthusiasts, stood at the centre of a movement to reintroduce 'exotic Japan' to the American public as a culture marked by homogeneity and harmony such as could be glimpsed in the simple beauty of a Zen garden or Nara-period sculpture. In many ways, the post-war rediscovery of Japanese art reconnected with Okakura's patronage of ancient Buddhist art and the spiritual principles he introduced to Americans with his enormously influential *The Book of Tea* (1906). More to the point, the promotion of a timeless, spiritual, resilient Japan through its arts – including the folklore movement of the interwar period – was part and parcel of America's politics of memory at the time, that is, the effort to convince the American public to forget about the Pacific War and embrace its (now non-threatening) ally in the Pacific. In a sense, while the late nineteenth-century Japan-craze ignored the present by celebrating Japan's past, the mid-twentieth-century version celebrated Japan's timeless present while ignoring its (wartime) past. The institutions founded around that enterprise – the Asia Society, the revived Japan Society, the US–Japan Friendship Commission etc. – were instrumental in re-educating the American public by funding Asian studies in the academies, schools and museums.

In Japan, meanwhile, struggles to overcome the very real social divisions rooted in the war experience and, perhaps even more, in the Allied occupation's interventions in Japanese politics and society, rendered the making of a national identity difficult. In the 1960s, however, two particularly visual events helped to articulate a sufficiently broad national memory that related Japan's modern past to the present in ways that could be celebrated – the 1964 Tokyo Olympics and the 1968 Meiji Centennial celebrations, both state-sponsored. For the historian of memory, the most useful visual sources are Kon Ichikawa's artistic film *Tokyo Olympiad* (1964) and Japanese catalogues of the many exhibitions and events that took place in every locality of the archipelago contributing to the larger narrative of '100 years of modernization'.[13] Ichikawa's film began with a long shot of a rising sun followed by beautiful images of the Olympic flame being carried from Greece via India, Southeast Asia, Okinawa, to Japan, where clips of rice terraces contrasted with the demolition of war-ravaged buildings until the flame arrived in spic-and-span modern Tokyo greeted by all the flags of the world. Close-ups of jets landing at the new Narita Airport and the American, then Russian teams of smiling blond athletes making their way off their planes mixed with special overtures given to the small, colourfully-dressed contingents from newly independent African and Asian nations, arriving at the state-of-the-art Olympic stadium.

This artful celebration of Japan having overcome the ravages of war and rejoining the world in peace, now ready to offer the most modern facilities to its international guests, was echoed at the Meiji Centennial with its exhibits, for example on 'Mutual influences between Japanese and Western arts'. But nothing spoke as eloquently to 'memory' than one of the Centennial's official posters, which featured a photo of an old, benevolent-looking man in Japanese dress looking down on his young granddaughter on his lap wearing a little pink dress who touches his chin with her small hand in a loving and curious way while his hand embracing her other hand holds a little Japanese flag. The caption read 'Embracing our wish for the future'. The great distance between the young child and the old man expressed through age and dress was nonetheless bridged by his support for her (the past for the present) and her curiosity towards him (the present towards the past), in which lay the nation's future.

Whereas Ichikawa did reflect on the arduous task of rebuilding after the war in Japan, the official Centennial celebrations conveniently left out the war disaster to directly connect Meiji – the hard work of jump-starting 'modernization' – with the post-war arrival at full modernity. Although the contentious memory of the war was never far below the surface in 1960s Japan (unlike, perhaps, in the United States), a national essence could nonetheless be visualized in terms of a more general overcoming of difficulties (in modernizing) at the core of present success.

One might legitimately claim a third historical moment around the turn of the millennium, when the authenticity of such efforts to articulate a national core or cultural essence began to be called into question on a large scale, in Japan and in America. As images of particular Japanese war crimes that had been left unresolved by both victors and losers began to flood not only Japan's but a global public culture attuned to issues of historical memory, the myths of cultural essences were harder to sustain. Exhibits such as *Splendors of Meiji*, the Leonard A. Lauder collection of Japanese early twentieth-century postcards at the MFA[14] or Japanese wartime propaganda textiles[15] questioned many of the cultural essentialisms that had enveloped Japan as memory and myth. Once we started seriously looking at Japan's modern popular arts, sometimes side-by-side with comparable contemporary works elsewhere, Japan began to look less exotic and a lot less spiritual and harmonious. Even though none of these stereotypes have died, the common conditions that Japan, the United States, and most of Europe share as late industrial societies within a global world may serve to deemphasize, for the time being, Japan's 'otherness'.

Of equal importance is surely the media revolution in the age of the internet, which has made Japan's visual record – and Asia's more broadly – incomparably more accessible in all its diversity. Perhaps no other academic initiative has capitalized on these new opportunities as deliberately as the multi-media web project *Visualizing Cultures: Image-Driven Scholarship* at the Massachusetts Institute of Technology.[16] Founded in 2002 by MIT professors John W. Dower and Shigeru Miyagawa, '*Visualizing Cultures* weds images and scholarly commentary in innovative ways to illuminate social and cultural history. ... *VC* is a gateway to seeing history through images that once had wide circulation among people of different times and places.'[17] The cultures being visualized here are those of everyday life in modern Japan and more recently modern China. They include commercial art, satirical art, commemorative art and propaganda art through prints, posters, postcards, photographs, sketches, paintings and drawings carefully integrated with text, close-ups and links to related or comparative materials.

The 41 exhibits (and counting) speak to 'memory' in multiple ways. The visual material presented here is meant to complicate older, received visualizations of Japan and China and in fact recover some of what had been missing in earlier visual renderings along the lines detailed above. The units on the highly modernist advertisements and posters of Japan's largest cosmetics company Shiseido between 1910 and 1940 rely on Shiseido's own extensive archives, virtually unknown outside Japan, and document a modern sophistication that rivals if not simply outperforms its counterparts in the West. Indeed, all units are based on already existing collections at archives, museums, in art catalogues or in published books. As such, the authors are keenly aware of the selectivity of the images that comprise each collection, the circumstances of their original production, and the new meanings the collection might acquire from today's perspective. Some are visual narratives that tend to be explicitly commemorative. The 'great encounter' between Commodore Perry and the Japanese in 1853–54 is presented through American eyes based on the official report of Perry's expedition,[18] as well as through Japanese eyes, which introduces a variety of artwork by many mostly unnamed artists.[19] Organized thematically and within this comparatively, the unit lets viewers contemplate not so much what exactly happened but how the events were interpreted and remembered through these two different cultural lenses. Other units function as artists' galleries that showcase critical, anti-mainstream struggles over war memory and foreign military bases in the 1950s. Most of all, the text accompanying each gallery or visual narrative explains in detail how one might 'read' these visual texts as memory.

Visualizing Cultures also demonstrates in frightening ways the destructive politics of memory that such easy access to potentially disturbing images on the internet can spur. A unit on Japanese woodblock prints of the first Sino-Japanese War in 1894–95 created at that time included several disturbing prints of valorous Japanese soldiers cutting down their Chinese enemies.[20] The text accompanying these prints carefully laid out the contemporary jingoistic and clearly racist public culture, to which these images contributed and of which they were evidence. This had been a historical reality the viewer was invited to study by way of the surviving visual record. In April 2006, a Chinese internet user lifted one of these prints out of context and circulated violent denouncements of *Visualizing Cultures'* directors, alleging they had posted the prints because they 'found killing Chinese people beautiful'. Within minutes, 'a torrent of vituperative e-mail and phone messages poured in' on the co-directors of the project, especially Shigeru Miyagawa, whose name identified him as Japanese. Insisting that the website 'insulted the Chinese people', Chinese students at MIT and elsewhere demanded that the unit be taken down.[21] What had happened?

The memory of Chinese suffering inflicted by Japanese militarism during World War II had emerged two decades earlier as a contentious factor in Chinese–Japanese relations and animated popular nationalism in China. After many decades of celebrating Maoist communism as the state-promoted core identity of mainland Chinese, an older national memory of China's humiliation at the hands of Western powers was reanimated by the newly relevant memory of suffering at the hands of Japan just as a 'rising China' began to rival Japan for hegemony in East Asia. Had the Chinese internet users read the text that accompanied these violent woodblock prints, they could easily have seen them as confirmation of – even empathy with – a Chinese memory of suffering by people outside China's national community. As it was, however, the very idea of non-Chinese treating icons of Chinese identity as part of a global public culture met with an emotionally charged push-back that owed much of its voracity to the medium in question – visual art.

Images function differently from text. We *see* with memory, whether framed by national identity, family or other group history, or individual experience. Images tend to tap into habits of mind (as distinct from critical thinking) – in this case an affronted nationalism – to make sense. The woodblock print, in its violent immediacy, served to heighten the rawness of a victimization consciousness as national memory, while the context in which it appeared seemed to negate such victimization: the people responsible for making it available to the global public came from outside China, indeed they represented those against whom China's national memory was directed, for both historical and contemporary reasons. Thus the response that the unit on Japanese woodblock prints of the first Sino-Japanese War 'insulted the Chinese people'. Here, one layer of memory was deliberately used to interfere with – or even hijack – another, turning the intended lesson on its head. It gives us reason to pause and reflect on the ways in which visual memory is habitual, contextual, selective and committed, for better or for worse.

Visualizing counter-memory: *The Story of Hanaoka*

The manner in which the politics of memory played themselves out in the *Visualizing Cultures* case – involving national memory in a global public context made immediately available via the internet – is unique to our contemporary times. But the political uses of diverse memories within Japan, and contested memories of World War II in particular, have a long and rich domestic history.[22] Japan's aggressive military expansion into mainland China between 1937 and 1945 (as well as its 35-year colonial rule of Korea) left an especially divisive legacy to the Japanese people in part because the Japanese government refused to face it through official apologies or reparations payments. As a United States' ally, Japan could not establish official relations after China's Communist Revolution in 1949, and when the two countries signed a peace treaty in 1978, the Chinese state relinquished its right to claim reparations. Nevertheless, since the 1990s and with the help of Japanese lawyers, Chinese individuals have sued the Japanese state for compensation for war crimes insufficiently prosecuted in the past, among them Japan's wartime use of Chinese forced labour.

In fact, Japanese citizens have, from the late 1940s on, actively resisted state-sponsored 'forgetting' of crimes committed against Chinese under Japanese militarism. One such early place of resistance was art. In 1950, when the Korean War began amid labour protests and a burgeoning anti-government peace movement in Japan, three woodcut artists from the Akita area in north-eastern Japan embarked on a collaborative project to document and commemorate through a series of woodcuts the uprising and massacre of Chinese forced labourers five years earlier at the nearby Hanaoka mine, owned by the national construction firm Kajima. The project was supported by the newly founded Japan–China Friendship Association, which published all 56 black-and-white woodcuts, each accompanied by a poem in local dialect, as a book entitled *Hanaoka Monogatari* (*The Story of Hanaoka*).[23] This collection will serve as an example of how historians might use a visual source to learn about memory, or, in this case, counter-memory, to borrow Michel Foucault's term.[24] For this was conceived of as resistance art, as remembering in the face of public forgetting, as local activism combatting the central government's negligence, as workers standing up to irresponsible capitalists, and of solidarity with Chinese residents who supported the communist People's Republic of China rather than the nationalist government on Taiwan.

These were dark images expressing a range of raw emotion, aided by the rugged bold lines of the black-and-white woodcut. Woodblock prints had been a major popular art in Japan since the seventeenth century and one whose original colour, style, and thematic repertoire have indeed made it virtually synonymous with 'Japan' in recent decades. It declined in the late nineteenth century only to be revived in the 1910s as a major vehicle for modernist styles and themes that spoke to the commercialization and industrialization of pre-war society more generally while also making use of Japanese folklore.[25] The prints that comprised *The Story of Hanaoka* connected more directly to the proletarian art movement of the 1920s and 1930s, but above all, the three artists under Maki Daisuke's guidance drew their inspiration from a style of woodcut that had come to visually define the anti-Japan resistance movement among Chinese left-wing artists in the 1930s such as the Shanghai-based revolutionary writer Lu Xun.[26]

Like their (artistically more accomplished) Chinese predecessors, the Hanaoka woodcuts conveyed powerful graphic messages in simplified form by way of strong value contrasts between the Japanese mining camp supervisors and the Chinese forced labourers.[27] They were full of dynamic movement, both in terms of physical action and emotional upheaval, suggesting disgust with the Japanese overseers' sheer brutality, breathless empathy with the Chinese victims' pain and despair, and a rooting for the labourers' solidarity and collective action. The critique of the mine owners was there from the start. The poem that accompanied the opening image, entitled 'Ballad of Hanaoka', read: '[e]very time there's war, they swell up: Mineworkers' ranks, mine-owners' purse. Hanaoka's copper mine is Hell's very worst'.[28] The next seven woodcuts detailed life at the mine under the pressures of war – rice paddies turned into 'metal shit'; families demanding the bodies of those who died in mine cave-ins; peasants, women, the sick, Koreans and even town merchants being 'dragooned' into working beyond their capacity to 'patriotically' produce copper and gunpowder.

The story of the Chinese forced labourers started with the ninth woodcut – a Japanese worker in the forefront leaning on a shovel watching a train come in from a distance, steam billowing ominously. Among the many trains bringing labourers to Hanaoka were three that brought Chinese POWs from Shandong, in July 1944, May 1945 and June 1945 ('Three trains', p. 18). The following three pieces ('Why were there Chinese in Hanaoka?' I, II, and III) textually shifted the narration to the Chinese, relating the story of their abduction and forced transport to their Japanese co-workers, while visually continuing the perspective of the Japanese worker as witness to the brutality to which the Chinese prisoners were subjected. There is a double act of witnessing going on here: the viewer is invited to bear witness to the Japanese workers listening sympathetically to the Chinese testifying to their suffering. In every picture, the Japanese overseers towered over the Chinese in shackles, packed into wagons like cattle, being thrown overboard from the transport ship or lying face down in the dirt. The overseers were well nourished in contrast to the scrawny, sunken-cheeked Chinese; they carried or swung weapons larger than themselves, their knees drawn up ready to strike with their oversized boots. This showed the continuation, if also intensification, of Kajima Construction's *modus operandi* at the Hanaoka mine during conditions of war (see Figure 5.1, 'Kajima Construction', p. 26).

There is no question that *The Story of Hanaoka* first and foremost documented the extreme physical brutality to which the Japanese mining camp personnel singled out the Chinese POWs. Being literally worked to death, denied adequate clothing, food and water while subjected to beatings with shovels, cudgels, swords and verbal abuse – all this was depicted in frightening candour. The

Figure 5.1 'Kajima Construction'.

extremely abusive treatment climaxed in the torture and massacre of more than 200 Chinese in response to the forced labourers' uprising and escape on 30 June 1945. After their recapture, they were tortured right on the town's square or inside Community Hall, strung up by their thumbs (see Figure 5.2, 'The Wire', p. 84). Today, there is enough historical evidence to corroborate these facts. For example, the trial records of a US military commission in Yokohama from 1947 to 1948, which prosecuted several Hanaoka camp guards and local policemen for conventional war crimes (abuse of prisoners) in connection with the massacre on 30 June, are indeed full of testimonies that speak directly to the abuses detailed in this woodcut series.[29] More recent oral histories with survivors of Chinese and Korean forced labour conducted in conjunction with compensation lawsuits in the 1990s confirm that this kind of treatment was far from exceptional in the last year of the war.[30]

At the time, however, this was only local knowledge. Maki Daisuke, the lead artist, was apparently motivated by the responsibility he felt to acknowledge what had taken place in his hometown. Growing up in difficult circumstances, he had spent some of his student years near the square in which the Chinese rioters were tortured after the uprising. Now he found himself back near Hanaoka having been laid off as a communist sympathizer in a labour strike at the electrical engineering company Hitachi and spent his time recording, through woodcuts, the Hitachi struggle, the farmers' movement, and finally *The Story of Hanaoka*.

Figure 5.2 'The Wire'.

A second, and in my reading even more important, memory theme was the Japanese workers' solidarity with the Chinese forced labourers, the betrayal of that solidarity in the face of coercion and its recreation in the post-war context. This was memory as confession or regret through which one glimpsed the possibility of redemption in the future. The artists devoted eight prints to the planning of the Chinese labourers' uprising against their Japanese captors: they were marked by as much tenderness as the previous ones were shot through with violence. Here the brave Chinese were in charge, Japanese and Korean workers joined hands with them in songs of liberation, shared the little food they had, and pledged victory not only for a free China but a new Japan relieved from the grip of fascists ('Pledge of Victory', p. 50). Indeed, hardly noticeable in the images, was the subtle flip over who joined whom in solidarity: suddenly it was the Chinese who rose up on behalf of their oppressed Japanese brothers: 'Now's the time/"to overthrow Japan's emperor system,/stop aggressive war,/set the people of Japan free –/for world peace/ for human happiness"' ('Secret Gatherings', p. 46). This surely was the language of post-war memory as it emerged in the crucible of left-wing democratic resistance. It was an attempt to retroactively make meaningful within a Japanese universe what had surely been senselessly violent actions from a Chinese contemporary standpoint.

The real tragedy to be mourned was the fact that the Japanese labourers ended up betraying their Chinese brothers by following orders to put down the uprising. Visually this was conveyed in a dull, subdued print, the ape-like figures of the Japanese workers only hinted at in the dark of night, faces almost invisible in favour of huge white-gleaming bamboo spears ('Bamboo Spears', p. 62). The poem read, '"They're armed!"/"They're uppity, those Chinks!"/"Kill 'em!"/Aping the officers,/officials and landlords filled our minds/ with malice./Wholly taken in by their glib talk,/you, I/took bamboo spears, drew swords,/swaggered into the woods,/took our stations.' Having become accomplices to the crime, the best the Japanese workers could do was bear witness and thereby rescue, in memory, the Chinese labourers' dignity as human beings. Whether intended or not, the piles of corpses in the square and in mass graves out in the fields made a visual link to Auschwitz, the grizzly pictures of which had travelled the world (see Figure 5.3, 'Bleached Bones', p. 88).

The story did not end here. Eleven more woodcuts followed on the legacy of Hanaoka: responsibility (or lack thereof), commemoration and lessons learned. The most important legacy was the political awakening of the Japanese workers through mourning the remains of the dead and listening to the voices of the survivors, even as they had to realize that justice was not being served where it was due. The ultimate responsibility for the employment of forced labour lay with the Kajima executives, who were released without a trial and went right back to their old game as capitalists: the print of three Kajima executives happily reading a newspaper announcement of their release, undisturbed by bad conscience – a murdered man hanging in a bubble unconnected to the three men – spoke powerfully to the artists' contention that the same criminals who

Figure 5.3 'Bleached Bones'.

had driven the country into war were still in charge (see Figure 5.4, 'Those Who Plan War', p. 94). In this dismal situation, hope was to be glimpsed in 'Learning from the example of those who came before' (p. 98), which made the surviving Chinese victims of the massacre the catalysts of Japan's as of yet unrealized anti-capitalist revolution. Tellingly the very last print – 'Never Forget!' (p. 110) – looked as if it had been lifted out of a collection of Chinese Communist Revolution woodcuts: a woman, man and children rushing forward with great determination, leaving the star-studded night behind. The close visual resemblance to contemporary Chinese woodcuts established this allegiance for anyone familiar with them.

'Never Forget Hanaoka' was above all a call to arms. As such it rested on a conflation of temporalities typical of the political uses of memory. The post-war present had altered the wartime past to create a sense of political solidarity that was mnemonically real but not historically true. Its very commitment to public protest Chinese-communist style resonated with the politics of the Japan–China Friendship Association, who made the memory of Hanaoka one of its first flagship activities. But in 1950s Japan, especially after the Stalin critique in 1953, critical memories of Japan's war crimes became tied to communism and as such had a precarious place in the political landscape of war memory in Japan. Such memories commanded a marginal public space that only broke up when Japan's domestic struggles over war memory had to contend with a global public eye. *The Story of Hanaoka* was reprinted in

Figure 5.4 'Those Who Plan War'.

1995, the 50th anniversary of the massacre, and served as evidence in the Hanaoka compensation trial against Kajima, which the survivors eventually won. It assumed broader public meaning in the early post-war and again in the late post-war contexts, whereas it remained virtually unknown for many decades in between.

Layers of memory: the work of Iri and Toshi Maruki

Thus far memorialization has emerged as selective, committed and disturbingly reductionist. To see with memory, including self-conscious counter-memory, has meant to celebrate or mourn the present on the basis of a narrowly defined past. The modern political woodcut with its bold, unambiguous, literally black-and-white contrasts illustrates this particularly graphically. But can visual art also aid in expanding the mental and ethical horizons of memory? The answer may lie in conceiving of memory and art's temporality more flexibly in relation to multiple contexts. For art has the capacity not only to direct or change minds but also to open hearts.

  The collection under consideration here is the 40-year collaborative work of Iri Maruki (1901–95) and Toshi Maruki (1912–2000), a husband-and-wife team of painters most famous for their 'Hiroshima Panels'. These consisted of 15 murals painted across eight-panel screens (each panel 1.8 by 7.2 metres in size) that explored the human consequences of the atomic bombings of

Hiroshima and Nagasaki. Six additional large panels turned to other twentieth-century mass atrocities, including Auschwitz and the Nanjing Massacre. Although not atomic bomb survivors themselves (they lived in Tokyo), they nevertheless witnessed the conflagration upon their trip to Hiroshima days after the bombing to help with relief efforts. *Ghosts*, completed in 1950, was their first response. Unlike the Hanaoka woodcuts, the Marukis' panels attracted much public attention through travelling exhibits and their permanent gallery near Tokyo, and they have inspired some of the best writing on visual memory.[31] Scholars such as John W. Dower and Kyo Maclear have argued that these panels show the power of art to break out of the reductionist tendencies of memory by experimenting with what I call *layers of memory*.[32]

Quite literally, the couple painted in layers. Both were accomplished artists before they met in 1939: Iri Maruki worked in the *nihonga* tradition, specializing in abstract landscape paintings in ink-and-brush, whereas Toshi Maruki was trained in Western-style figurative oil paintings. Their collaborative work drew upon an eclectic repertoire of artistic traditions that defied the modernist or postmodernist trends of their days. Their relationship, Iri once said in an interview, resembled, quite literally, 'oil and water'.[33] Painting from live subjects, Toshi's realistic, detailed human figures would be obscured by Iri's ink splashes, upon which she would repaint her bodies, until the multiple layers of concealing and repainting gradually produced a depth out of which emerged traces of the dead, survivors as phantoms of themselves, fragments of the past and irreconcilable fissures of the present. 'The ghosts of atrocity are everywhere, the Marukis tell us, but because they are vaporous, it is left to us to ensure that their claims on the living do not dissipate like smoke.'[34] Rather than simply representing a preconceived idea, commemorative art, Maruki-style, was a collaborative process that depended on the dynamics of adding layer upon layer of meaning, thereby offering multiple possibilities of what kind of 'whole' would emerge in the eye of the viewer.

The murals suggest jarring paradoxes that John Dower has described as a transmogrification of classical motifs: water, usually life-giving, carried death for many people in Hiroshima, who tried to quench their thirst in Hiroshima's rivers ('Water', pp. 38–41); mothers nursing dead babies or babies trying to nurse on dead mothers exploded the image of security and protection and turned it into despair ('Mother and Child', 1959, pp. 70–73); a bamboo grove, the symbol of resilience in Asia, so charred it only emphasized the nakedness of the victims, dead or alive ('Bamboo Grove', 1954, pp. 54–57). The 1969 mural 'Floating Lantern', perhaps the best known and certainly the most beautiful, addressed commemoration practices in Hiroshima directly. Here the older tradition of floating candle-lit lanterns down the river to invite back the dead took on more specific meanings. In their vision, the dead had never left; instead, Hiroshima's seven rivers had become 'gorged arteries of memory ... clogged with images' represented by a sea of lanterns, each of which bore a fragment (a skull in one lantern, an outstretched hand in another), whose detailed precision faded into abstractions when seen as a whole.[35] The Marukis' short comment read: 'The tide shifts before the lanterns reach the sea, and they are swept back to the city by the swell. Extinguished now, the mass of crumpled lanterns drifts in the dark currents of the river. In 1945, these same rivers flowed dense with corpses' ('Floating Lanterns', 1969, pp. 74–77).[36]

Over the Marukis' 40 years of collaboration, other layers of memory emerged. On an exhibition tour in America in 1970, they were asked if they could conceive of a Chinese artist touring Japan with paintings of the Rape of Nanjing.[37] This spurred a new phase of productivity in which they delved into new depths of what it meant to confront a more complex reality of victimization, indeed the human capacity for extraordinary destruction and suffering in the modern age writ large, transcending Japan's victimization in Hiroshima and Nagasaki. The murals of the early 1970s considered Hiroshima with an expanded vision: they discovered American prisoners of war who had died at the hands of locals seeking revenge before they succumbed to the effects of the bomb. They were painted in the imagined company of wives and lovers looking for them, as well as heaps of skulls. Then attention was turned to the Korean atomic-bomb victims, brought to Nagasaki as forced labourers, whose corpses, discriminated against even in death, were barely visible underneath a ravaging flock of crows picking out their eyeballs ('Crows', 1972, pp. 82–85). Iri's black-ink drawings of the crows blocked out much of the Korean corpses, thereby further underlining the mnemonic invisibility of the Koreans.

From then on, the Marukis branched out in ever widening circles while retaining their signature style of meticulous layering of images until a depth of meaning was achieved that exploded what had previously been visible. In 1975 they painted the Rape of Nanjing (having discovered that neither Japanese nor Chinese artists had ever rendered this atrocity visually), then Auschwitz, before turning to Japan's worst environmental disaster, the mercury poisoning of the fishing village Minamata by a nearby chemical plant. They returned to World War II with their mural 'The Battle of Okinawa' (1984), a military event that foreshadowed the complexity of competing communities of memory under American, then Japanese structures of dominance. Each part of this collection of murals, produced over four decades, speaks to the others powerfully. To ponder these linkages means to confront present varieties of human destructiveness in relation to past incarnations of it. As Kyo Maclear has suggested, '[a]rt, in this sense, opens us up to events whose value and meanings have not been exhausted. If art has a vocation, it is to remind us of the role we play in constructing a living memory.'[38]

Conclusion

For my (American) students, the Hiroshima Panels are jolting. The paintings fail to confirm the only way they have ever 'known' the atomic bombs – as successful tools to end an atrocious war. They express embarrassed disbelief that they never thought to consider what happened to the people of Hiroshima. While the panels do seem to suggest that the Japanese see themselves as victims of war, the figures do not look particularly Japanese (the Marukis drew them mostly naked, as the intense heat had melted away their clothes), and there is little else that is recognizably 'Japanese' in style. This art disavows my students' habits of seeing both the bomb and Japan, and in the company of the 'American POWs' and 'The Rape of Nanjing', even the trope of Japanese victimization crumbles. The absence of certainties afforded by earlier visions of *Japan as memory* first redirects their gaze to examine their own received narratives, and then convinces many to add in a different perspective or even commit to the need of a counter-memory in American public culture. Furthermore, if we linger and draw visual connections to other nuclear disasters or mass atrocities, the Japan/America or victim/perpetrator binary tends to vanish and other *layers of memory* make themselves apparent. I ask them: 'What kinds of witnesses will you be?'[39] This is our own memory work, and art can be a powerful resource.

Notes

All illustrations are from the book of woodprints, *The Story of Hanaoka*. The latest edition is Nozoe Kenji (ed.), Nii Hiroharu, Takidaira Jirō and Maki Daisuke, *Hanaoka Monogatari*, Tokyo: Ochanomizu shobō, 1995.

1 C. Benfey, *The Great Wave: Gilded Age Misfits, Japanese Eccentrics, and the Opening of Old Japan* (New York: Random House, 2003), p. 85.
2 E. Said, *Orientalism* (New York: Vintage Books, 1978).
3 John Dower makes this point in 'Sizing up (and breaking down) Japan' in H. Hardacre (ed.) *The Postwar Development of Japanese Studies in the United States* (Leiden: Brill, 1998), pp. 1–4.
4 I take this idea from K. Maclear, *Beclouded Visions: Hiroshima–Nagasaki and the Art of Witness* (Albany: SUNY Press, 1999), pp. 75, 82.
5 J. Earle, *Splendors of Meiji: Treasures of Imperial Japan – Masterpieces of the Khalili Collection* (St. Petersburg, Fl.: Broughton International Publications, 1999).
6 Ibid., 'Foreword' and 'Preface', pp. 8–9.
7 See the popular woodblock prints of Japan's remarkably fast 'Westernization' in the Jean S. and Frederic A. Sharf Collection at the Museum of Fine Arts in Boston. See the web exhibit 'Throwing off Asia I' on *Visualizing Cultures*, http://ocw.mit.edu/ans7870/21f/21f.027/throwing_off_asia_01/toa_essay02.html (accessed 25 August 2012).
8 Ibid., 'Revolutions and exhibitions', pp. 31, 35.
9 Ibid., 'Exotic goods for globetrotters', p. 93.
10 A. Hockley, 'Felice Beato's Japan: places/people – album by the pioneer foreign photographer in Yokohama', units on the *Visualizing Cultures – Image-Driven Scholarship* website http://ocw.mit.edu/ans7870/21f/21f.027/home/vis_menu.html (accessed 23 August 2012).
11 For a theoretical discussion of this, see J. Clark, 'Okakura Tenshin (Kakuzo) and aesthetic nationalism' in J.T. Rimer (ed.) *Since Meiji: Perspectives on the Japanese Visual Arts, 1868–2000* (Honolulu: University of Hawaii Press, 2012), pp. 212–56.
12 A fascinating account of the Fenollosa-Okakura collaboration is 'The Boston Tea Party' in Benfey, *The Great Wave*, pp. 75–108.

13 An overview of the centennial celebrations is provided in Naikaku sōri daijin kanbō [Office of the Minister of the Interior], *Meiji hyakunen kinen gyōji no kiroku* [Record of the Meiji Centennial Events], Tokyo, 1969.

14 Museum of Fine Arts, Boston, *Art of the Japanese Postcard*, 2004.

15 J.M. Atkins, *Wearing Propaganda: Textiles on the Home Front in Japan, Britain, and the United States, 1931–1945* (New Haven: Yale University Press, 2005).

16 The website can be found at http://ocw.mit.edu/ans7870/21f/21f.027/home/index.html (accessed 25 August 2012).

17 'About *Visualizing Cultures*', http://ocw.mit.edu/ans7870/21f/21f.027/home/vc01_about.html (accessed 25 August 2012).

18 M.C. Perry, Narrative of the Expedition of an American Squadron to the China Seas and Japan, Performed in the Years 1852, 1853, and 1854, Under the Command of Commodore M.C. Perry, United States Navy, by Order of the Government of the United States, compiled by F.L. Hawks, D.D., L.L.D. (Washington, DC: Published by order of the Congress of the United States, 1856–58).

19 'Black ships and Samurai II: facing east, facing west', http://ocw.mit.edu/ans7870/21f/21f.027/black_ships_and_samurai_02/bss_visnav01.html (accessed 25 August 2012).

20 'Throwing off Asia II', http://ocw.mit.edu/ans7870/21f/21f.027/throwing_off_asia_02/index.html (accessed 25 August 2012).

21 P. Perdue, 'Reflections on the "*Visualizing Cultures* incident"', *MIT Faculty Newsletter*, 18(5), 2006, http://web.mit.edu/fnl/volume/185/perdue.html (accessed 26 August 2012).

22 I have traced this history in some detail in F. Seraphim, *War Memory and Social Politics in Japan, 1945–2005* (Cambridge, MA: Harvard University Asia Center Press, 2006).

23 The latest edition is Nozoe Kenji (ed.), Nii Hiroharu, Takidaira Jirō and Maki Daisuke, *Hanaoka Monogatari* (Tokyo: Ochanomizu shobō, 1995).

24 M. Foucault, *Language, Counter-Memory, Practice: Selected Essays and Interviews*, ed. D.F. Bouchard (Ithaca: Cornell University Press, 1977).

25 L. Smith, 'Japanese prints 1868–2008', in J.T. Rimer (ed.) *Since Meiji: Perspectives on the Japanese Visual Arts, 1868–2008* (Honolulu: Hawaii University Press, 2012), pp. 361–407.

26 L. Rotondo, *Chinese Revolutionary Woodcuts, 1935–1948: From the Herman Collection, the Picker Art Gallery, Colgate University* (Middletown, CT: Davison Art Center, 1984).

27 Adapted from Ellen D'Oench's preface in ibid., p. 3.

28 Ibid., p. 2.

29 RG 153 Records of the Judge Advocate. Reviews 8th Army – Yokohama, Box 2 (2 May 1949), National Archives and Records Administration (USA).

30 For example Shōgen suru fūkei kankō iinkai (ed.) *Shōgen suru fūkei: Nagoya hatsu Chōsenjin Chūgokujin kyōsei renkō no kiroku* [The landscape of giving testimonies: Records of Korean and Chinese forced labourers from Nagoya] (Nagoya: Fūbaisha, 1991).

31 In particular, J.W. Dower and J. Junkerman (eds) *The Hiroshima Murals: The Art of Iri Maruki and Toshi Maruki* (Tokyo: Kodansha International, 1985), as well as Dower and Junkerman's documentary *Hellfire: A Journey from Hiroshima* (1986); Maclear, *Beclouded Visions*.

32 J.W. Dower, 'Crossing boundaries: an introduction' in H. Isaacs and J. Junkerman (eds) *Surviving Visions: The Art of Iri Maruki and Toshi Maruki* (Boston: Massachusetts College of Art, 1988), pp. 6–7; Maclear, *Beclouded Visions*, pp. 159–80.

33 J. Junkerman, 'Oil and water: an interview with the artists', in Dower and Junkerman, *The Hiroshima Murals*, pp. 121–28.

34 Ibid., p. 124; Maclear, *Beclouded Visions*, pp. 166–67.

35 Maclear, *Beclouded Visions*, p. 171; Dower and Junkerman, *The Hiroshima Murals*, pp. 19–20.
36 References are to Dower and Junkerman, *The Hiroshima Murals*, both art plates and Dower's introduction.
37 The brutal destruction of the city of Nanjing by the Japanese army in 1938 in which up to 300,000 Chinese died.
38 Maclear, *Beclouded Visions*, pp. 176–77.
39 Ibid., p. 9

6 The contested memorial cultures of post-Liberation France

Polemical responses to the legal purge of collaborators, 1944–c.1954

Joan Tumblety

In early November 1951, a Catholic mass was held in the cathedral of Notre-Dame in central Paris to honour the memory of Marshal Pétain, head of state of the collaborating Vichy regime (1940–44). It sparked energetic popular protests that had been encouraged by Resistance veterans' groups, where angry crowds shouted 'Pétain assassin!' and 'Death to collaborators!' For historians of memory, there are at least two sets of source material here. On the one hand there are the rituals – the religious ritual designed to build a sense of solidarity among those who valued a military hero and political leader and who mourned his passing; and by contrast the familiar ritual of the counter-demonstration, similar in function to the first while being pitted against it. On the other hand there are the newspaper articles in which these events were reformulated by a mass press that competed to give them meaning. Thus the pro-Pétain publication *Rivarol* complained that the authorized news agencies had issued no photographs of the mass, so that the French reading public were left with the impression that the 'popular' – and therefore legitimate – event had been constituted only by the protest, despite the fact that some 6,000 people had crammed into the cathedral for the occasion.[1]

Both sets of sources suggest how 'memorial cultures' – in this case the public commemoration of France's experience under occupation by Germany during the Second World War – are created and maintained.[2] This chapter will consider the role in that process of a set of interlinked sources that show similar interactions between ritual and text – legal testimony and legal polemic, the activities of 'memory' associations, the periodical press and the hybrid genres of memoir-history and 'history novels'. In discussing these sources I want to examine the problem of how memorial cultures operate, and to highlight the political stakes that are invariably involved in such memory work. What I want to emphasize is how these processes of memorialization are multiple and conflict-ridden; they usually involve the interplay of rival visions of past and present, constituting a struggle among rival groups to lend legitimacy to private or sectarian grievances by influencing the dominant stories that are told about the events in question.

The year 1951 was a crunch year where commemoration of France's recent wartime past was concerned. It brought not only the death of the former

Vichy head of state, Pétain, but was also the year in which the long legal purge of Vichy political elites and other collaborators ended. Pétain himself had been put on trial for 'intelligence with the enemy' (the German occupying forces) in summer 1945: his death sentence was commuted and he spent the rest of his life imprisoned on a small island off the west coast of France. The end of this purge, that had handed down almost 40,000 prison terms and up to 1,500 executions, coincided with a number of legal amnesties voted for by elected deputies, allowing the early release from prison of many among the condemned.[3] In the early 1950s, then, it would seem that the French justice system, and the political authorities who shaped its mechanisms, had extinguished its persecutory drive in favour of some kind of national reconciliation. One of the strongest advocates for that shift was Jacques Isorni, the high-profile lawyer of the most famous purge defendants – Pétain himself and collaborationist intellectual Robert Brasillach – who was elected to the French parliament as a deputy in 1951. Isorni had foregrounded demands for amnesty and the release of Pétain in his electoral campaign, and he devoted the rest of his career to a spirited attack on what he saw as the hypocrisy and injustice of the 1944–51 purges. Along with a number of like-minded cultural elites, he developed a critique aimed at both the legal and judicial mechanisms of the Liberation era, and at the new republican authorities who – to his mind – manipulated the recent past to fit political objectives in the present. They were charged with telling skewed stories about what the French had experienced between 1940 and 1944, forging an officially sanctioned culture of commemoration that valued the experience of resistance to the German occupiers rather than collaboration with them. I will explore how this so-called 'counter-orthodoxy' (or 'national opposition') worked at the level of the sources that historians can use to analyse it, highlighting some of the attempts in the years after the Liberation to galvanize a memorializing narrative that was counter to the imagined dominant and 'official' one.[4]

That dominant memorial culture was constituted through its own interlinked rituals and texts, including the purge process itself: the arguments rehearsed by the prosecution in the serious play of the courtroom were reiterated in mainstream newspapers, so that the overall narrative of a just and necessary purge was reinforced. That the wider public endorsed the punishment of former collaborators is suggested by the overwhelming support for the trials found in the semi-official public opinion surveys of the period.[5] Memorial culture also encompassed ceremonies, often involving military parades, which were organized by state and municipal authorities who claimed to be acting as custodians of the nation's heritage. Key anniversaries of the Liberation of France were marked in this way, the involvement of private veterans' groups adding to the authority of such occasions. The date of 8 May (for the German surrender in 1945) was the official national day for commemoration of the war after 1946, thereby emphasizing how the French experience was part of the wider, successful Allied struggle.[6] But 25 August (for the triumphant march of de Gaulle's FFI down the Champs-Élysées in central Paris in 1944) was also widely celebrated. In 1948, for example, a commemorative plaque was unveiled at the Hôtel de Ville by the leader of the Paris municipal council in a ceremony in which war veterans took part.[7] The proximity of VE day (8 May) and the feast day of Joan of Arc – a medieval martyr honoured in both ultra-nationalist and republican traditions – meant that on at least one occasion these two 'liberating epics' were celebrated together, presented in the press as intertwined anniversaries of French military honour.[8] This sort of juxtaposition was commonplace in post-war commemorative acts: it had the effect of displacing uncomfortable memories of military defeat (in 1940) and the political division of the Vichy period by emphasizing a story of national unity, continuity and triumph.

In addition, the courage and initiative of Resistance fighters was celebrated through the genre of film, often publicly funded and controlled. In 1946, there were at least a dozen feature films on the French Resistance shown in cinemas. Some achieved immense popular success; others were used as teaching aids in schools. For historian Suzanne Langlois, it was the drive to create 'visual documents' of the Resistance struggle that underpinned this production: the films functioned as historical sources in the absence of much written material about work that had been of necessity secret, thus playing a role in 'the reconstruction of wartime memory'. In fact, Langlois argues that the reiteration of stock images of the resistance struggle on screen became 'an important source of general knowledge about the Resistance' in the years after 1944.[9] That is certainly what the embittered supporters of the condemned collaborators thought.[10] However, it should be recognized that it was not only those who were critical of the purges who felt excluded from this memorial culture. Jewish survivors, whether those who had been deported or those who remained in France, found themselves living in a country that failed to appreciate either the scale of anti-Semitic violence inflicted across the continent or the part played by Vichy authorities in the fatal deportation of around 76,000 Jews from France. Survivors often returned to Paris to find their homes had been expropriated or their household goods stolen by neighbours; the process of seeking restitution was long and often fruitless. Leora Auslander suggests that the loss of such personal objects may well have signalled a wider loss of home for these men and women, even 'the loss of memory itself'.[11] Furthermore, the very Resistance fighters whose collective actions facilitated the post-war cult of Resistance were often honoured in rather abstract terms, the sweat and sacrifice of individual men and women often overlooked in favour of a homogenized narrative of heroism.[12] Sectional memories were in any case always present under the veneer of surface unity. Associations set up to represent specific interest groups, such as those created by Resistance veterans or deportees, anchored their campaigns in competing appeals to history in order to secure pensions, compensation or social recognition for their members. We need to be aware of the moving waters that lie beneath 'official' memorializing narratives that might otherwise appear to fix memories of Occupation as a singular thing: this is not so much the failure of 'official memory' as an unavoidable part of the memorializing process. I would venture that the above examples collectively suggest not only that historians need to take into account the plural nature of memory and memorialization, but also that we need to be attuned to the relationship between 'collective modes of remembering' and power.[13]

From the courtroom to public life: Jacques Isorni and legal polemic

The purges (1944–51) lay at the heart of the memorial culture built by those who rejected the orthodox commemoration of the war, and at the heart of the purges loomed the figure of the lawyer. Inside the courtroom the prosecution and defence in each case were – in part – charged with the task of harnessing the available evidence to emerging national narratives likely to secure the desired verdict from the jury. By paying attention to the rhetorical strategies of lawyers as well as the testimony provided by witnesses and defendants, the trial transcripts of collaborators themselves provide a source for the study of memory politics. It was here that the onslaught against the memorializing narratives being cultivated by the political authorities began. Defence lawyers claimed (not unreasonably, in fact) that far from resurrecting the democratic credentials of the republic, the purge process was arbitrary and hypocritical (the severity of sentences depended on the timing of the trial, some professions were pursued more systematically than others, many of the presiding judges had served the Vichy regime), and that it flew in the face of juridical conventions by applying laws (especially the new crime of national degradation) retroactively. Another common technique was to argue that collaboration had provided not proof of France's treasonous shame but a 'shield' against greater German brutality. The case of Bernard Faÿ was typical in this respect. A Catholic intellectual and academic who became head of the French national library in 1940, Faÿ was sentenced to forced labour for life in December 1946, although he managed to escape after several years of incarceration.[14] The defence counsel presented Faÿ as a loyal servant of the Vichy state – not the Germans – for his work against 'secret societies' (Freemasons). Against claims that Faÿ had had intelligence with a 'foreign power' it was argued that the defendant had prevented the Germans getting their hands on a single volume in the national library.[15] This defence strategy may not have been powerful enough to secure acquittal, but it is a measure of its wider resonance that, once the fury of the purges had dissipated, the view of the Vichy regime as a protective 'shield' became established even in mainstream scholarship.[16]

Another widespread technique was to draw parallels between the purges and the Terror of 1793. This rhetorical strategy was deployed by the lawyer of Fernand de Brinon, Paris ambassador to Germany after 1940 who was executed for treason in 1947. The defence counsel, Bizos, complained that the case against his client had been made without due process: he saw in the trial echoes of the 'partisan justice' to which the French Revolution had descended through the 'Tribunals of Prairial' (a reference to the notorious law of June

1794 that withdrew defendants' right to witnesses and a thorough examination of the evidence).[17] The injustices carried out in the courtroom were magnified as far as these critical voices were concerned by the violence of the so-called wild purges, the summary executions and other extra-judicial punishments that were meted out to suspected collaborators by local Resistance fighters all over the country in the chaos of regime change in summer and autumn 1944. It became increasingly routine in these oppositional narratives to claim that a 'red terror', promulgated by communist resisters, was at work during this time, and that it had taken more than 100,000 lives.[18] This wider context of popular violence helps to explain why the historical parallel with the French Revolution was so widespread.

Trial transcripts were not just kept for posterity in archival vaults. Several were published soon after the judgment had been decided, forming a genre for which the reading public seemed to have a keen appetite in the years after Liberation.[19] Jacques Isorni, the lawyer-memoirist-polemicist-deputy who remained a tireless (if unsuccessful) campaigner for the pardon of Pétain, and who was also a force behind the passage of the 6 August 1953 amnesty law in the French parliament, was a central figure in this respect.[20] His campaigns plugged Isorni into the activities of the kind of 'memory' associations discussed in the next section, but he also published a good many books that served to popularize his legal polemics among a wider audience. Among these were *plaidoiries* (defence pleadings) from Isorni's wartime and Liberation-era career, including the defence arguments he presented for his two most famous clients. In Pétain's trial, Isorni too had argued that Vichy had provided a protective 'shield' for France. And he painted Brasillach as a naïve but talented writer who did not deserve to die for expressing his opinions, especially when equally culpable collaborators (including purge-era lawyers and judges who had previously served the Vichy regime) had escaped the reach of the law.[21]

These themes echoed in his other books, some of which were specifically designed to swing public opinion behind the request for a judicial review of Pétain's trial. In 1948, for instance, Isorni facilitated the publication of a volume of testimonies by politicians and intellectuals whose purpose was to show that Pétain's actions under the Occupation had benefited France.[22] And to coincide with the 50th anniversary of the battle of Verdun, he published a collection of correspondence with Pétain's wife that stretched over the Marshal's long period of incarceration. In stoking the memory of Pétain the celebrated army commander of 1916, Isorni wanted the public to doubt the justice of letting a First World War hero pass his extreme old age in prison.[23] Isorni invited other kinds of juxtaposition, too. In one text he underlined the political neutrality with which he (a man of the right) had defended communists before the special courts set up by the Vichy government to prosecute its political enemies in 1942. By contrast, the recent purges had to his mind made criminals of thousands in politically motivated trials, the fate of defendants decided in minutes by prejudiced juries whose minds were already made up.[24] Other works offered a more allusive critique of the purges.

In 1949 Isorni republished the ill-fated 'appeal to the nation' that Louis XVI's defence counsel had written in early 1793 in an attempt to save the king from the guillotine. He articulated no analogy with the contemporary situation, but against the almost routine parallels being drawn between the brutality of the purges and the Terror of 1793 inside and outside the courtrooms of France, this connection was surely intended. (Elsewhere, Isorni in fact asserted that the three greatest trials in French history were those of Louis XVI, Joan of Arc and Philippe Pétain.[25]) It seems clear from these examples that Isorni's arguments – first rehearsed in court and then reiterated for the reading public – constituted a kind of historical revisionism, an attack on the consensual (his)story of France's recent and distant past that was endorsed by the ruling authorities.

The work of 'memory' associations and the popular press

This assault on the dominant memorial culture was also expressed through the work of several long-lived societies set up literally to 'defend the memory' of political and literary figures who had fallen victim to the purges. The most significant of these was the Association pour Défendre la Mémoire du Maréchal Pétain (ADMP) established in November 1951. Jacques Isorni was a statutory member. Its main purpose was twofold. First, it tried to rally the like-minded behind a campaign for the transfer of the Vichy leader's remains to the military cemetery at Douaumont, close to the First World War battlefields of Verdun where he had forged his reputation as a public figure.[26] Secondly, it functioned in parallel to the ongoing efforts of Isorni for Pétain's legal rehabilitation. Its high-profile leaders also wanted to popularize the arch-conservative values of the Vichy regime as an antidote to contemporary political preferences. Like Isorni, they were intent on gathering evidence of the good that Pétain had done as head of state, such as the testimony of one former soldier who had been immensely grateful for the 1940 armistice, organized by Pétain, which had ended his period of anxiety.[27] One could also mention the Association des Amis de Robert Brasillach (ARB) founded in Switzerland in 1948 that set about eulogizing the executed collaborationist as a martyr of purge injustice through its semi-regular magazine, or the tiny 'club' and monthly bulletin created in 1981 in support of collaborationist Catholic intellectual Alphonse de Châteaubriant, who had been condemned to death in absentia by the courts in 1948 and who died in exile in 1951.[28] The popular reach of these societies was limited but the publications that they produced, the publicity flyers they distributed and the speeches their leaders made at social events, provide historians with important evidence of 'memory work' in action.

The periodical press also provides historians of these memory politics with a crucial source. Even before the purge process was complete a rash of weekly and monthly newspapers or magazines erupted onto the scene in an attempt to reach out beyond the membership of such small associations, presenting oppositional and intertwined narratives about the present and the past. Collectively, backed by powerful right-wing financiers, they helped to build what Nicholas Hewitt describes as a 'reactionary culture'[29] in the post-war years, rooted in a sense of outrage at the manipulation of collective memory by the ruling authorities.[30] The most successful of these publications was *Rivarol*, whose very title evokes the memorialization impulse at the heart of political struggle: it honours the iconic royalist journalist *émigré* of the 1790s, Antoine de Rivarol, who stridently and wittily rejected the French Revolution and the democratic values on which all the French republics had thereafter been built. It first appeared in January 1951, with a circulation of around 45,000 in the middle of that decade.[31] It is worth noting that the activities of this oppositional press and the 'memory' associations referred to above were mutually reinforcing, since subscribers and members were sometimes shared and frequent support of each other's campaigns forged something of a coherent community of complaint.[32] Similarly, the periodical press played a role in popularizing the legal efforts of maverick Jacques Isorni, for example celebrating the rapturous applause the lawyer received in 1951 when he spoke to a 2,000-strong audience at a human rights meeting in Marseilles. Isorni's mission supposedly to heal divisions among the French was reiterated; his claims of a million purge suspects and 150,000 summary executions were repeated and thus endorsed, helping to build an alternative body of social knowledge about the recent past.[33] *Rivarol* often criticized political and judicial elites opposed to more generous amnesty laws, and in late 1951 claimed to have garnered more than 200,000 signatures for its own petition in favour of the transferral of Pétain's remains to Verdun.[34]

Certainly, *Rivarol* not only attacked the democratic ethos of the nascent Fourth Republic, but railed against the memorial culture over which it presided. The polemical articles, historical accounts and fiction published in the newspaper negotiated both the recent and the more distant past, so that in effect the political position of the editors was explained and justified through an appeal to a shared appreciation of elements of the national past that were allegedly being repressed in public discourse. In all of this, it was the legitimacy of certain stories about the national past that was being contested as much as the events of that past themselves; and under particular scrutiny was the way that these stories – of unqualified national support for resistance, of the nobility and humanity of resistance fighters, of widespread popular hatred for all that collaboration and the Vichy regime had stood for, of the even-handed and necessary justice of the post-Liberation purges – functioned as political capital for the leaders of the new republic, helping to shore up their control over the present. In short, the attacks on this presumed orthodoxy proceeded through comparison and analogy, through a juxtaposition of wars and legal judgments across time that had the effect of naturalizing the violence involved in the rise and fall of all regimes and empires, and thus relativizing the crimes punished in the post-Liberation purges. If, as one contributor put it, 'we are in the century of treason', then why single out one set of transgressions for punishment and not others?[35] Philip Watts has asserted that this kind of allegorical technique was a deliberate rhetorical strategy in building a counter-narrative of purge injustice among oppositional literary elites in general.[36]

The pages of *Rivarol* were saturated with such attempts to mobilize the past in a bid to problematize and ultimately reshape the memorial culture of the present. The purges of the 1940s were first and foremost compared to the Terror during the French Revolution: testimony from purge defendants themselves was used to substantiate the general claim that the violent Liberation had produced more victims than the revolutionary tribunals of 1793–94.[37] It was also pointed out that the purge of 1816 that followed the restoration of the Bourbon monarchy after the fall of Napoleon was also less bloody and extensive than the present one; just as the 'civil war' of the 1940s had allegedly created more victims than the wars of religion in the sixteenth century.[38] A parallel was drawn between Marshal Pétain and Marshal François Bazaine, who was condemned to death for surrendering the town of Metz to the enemy during the Franco-Prussian war of 1870: if generations had been taught that Bazaine was a traitor, the author argued, that was because no one had been courageous enough to 're-establish the truth'.[39] Instead of celebrating Bastille Day, the publication marked other occasions such as the centenary of Pétain's birth and the anniversary of the execution of Robert Brasillach, which by coincidence was also the date – 6 February – of the right-wing anti-government protests of 1934, celebrated by journalists as a great earlier instance of 'national opposition'.[40] Such figures were routinely compared to iconic national martyrs such as Joan of Arc (burned at the stake as a heretic in 1431) and André Chénier (the poet guillotined during the Terror of 1794), which had the effect of de-emphasizing and sanitizing their actions during the war.[41] *Rivarol* marked the anniversaries of the Liberation of Paris, and their officially orchestrated parades and ceremonies, by underlining the lack of popular involvement in the original events and by painting communist Resistance fighters as brigands who were usurping and alienating the voice of 'real' resisters.[42]

Indeed, every effort was made to burst the bubble of 'official' memorializing practices by arguing for the brutality of individual Resistance fighters, especially communist ones. On one occasion a supportive letter from a female reader was published, attesting to the desire of local communities to uncover the truth about the 'red terror' that was perpetrated in their midst.[43] Articles that decried Liberation violence were sometimes illustrated with large photographs of the so-called *tondues*, the 20,000 or so suspected female collaborators whose heads had been shaved all over France in a ritual display of local Resistance muscle. Postcards depicting this phenomenon had been sold commercially in 1944–45 as rather grisly souvenirs: *Rivarol* was here harnessing the voyeurism at the heart of this phenomenon for new purposes, exposing the atrocities committed by communists who were perceived as most guilty of popular (sexual) violence and the most zealous supporters of the purge.[44]

Thus did the contributors to *Rivarol* turn the narrative of a just Liberation back on itself. Perhaps most ironically, given its hostility to the 'universalist' republican values that underpinned the Fourth Republic, *Rivarol* configured the purges as a human rights abuse, arguing that to honour its own commitment to the defence of the human person taken by delegates to the United Nations in 1948, the French regime ought to reinstate political elites barred from office under the purge.[45] And when news of Pétain's final illness became public knowledge in spring 1951, the editorial team commented sarcastically that it was a 'nice regime of defenders of the human person' that would let an extremely elderly man languish in a dungeon.[46] Similarly, in occasionally championing leftist victims of laws against censorship (such as anarchist Jean Grave who was imprisoned for his published opinions in the 1890s[47]), and by reminding their audience of leftist campaigns for amnesty in earlier times (as when the novelist Victor Hugo, as senator in the 1880s, had worked towards an amnesty for the imprisoned and exiled Communards of 1870[48]), the contributors to *Rivarol* sought to destigmatize the transgression of collaborators by emptying it of ideological content and casting it purely in terms of freedom of expression.

From memoir-history to 'history novel'

This challenge to the dominant memorial culture took many forms, and it ranged beyond controversies over the legal purge of collaborators and challenges to national anniversaries. In this section I want to show how two hybrid genres – 'memoir-history' and so-called 'history novels' – can be read as attempts to build a multifaceted edifice of historical revisionism that would challenge conventional accounts of the war. Many of these texts were released by small houses specifically set up for the purpose of rehabilitating unfashionable views of the Occupation, for example Les Sept Couleurs, established by Maurice Bardèche and named after one of his brother-in-law Robert Brasillach's novels.[49] But mainstream publisher Fayard, whose history collection was directed for a time in the early post-war years by monarchist historian Pierre Gaxotte, also published this kind of material and brought it to a wider audience. Paying attention to the question of who published these works allows the historian to identify tangible vehicles for memory work and to gain a sense of how widely these ideas travelled.

The rash of autobiographies that were published shortly after the incarcerated left prison as a result of the amnesties of the early 1950s can be read as 'memoir-histories', written by self-identified victims of injustice with an axe to grind about the present regime and its alleged manipulation of the past. Pierre-Antoine Cousteau – brother of the more famous scientist and marine explorer Jacques Cousteau and former editor of the collaborationist newspaper *Je suis partout* – was released from prison in 1953. In a self-exonerating text published three years later, Cousteau expressed the sense of outrage he felt coming out into a city remapped by the victors, scarred with public landmarks named in honour of Churchill, Roosevelt and Stalin. He found a country 'occupied' once again, this time by a combination of American capital and Resistance-controlled doublethink: 'In the same breath, they tell us that triangles have four sides, that de Gaulle is intelligent, that men are naturally good, that Paris liberated itself, that the Russians are protecting Hungary, that the *Boches* [Germans] have square heads, that a cannibal is as good as a Breton, that parliament is an august institution, that the British are our friends, that the war of '39 was necessary ...'[50]

Sometimes these memoir-histories specifically rebutted the trial narratives that had condemned their authors. The memoirs published by Bernard Faÿ in 1952, for example, reiterated the shield theory articulated in his trial. Faÿ – who suspected his jurors had all been communists – also emphasized his victim status by describing his captivity in the Drancy internment camp outside Paris and in Fresnes prison: these establishments were well known as German-run detention centres for Jews and political prisoners during the war. Unrepentant, he set himself up as a man on the losing side of history, positioning himself as a martyr of a 'spiritual cause' attacked unjustly after 1944 by reigning materialist, communist and Masonic forces.[51] And Fernand de Brinon's posthumous memoirs reiterated part of the trial defence, too, situating his Occupation-era acts within the longer French diplomatic tradition of seeking *rapprochement* with Germany. The purge court had understood de Brinon's interwar liaisons with German elites as a precursor to his later collaboration with the Nazis (de Brinon had met Hitler personally five times in the mid-1930s), but de Brinon insisted that it should be seen the other way around: his collaboration was merely a continuation of an earlier quest for reconciliation that many republican political elites had supported.[52] Both men sought in their memoir-histories specifically to correct the courtroom narrative that had condemned them. Their self-serving texts were, in that process, attempts to rewrite the public story of the Liberation era as well as their own individual ones.

Sometimes the historical revisionism at the heart of this literature was overt. Arguably its most vitriolic proponent was Maurice Bardèche, brother-in-law of Robert Brasillach and post-war convert to the radical right. Bardèche was briefly imprisoned in 1954 for the crime of 'apology for murder' by disputing German war crimes in a book about the Nuremberg trials.[53] He complained about the 'falsification of history' that characterized the era of the purges, arguing that the Allied governments were prosecuting Nazi leaders in order to deflect attention away from their own alleged war crimes, especially the civilian bombing of Dresden and the deployment of atomic bombs in Japan. As he put it in a different book, '60,000 Japanese were destroyed in 14 seconds for the "defence of the human person"'.[54] He accounted for the savagery of the war in east-central Europe by construing it as part of a necessary crusade against anti-Nazi partisans, and he also refused to believe that large-scale extermination had taken place in German camps.[55] Bardèche deployed similar rhetorical techniques to Jacques Isorni, the leaders of the ADMP and the contributors to *Rivarol*, drawing attention towards the widespread popular support for the armistice of June 1940 that Pétain had orchestrated, thereby deflecting attention away from the subsequent political compromises of collaboration. He also used the well-worn parallel between the wild purges and the Terror of the French Revolution, referring to the communist-driven 'September massacres' of 1944 (rather than 1792) in which innocent civilians had been tortured and killed, and repeating Deputy Pierre-Henri Teitgen's 1946 comment that the wild purges claimed more victims than the Terror.[56] Bardèche's intention was to cast seeds of doubt on the judicial and political legitimacy of the Allied position by appealing to popular anti-communism and drawing attention to the unsavoury aspects of the Allied war effort – civilian bombing in particular – that were being passed over in silence in the mainstream commemoration of the era. Bardèche's critique may have been strident and long lived, but there is no doubt that his was an extremist voice, preaching to a small audience of the converted.

Arguably the most demographically penetrating of all the genres serving this counter-construction of historical 'truth' was popular fiction, which at times took such views to a very wide audience indeed. Perhaps the most well-known example of such novelistic intervention was the publication of *Uranus* by collaborationist fellow-traveller Marcel Aymé, whose use of humour and fantasy resulted in a subtle polemic against the purges.[57] Aymé had contributed his fiction to the collaborationist press under the Occupation and had followed the legal purges closely. He signed the petition against Robert Brasillach's death penalty in early 1945; he attended the trial of *Je suis partout*'s editors in November 1946, and supplied the court with written testimony in favour of one of the defendants; he wrote a full-bodied critique of the purges in the magazine *Le Crapouillot* in 1950; and he drew on his observations of purge trials in putting together a play that was performed in Paris in 1952.[58]

Set in the fictional town of Blémont shortly after the Liberation, *Uranus* engages directly with the purge process: the story hinges on the experience of Maxime Loin, an ideologically-motivated fascist writer who is being sheltered from vengeful and violent local communists by one of the town's bourgeois elites. Many scholars have pointed out that Maxime emerges as one of the most morally upright and ideologically pure individuals in a story populated with self-serving, politically compromised men and women who lack integrity (many had dealings with the black market during the Occupation, some are involved in cowardly denunciations) and who do not therefore tug at the reader's sympathy. In contrast, Maxime had stayed loyal to his principles. The physical landscape itself implicitly undermines Liberation-era triumphalism, as the reader is frequently reminded that the streets and houses of Blémont have been devastated not by the occupying Germans but by Allied bombing.[59] As Anne Simonin has put it, novels like these put forward 'a vision of History as seen by the conquered'.[60] Furthermore, in engaging the emotions and appealing to a shared awareness of human frailty, novels could function particularly effectively as instruments of cultural contestation.

Alongside the other examples cited above, they helped to forge a fairly coherent historically revisionist account of the war and Occupation period that had its roots in an ideological assault on the purges and their place in the growing memorial culture of post-Liberation France. This was a process by which autobiographical memory fused with a sense of political grievance in a bid to create not only a social counter-memory among those who remembered the war but a new historical memory for posterity.

Conclusion

I have tried in the above discussion to shed light on how historians can use certain kinds of source material to illuminate the memory politics at work in a given time and place. I have presented a view of memorialization practices that is at heart a conflict-ridden one in which rival claims about what was true and what is worth remembering about the past were pitted against each other in the service of a present-day jostling for position about other things; commemorative practices are thus not only multiple and dialogic, but bound up with relations of power. There are, however, limits to how close a reading of such source material can bring us to grasping the lived experience of the 'memorial cultures' of the time, or the meaning they held for those who engaged in them. Indeed, we should not forget that however politically driven memorialization practices have been, these appeals to the past amount to more than mere strategies to 'sell or justify policy preferences': they give individuals 'an important frame of reference for judging the meaning of these events and issues, and for formulating responses to them'.[61] What the sources presented in this chapter do illuminate are the intentions of cultural elites to engage an imagined shared remembrance of the recent past as a way of fighting political battles in the present, simultaneously firming up an alternative general knowledge of history; and they give us an insight into the rhetorical strategies that were deployed in that process. These sources, which point in many ways to the outside world in which they were created, may even provide us with evidence of how memorial cultures are established in the first place – through shared stories and shared rituals performed and reiterated in public spaces.

What they can tell us much less about is the reception of these attempts, and indeed whether the systematic endeavour to forge an oppositional memorial culture about the Occupation period, which stood in contrast to that forged through officially sanctioned anniversary celebrations or publicly funded filmic representations of the war years, actually shaped or altered the 'collective memory' of the Second World War in France. It is difficult enough to make firm connections between individual remembrance and communal memorialization practices. (The tangible links between what Susan Suleiman calls personal memory, social memory and historical memory remain elusive for historians.[62]) But we are also left with the problem of how it is that these social processes of commemoration result in a discernible – or measurable – 'collective memory'. Indeed, scholars of post-war France often seem to use this term metaphorically, conveying little sense of what such a thing might be or how it might function. The elusiveness of the term is one reason why sociologist Jeffrey Olick has taken the concept of 'collected memory' so seriously: it conjures up a prosopography of known individual remembrances of lived experience rather than a meta-entity (an intangible 'metaphysics of group mind') in which individual mentality and motives are not only submerged but unknowable.[63] What I have offered in this chapter is perhaps an exercise in collected memorialization, privileging some voices – and sources – more than others in the noise of the post-Liberation contestation of the past. It was precisely the battle to ensure which version of that past predominated in French public life in the years after the end of the war that engaged the aggrieved protagonists discussed in this chapter. It was a battle in which they were categorically defeated, their views remaining minority opinions throughout, but their efforts help to illuminate the mechanisms by which individual memories are harnessed through social acts of commemoration in a quest to craft an alternative historical knowledge that serves to justify distinct political needs in the present.

Notes

1 'Le Peuple de Paris a prié pour le Maréchal', *Rivarol*, 1 November 1951, p. 1. A blank space appeared on the front page of the newspaper to underline this point about censorship by default.

2 I have chosen 'memorial culture' rather than 'myth' – the term of preference among scholars of this subject – because the former evokes questions about *how* things are remembered rather than *what* is being remembered. It is a term that thereby prompts historians to consider the role of human agency in the transmission from private memory to social commemoration – to think about who is doing what to whom, when, where and why.

3 H. Rousso, *The Vichy Syndrome: History and Memory in France Since 1944*, trans. A. Goldhammer (Cambridge, MA: Harvard University Press, 1991), pp. 6, 49–54.

4 The terms are used by Rousso, *The Vichy Syndrome*, and N. Hewitt, *Literature and the Right in Postwar France: The Story of the 'Hussards'* (Oxford: Berg, 1996), respectively.

5 Surveys published in *Sondages: Bulletin d'informations de l'Institut français d'opinion publique*, October 1944 to May 1947.

6 On the complex history of the VE day commemoration, see Rousso, *The Vichy Syndrome*, pp. 221–26.

7 'Le Quatrième anniversaire de la libération de Paris', *Le Monde*, 26 August 1948, p. 8.

8 'Sous un soleil éphémère Paris a célébré Jeanne d'Arc et l'anniversaire de la victoire', *Le Monde*, 11 May 1948.

9 S. Langlois, 'Images that matter: the French Resistance in film, 1944–46', *French History*, 11(4), 1997, pp. 461–90.

10 Robert Brasillach's brother-in-law complained that cinema was creating the illusion of a 'truth' from which he desisted. M. Bardèche, *Lettre à François Mauriac* (Paris: La Pensée Libre, 1947), p. 82.

11 L. Auslander, 'Coming home? Jews in postwar Paris', *Journal of Contemporary History*, 40(2), 2005, pp. 239, 253.

12 N. Bracher, 'Remembering the French Resistance: ethics and poetics of the epic', *History & Memory*, 19(1), 2007, pp. 39–67; D. Sherman, 'Commemoration', in E. Berenson et al. (eds) *The French Republic: History, Values, Debates* (Ithaca, New York: Cornell University Press, 2011), p. 328; H. Footitt, 'Women and (Cold) War: the Cold War creation of the myth of "La Française résistante"', *French Cultural Studies*, viii, 1997, pp. 41–51. It is true that the contribution of a select band of communist and Gaullist martyrs was widely recognized – Danielle Casanova, Gabriel Péri, Jean Moulin, Pierre Brossolette, Berty Albrecht, for example – but those who survived appear not to have been honoured in the same way.

13 N. Wood, *Vectors of Memory: Legacies of Trauma in Postwar Europe* (Oxford: Berg, 1999), p. 2. See R. Gildea, *The Past in French History* (New Haven & London: Yale University Press, 1994) for a general account of the political stakes of commemoration in modern France.

14 J. Verdès-Leroux, *Refus et violences: politique et littérature à l'extrême droite des années trente aux retombées de la Libération* (Paris: Gallimard, 1996), p. 419; J. Jackson, *France: The Dark Years, 1940–1944* (Oxford: Oxford University Press, 2001), pp. 190, 211.

15 For the full trial transcript, including the words of defence attorney Chresteil, see the Fonds Bluet, Archives Nationales, Paris (AN) 334 AP 22.

16 Most famously in the apologia offered for the regime by R. Aron in *Histoire de Vichy, 1940–1944* (Paris: Fayard, 1954).

17 Transcript of the Brinon trial, 4–6 March 1947, Fonds Bluet AN 334 AP 37.

18 Historians think the figure is closer to 9,000. P. Watts, *Allegories of the Purge: How Literature Responded to the Postwar Trials of Writers and Intellectuals in France* (Stanford: Stanford University Press, 1998), p. 3.

19 Watts, *Allegories of the Purge*, p. 7. He cites the series on 'great contemporary trials' released by Albin Michel, the publication of Action Française leader Charles Maurras' trial, and lawyers' defence briefs published by Gallimard.

20 Bardèche, Maurice, *L'Épuration* (Editions Confrérie Castille, 1997), p. 140. For Isorni's attitude to the purges, see A. Kaplan, *The Collaborator: The Trial and Execution of Robert Brasillach* (Chicago & London: University of Chicago Press, 2000), pp. 108–21.

21 J. Isorni, *Plaidoirie … pour le maréchal Pétain, prononcée par le bâtonnier F. Payen, Mes J. Isorni et J. Lemaire* (Paris: Imprimerie de J. Haumont, 1946) and *Le procès de Robert Brasillach: 19 janvier 1945* (Paris: Flammarion, 1956); also Kaplan, *The Collaborator*, pp. 170–84.

22 Isorni, preface to A. Martel, *Après le procès du Maréchal Pétain pour la révision*, 1948, pp. 10–11.

23 J. Isorni, *Correspondance de l'Ile d'Yeu* (Paris: Flammarion, 1966).

24 J. Isorni, *Témoignages sur un temps passé* (Paris: Flammarion, 1953), pp. 8–20, 32–44.

25 J. Isorni, *Pétain a sauvé la France* (Paris: Flammarion, 1964), p. 7.

26 Rousso, *The Vichy Syndrome*, pp. 43–49.

27 An official bulletin, *Association pour défendre la mémoire du Maréchal Pétain*, was published after 1952. For the testimony in question, see the October 1952 issue, p. 11.

28 P. Favre, 'Brasillach est vivant', *Cahiers des amis de Robert Brasillach*, 1, June 1950, p. 3; K. Chadwick, 'Alphonse de Châteaubriant, collaborator on retrial: *un non-lieu individuel d'une portée nationale*', *French Historical Studies*, 18(4), 1994, pp. 1067, 1071.

29 N. Hewitt, 'Non-conformism, "insolence" and reaction: Jean Galtier-Boissière's *Le Crapouillot*', *Journal of European Studies*, 37(3), 2007, pp. 277–94.

30 Titles included *Aspects de la France*, founded June 1947 by supporters of the royalist ultra-nationalist Action Française; *Ecrits de Paris*, first published in January 1947; and *Défense de l'Occident*, set up by Maurice Bardèche in 1952.

See Verdès-Leroux, *Refus et violences*, p. 440; Hewitt, *Literature and the Right in Postwar France*, p. 46.

31 Hewitt, *Literature and the Right in Postwar France*, pp. 51, 34. Purge 'victims' Pierre-Antoine Cousteau (1954–58) and Lucien Rebatet (after 1958) were closely involved with the newspaper after the amnesties of the early 1950s. P.-M. Dioudonnat, *Les 700 rédacteurs de* Je suis partout, *1930–1944: dictionnaire des écrivains et journalistes qui ont collaboré au* grand hebdomadaire de la vie mondiale *devenu le principal organe du fascisme français* (Paris: Sedopols, 1993), p. 31.

32 Chadwick, 'Alphonse de Châteaubriant, collaborator on retrial', pp. 1074–75, referring to the 1980s.

33 *Rivarol*, 1 February 1951, p. 2.

34 J. Ricard, 'La Première tâche de la législature sera d'apurer les comptes de l'épuration', *Rivarol*, 21 June 1951, p. 2; 'La pétition de Rivarol "Pour le Maréchal à Douaumont"', *Rivarol*, 15 November 1951, p. 3; Michel Dacier (pseudonym of René Malliavan), 'Le 28 novembre 1951, 203 357 Français avaient signé notre pétition-plébiscite pour "Le Maréchal à Douaumont"', *Rivarol*, 29 November 1951, p. 3; one article communicated the minutiae of the August and December 1953 amnesty laws to encourage eligible readers to reclaim their pensions, *Rivarol*, 7 January 1954, p. 9.

35 A. Thérive, 'L'époque tout entière respire la trahison puisqu'elle respire sans cesse le sang et la poudre', *Rivarol*, 25 January 1951, p. 6.

36 Watts, *Allegories of the Purge*, p. 11.

37 J. Ricard, 'Xavier Vallat: La Terreur de 1793 a fait 20 morts dans mon département, la Libération en a tué huit cents', *Rivarol*, 22 February 1951, p. 1.

38 P. Dominique, review of Pierre Gaxotte, *L'Histoire des Français*, *Rivarol*, 5 July 1951, p. 4; and 'Les haines entre Français n'étaient pas moins fortes sous Charles IX que sous Charles de Gaulle', *Rivarol*, 2 August 1951, p. 2.

39 Admiral Auphan, from *Les Grimaces de l'histoire* under the title 'Les procès politiques font du condamné d'aujourd'hui le héros de demain', in *Rivarol*, 15 February 1951, p. 7. Auphan, a navy minister under the Occupation, had been tried for collaboration.

40 J.M., 'Que reste-t-il du 6 février 1934?', *Rivarol*, 5 February 1954.

41 E. Delamare, 'L'Éternel visage des révolutions', *Rivarol*, 12 February 1954, p. 8.

42 J. Guernec, 'À Paris, "le peuple unanime" n'a tenu la rue que le 25 août', *Rivarol*, 23 July 1951, p. 5; 'Anniversaire communiste d'une libération "patriotique"', *Rivarol*, 26 August 1954, p. 3.

43 J. Ricard, 'Dans les charniers de l'Ardèche il y aurait aussi des cadavres de résistants liquidés par les FTP', *Rivarol*, 5 April 1951.

44 F. Virgili, *Shorn Women: Gender and Punishment in Liberation France*, trans. J. Flower (Oxford & New York: Berg, 2002); B. Dufour, 'Dans la guerre franco-française, l'épuration a été le cheval de Troie des communistes', *Rivarol*, 7 June 1951, p. 7; Guernec, 'À Paris'; Fabricus, 'La Terreur, si terreur il y eut … ', *Rivarol*, 15 November 1951, p. 1.

45 Ricard, 'La Première tâche'.

46 'Les Yeux du plus vieux prisonnier du monde', *Rivarol*, 19 April 1951, p. 1.

47 M. Dacier, 'Ne brûlez pas l'hérétique', *Rivarol*, 1 February 1951, p. 1.

48 P.-A. Cousteau, 'Prise de la Bastille', *Rivarol*, 17 July 1954, p. 1.

49 M. Bardèche, *Souvenirs* (Paris: Editions Buchet, 1993), pp. 227, 261.

50 P.-A. Cousteau, *Après le déluge* (Paris: La Librairie Française, 1956), pp. 39, 8–10.

51 B. Faÿ, *De la prison de ce monde: journal, prières et pensées, 1944–1952* (Bulle: Imprimerie Jules Perroud, 1952), pp. 40, 14–15, 19, 26.

52 F. de Brinon, *Mémoires* (Paris: LLC, 1949), pp. 28–38.

53 Hewitt, *Literature and the Right in Postwar France*, p. 63: Bardèche was in breach of an 1881 press law. See also Bardèche, *Souvenirs*, p. 228. Jacques Isorni had been the defence lawyer.

54 Bardèche, *Lettre à François Mauriac*, pp. 23, 27, 49, 144, 58, 183, 133.
55 M. Bardèche, *Nuremberg, ou la terre promise* (Paris: Les Sept Couleurs, 1948), pp. 9, 17, 128, 133.
56 Bardèche, *Lettre à François Mauriac*, pp. 20, 51, 59, 107; and in *L'Épuration*, p. 8.
57 Hewitt, 'Non-conformism, "insolence" and reaction', pp. 280–81.
58 For Aymé's contribution to the trial of *Je suis partout* see the Fonds Bluet AN 334 AP 82, and the report in *Combat*, 23 November 1946; Watts, *Allegories of the Purge*, pp. 51–57; A. Simonin, 'The right to innocence: literary discourse and the postwar purges (1944–53)', trans. J. F. Austin, *Yale French Studies*, 98, 2000, pp. 24–25.
59 First published as *Uranus* in 1948, an English translation was issued by Bodley Head, London, in 1950 under the title *Fanfare in Blémont*. For a recent discussion of the novel see A.L. Merfeld-Langston, 'From text to screen: portraits of collaboration in *Uranus*', *French Cultural Studies*, 21(3), 2010, pp. 178–91.
60 Simonin, 'The right to innocence', p. 12.
61 R.N. Lebow, 'The memory of politics in postwar Europe', in R.N. Lebow, W. Kansteiner and C. Fogu (eds) *The Politics of Memory in Postwar Europe* (Durham: Duke University Press, 2006), p. 3.
62 S. Rubin Suleiman, *Crises of Memory and the Second World War* (Cambridge, MA: Harvard University Press, 2006), pp. 1–11.
63 J.K. Olick, 'Collective memory: the two cultures', *Sociological Theory*, 17(3), 1999, pp. 337–41.

7 The pictures in the background

History, memory and photography in the museum

Susan A. Crane

> ... in fact no museum can exhibit photography without also exhibiting its character as exhibit medium ... Can photography be exhibited, without also exhibiting the thematic of 'exhibit' itself?
>
> Wolfgang Ernst[1]

History and photography came of age together in nineteenth-century Europe, during the same era that witnessed the creation of the modern museum. These developments were not coincidental, which encourages the question: how did the inclusion of photographs in museums shape the way that diverse audiences, from curators to scholars to the visiting public, interacted with the visual presence of the past? It is important to understand how photographs first appeared in European and American museums, and to what purposes, in order to investigate how both memory and history were served by the presentation of this new visual media in the most popular cultural venue for instruction, the museum. Photographs in museums have served two distinct purposes: as art objects on display and as documentary evidence. As documents, however, it is important to realize that photographs have also served as pictures in the background, establishing historical context for other objects or staging a visual argument. How then has the presentation of photographs in the background shaped collective memories about themes and objects presented in museums, and about museums themselves? Was there a particular role to be played in creating a context of authenticity, legitimacy or historicity that photographs uniquely could fulfil? Inquiring into the supplemental use of photographs in museums illuminates their distinctive dual roles as elements of museum display design. Photographs create contexts for collective memories – those memories shared by museum visitors prior to their visit, as well as those derived from viewing museum displays in the past as well as the present. In museum displays, photographs both illustrate the pasts they represent, like any other artefact, and, working in the background, offer a highly flexible platform from which to launch interpretations.

To pursue the interlaced histories of photographs and museum display, I turn first to the evolution of exhibit design. For more than 150 years, photographs' distinctive capacity to illustrate historical context has made them ideally suited to museum display enhancement. But their presence was never merely decorative; 'background' implies design choices that enhance the intentions of the designers. 'Background' also implies 'backdrop', where a wall of photographs may offer evidentiary ballast. Photographs have shaped the memories of museum visitors for generations, as well as challenged visitors who resisted the implications of the photographic arguments being staged in exhibition. The more photographic background display became common in the twentieth century, the more fraught the public response became as collective memories, particularly of World War II and the Holocaust, confronted the visual archive. The second part of the chapter elaborates on photographs from that visual archive in historical exhibition at American and German museums, and the repercussions of staging arguments through photographs, where the images are presented less as inherently worthy of museum display and more as pedagogical tools for reinterpretation of the past. The twentieth century witnessed dynamic developments in the use of photographs in museums. Inquiry into the dramatic responses generated by 'the pictures in the background' can illuminate how memory and history are dynamically and simultaneously engaged through photographs in museum display.

Photographs in museums: a brief exhibit design history

Photographs entered museum displays by a variety of means in the nineteenth century, but one of the most influential routes was through popular expositions and fairs. The first public display of photographs occurred in Paris at the universal exposition of 1855.[2] Within the first decades of their existence, daguerreotype and albumen print technologies were regularly featured in national exhibitions, industrial fairs and world's fairs. Through the second half of the nineteenth century, public audiences were more likely to encounter displays of photographs in expositions than in museums. According to Ann McCauley, '[d]uring most of the nineteenth century, the photograph remained what it had been since its invention: the handmaiden of the arts, but never allowed into the royal court (or onto the gallery walls)'.[3] Curators began to consider photographs as museum-worthy objects and to collect them, but the new technology was primarily considered worthy of display as evidence of economic and craft development, and worthy of museum use primarily as a tool for preservation. At the Muséum National d'Histoire Naturelle in Paris, museum curators teamed with the Académie des Sciences in 1852 to photograph natural historical specimens and publish a catalogue.[4] Henry Cole's staff at the South Kensington Museum (forerunner of the Victoria & Albert Museum in London) ensured that the expositions themselves were preserved in photographs, hiring photographers to document exhibitions beginning with the Crystal Palace exposition in 1851.[5] In addition to being marvelled at as evidence of technical innovation and surprising, pleasing verisimilitude, photography contributed to a documentary record of exhibit practices, well before becoming an element of exhibit design.

As museums began to exploit the potential of photography for preservation, they also considered the use of photographs as supplements for display and even as substitutes for genuine specimens, art or artefacts. At the turn of the century, a heated debate developed among influential curators such as Alfred Lichtwark at the Hamburg Kunsthalle and Benjamin Gilman at the Boston Museum of Fine Arts about whether copies of art should be displayed in the same space as authentic works of art, and whether photographs of art could ever do more than provide study aids and catalogue records. Merry Foresta, a senior curator of photography at the Smithsonian Institution, notes that museums' preference for using cameras to catalogue specimens was also applied to inventories of human populations in the Smithsonian's first photographic project. Appallingly by today's standards, at the American museum 'scientists adapted the idea of the Photographie Zoologique as part of an effort to record America's native populations ... making a photographic record of members of the Indian delegations that visited Washington to finalize treaties'.[6] The new tool for conservation, the camera, was deployed in anticipation of future loss – whether of a specimen or an entire population, a memory or a memory object. Impetus for the Smithsonian's inaugural exhibition of photographs was another loss, an 1865 fire that destroyed the bulk of more than 150 previously commissioned and collected painted portraits of native delegates. Local photographers were hired to take pictures to replace the paintings as new groups of delegates appeared. The photographs were 'more faithful in appearance ... could be created in multiples, so any future loss could be remedied quickly and inexpensively. As substitutes for the Indians, they could be labelled, catalogued, and studied.'[7] The camera allowed the photographer to become a portrait artist, and the photograph to find a place in museum display. A 'likeness' can be taken in any portrait, whether painted, photographed or written; but the production of a 'far more authentic and trustworthy collection of likenesses of the principal tribes of the U.S.', as Smithsonian's first Secretary, Joseph Henry, desired, allowed the kind of copy produced by a camera to have a legitimate place in the museum.[8] That indigenous human populations could be photographed to be catalogued and studied as a disappearing race appeared only to heighten curatorial interest in photography's documentary capacity.

Photography continued to be a popular display in the universal expositions of the 1860s and 1870s, as evidence of advances in camera technology and the skills of photographers. The verisimilitude achieved by photographs was considered a hallmark of the technology. At the same time, museums began to experiment with borrowing on the verisimilitude of photographs to create historical, archaeological or natural historical context around objects on exhibit. At the Museum of the American Antiquarian Society in the 1880s, a collection of Central American photographs was exhibited in revolving cases alongside the display of indigenous artefacts. These were, in turn, considered insufficient to provide context, and so a plaster cast of a Mayan temple was added in 1887.[9] As an element of context, the photographs were being displayed less with an interest in their unique aesthetic properties than with a concern for their ability to attest to contextual authenticity. As such, they were elements of the background: the qualities of the photograph that made it worthy of display were not its uniqueness, exemplarity or the individual genius of its maker – qualities that designated art, natural historical or anthropological artefacts for museum collection – but rather its representativeness.

Over the course of the nineteenth century, museum display designers debated the most appropriate backgrounds and lighting for effective exhibition. In the museum, as Marion Ackerman writes, 'the naked wall basically was nowhere to be seen before 1900'.[10] Science museums tended to make greatest use of a popular nineteenth-century visual culture attraction, the panorama, and its cousin, the diorama. As contemporaries marvelled, the diorama and panorama afforded the viewer a sensation of approximate reality, a sense of 'being there' in the natural environment of a gorilla or flock of birds, which was all the more enjoyable for the appreciation viewers could feel for the skill of the artisans in creating such excellent artificiality. While museums ironically collected nature in order to display it unnaturally, photographs began to be considered as bridges between the artificial setting of the museum and the desire for representation of the natural habitat. Photographs were made of scenery on location, for instance, so that artists could craft more realistic background paintings of Native American peoples.[11] The wilful dislocation of objects, in this case, included imperialist displacements of human populations, not only from native lands to reservations, but also from natural habitats to museum display.

Although innovations in exposition and museum display widened the scope of photographic representation, the widespread use of photographic backgrounds does not appear to have taken root among public museums prior to the 1930s. As the costs of reproducing photographs in formats amenable to large-scale museum display came down, exhibit designers began to exploit their multimedia possibilities. Herbert Bayer, an influential graphic designer associated with the Bauhaus school, who emigrated to the United States and designed museum exhibits for the Museum of Modern Art in New York in the 1940s and 1950s, attributes El Lissitzky with the introduction of large-format photographs into exhibition design.[12] El Lissitzky's groundbreaking work on the Soviet pavilion of the International Press Exhibition ('Pressa') held in Cologne, Germany in 1928 showcased photographs as backdrops for an installation presenting Soviet media technologies. The images feature close-ups of people with cameras, Soviet citizens at work and collectively enjoying leisure or representing ethnic minorities within the greater Socialist society. A photomural, 11 feet high and 72 feet long, entitled 'The Task of the Press is the Education of the Masses', prominently featured Lenin, and yet none of the included images are portraits per se; rather, Lissitzky selected candid photographs and created montages that juxtaposed action and reaction in their human subjects.[13] El Lissitzky was also innovative in the angle and height at which he displayed the photographs, using tilted exhibit elements to hold photographs and hanging other elements from the ceiling. Soviet and fascist states of the 1920s and 1930s recognized that the propaganda value of photographic background display was huge; but its ramifications were not limited to propaganda.

In the early 1930s, Italian exhibition designers were similarly experimenting with breaking apart the field of vision and creating display elements that followed the dynamic imperatives of fascist exhortation. Soviet, Italian fascist and Nazi aesthetics evolved on parallel tracks, influenced by the very *avant-gardes* that the regimes found ideologically suspect, and producing exhibits that excited designers who found the politics abhorrent. Italian display designers such as Marcello Nizzoli and Nicola Mosso installed modular temporary exhibits in Bologna, Milan and Turin using open fretworks to hang oversize photographs and 'wall pages' illustrating exhibition topics such as agricultural technology or the history of flight. In Rome, Nizzoli's 1932 exhibition design for the 'celebration of the fascist revolution' featured a fanned-out, three-dimensional flag surrounded by photographic collage elements reminiscent of the first Dada exhibiton.[14] Like El Lissitzky, the Italian designers tilted display elements at angles from the ceiling and suspended display frames in enormous elliptical curves from the wall. Visitors walked through, around and into displays surrounded by photographs. The images fostered a sense of being enveloped in a familiar world, both recognizably human and super-human scaled, in the service of a political agenda, much as they had in El Lissitzky's exhibits.

An interest in redesigning museum exhibit spaces to facilitate eye-level viewing had been brewing since the turn of the century, but in this practice as well, exhibition design innovation preceded and influenced museum design evolution. Nineteenth-century art museums, following a long tradition of princely and church collection display, had hung art objects to cover an entire wall, thus straining the viewers' eyes to accommodate short- and long-distance vision. Natural history, ethnographic and historical museums were famously cluttered in the Victorian style, their glass vitrines stacked with objects or the display cabinets themselves stacked from floor to ceiling. At the Boston Museum of Fine Art, Benjamin Gilman argued that 'museum fatigue' demanded a physically more salubrious solution to exhibition design: the strain of viewing the objects, as well as their superfluity, impeded the pedagogical intentions of the museum curator. Gilman illustrated a 1916 article with what now seem rather comical photographs of a man trying to accommodate himself to the objects on display in typical museum glass cabinets, even those practically situated on the ground level. The museum visitor was expected to crouch, lean, stretch and strain to read small labels or see small objects. Coins, relics and other small objects were thus harder to appreciate, much less learn about, than the more monumental museum exhibits.[15] But larger objects such as paintings were also difficult to see. Art museums only began to hang paintings in a single, horizontal row in the early twentieth century.[16] The visibility of museum exhibits remained a fundamental concern. Herbert Bayer, having had a revelation of the future in El Lissitzky's Pressa pavilion, experimented the following year with what he called 'extended vision' at the Werkbund exhibit of 1930. Bayer reasoned that a museum visitor's field of vision extended up and down as well as straight ahead. Exhibit design, he argued, had focused previously on the horizontal field of view; to take advantage of the vertical, he hung chairs from the walls above eye level, and tilted exhibits down from the ceiling.[17] Bayer's influence on American museum display design was substantial, particularly in the presentation of photographs as background.

Museum architecture and exhibit design only go so far to constrain the possible meanings, and therefore memories, visitors will take away from even a highly politicized exhibit in a totalitarian society, where intentional constraint attempted to control reception. Compare the introduction of photographs in displays to the influence of evolutionary thought on late nineteenth-century museum exhibits. As Carla Yanni argues:

> Although ideas about transmutation had been circulating for decades, the *Origin of Species* was published in 1859, and it is likely that afterward more visitors saw natural specimens as emblems of evolution – but these interpreters did not replace the people who visited natural history museums in order to see God's work; religious visitors were not going to recant their creed after one afternoon in the dinosaur gallery ... The architecture of museums can only *suggest* a particular view; it cannot determine meaning, and it cannot separate people from their beliefs.[18]

Photographs are bearers of possible meanings, such as evolutionary thought; arguably, no single photograph is inscribed with immutable and monolithic meaning. It will be received by viewers in the context in which it is presented, but each viewer will see the image through a personal lens imbued with multiple memories, knowledge and experience. As more modern museum-goers repeated visits to museums and began to form expectations for their experiences, they became more savvy about the kinds of visual interactions they preferred.

In her pioneering study of museum practices, *The Museum: Its History and its Tasks in Education* (1949), the art historian Alma Wittlin made recommendations for improvements that emphasized the use of photographs. The book was well received and read widely by generations of museum practitioners; in 1970, Wittlin published an updated survey, *Museums: In Search of a Usable Future*. Trained in Vienna in the 1920s, Wittlin began learning about museum practice at the Kaiser Friedrich Museum in Berlin but had to leave as a Jewish and intellectual refugee in 1937; she eventually found work at the Cambridge Museum of Anthropology and Archaeology.[19] Wittlin was committed to museum reform, particularly with the education of youth in mind. In the midst of World War II, Wittlin curated dual exhibitions on 'Money – What is it?' at the Cambridge museum in which she pitted conventional display methods (copious amounts of small objects, exhibited floor to ceiling) against more progressive models of smaller, more focused and contextualized exhibits, and then interviewed visitors to compare and contrast their reactions to both. Visitors to Wittlin's experimentally designed exhibits informed her that the addition of photographs made a substantial improvement in their experience. The newer model exhibit included photographs of people who produced and used the currency displayed. This feature was remarked upon by several of the interviewees, who further wished that the more conventional exhibit had included photographs as well.[20] That so many of the visitors responded positively to the photographs was striking to Wittlin. She summed up her findings with the recommendation that art museums in particular would benefit from adding photographs as background to their displays. Illustrative materials, particularly photographs, should be added to art exhibitions 'presenting the scenery and the people in whose environment the paintings and sculptures were created'. She thus specifically called for photographs to appear as contextual display supplements, without urging any particular care in the selection of images or their particular connection to the art.

By the 1970s, photographs were being integrated into museum exhibit display design on a routine basis, although art museums were the slowest to adopt this new display regime. In the contemporary Western museum, photographs are an acceptable alternative to original objects, much as plaster casts of sculptures had sufficed 100 years before. Lacking authentic artefacts, photographs would 'do' for display in their stead – even though, by the mid-twentieth century, photographs were being collected and displayed as authentic art objects in museums and galleries, and collected and preserved as unique historical artefacts in libraries and archives. Although photographs were clearly seen as valuable in themselves, both as evidence of technological achievement and for their artistic merit, photographs also came to be seen, by the end of the twentieth century, as second-best approximations of absent originals. As Michael Belcher notes, '[o]ne of the most frequently used and cheapest substitutes for reality is the photograph. If any original object is not available for display, nor a replica, then a photograph is often regarded as the next best thing.'[21] The photograph offered, finally, not verisimilitude, or not only that, but the third iteration of an absent original. Photographs thus exponentially increased their exhibition value. Since each print was an original, curators could display them as unique but also representative objects. However, curators could also use photographs as suppliers of background context, where the photographs themselves were reproduced not to demonstrate their unique and original qualities, but to illustrate historical, biographical or cultural background for other objects: literally, photographs provided background as aesthetically pleasing exhibit backdrops; figuratively, photographs presented background information.

By the end of the twentieth century, photographs figured regularly as background elements, providing illustrative contextual images to supplement other kinds of objects. This is a far less heroic role than the one most commonly, perhaps, assumed – where photographs are works of art or documentary produced by camera-operating photographers – but has become so fundamental to the modern museum experience as to be virtually unquestioned. Apart from the discussion among designers who see photographs as aesthetic elements among others to be used in creating displays, or critical interest in popular cultural adaptations of iconic images for consumer products, I have found no other discussion of the unique dual role that photographs play in museum displays. As Wittlin discovered, publics want them, notice them, remember them. Is this because viewers respond to contextual information as much as to the object they are being directed towards viewing? Or because curators, like historians, museum-goers and other publics, see no need to distinguish between the photograph as unique historical object, and the photograph used as illustration of a larger theme that the display designer wishes to highlight?

Arguing through photographs

It is surely not coincidental that the first major museum blockbuster exhibition of the twentieth century was comprised of photographs – 'The Family of Man' exhibit, which opened at the Museum of Modern Art in New York in 1955.[22] The exhibit presented contemporary photographs representing the gamut of human life and social interaction as a common, shared experience. Images of people from all stages of human life and from across the globe were hung on large wall-sized panels, and the absence of attribution or identifying captions encouraged a shared, universally human response to emotionally evocative images. Critics and historians alike agree on the foundational significance of 'The Family of Man'. The exhibit spawned an eponymous catalogue that has been continuously in print and appeared in numerous languages, and the exhibit itself toured internationally for eight years; in 1996, a permanent installation was created in a purpose-built museum in Clervaux, Luxembourg. UNESCO's inclusion of the exhibit in its 'Memory of the World' project in 2003, using 'selection criteria regarding world significance and outstanding universal value', attests to the humanist, transhistorical appeal of this photographic exhibition and its enduring popularity. 'The Family of Man' exhibit presents a pivotal moment in twentieth-century museum design: its embrace of the use of photographs in museum display conflated celebration of the artistic value of photographs and their value as documentary evidence. While historians of photography and museums have focused on the ideological implications of curator Edward Steichen's vision, attention should also be paid to the ways in which the exhibit sustained mid-century exhibition practices and demonstrated the impact of photographs as desirable media of museal memory.

Critics such as Roland Barthes and Alan Sekula have argued that 'The Family of Man' exhibition abandoned acknowledgement of the unique contribution of the individual photographer and the artistic value of a single print in favour of pandering to popular audiences' interest in universal human values and humanity's common traits. However, 'The Family of Man' used photographs as background in ways that drew on exhibition practices developed over the past century, and gave them a new twist. As Christopher Phillips notes, exhibition practices associated with El Lissitzky and Herbert Bayer that had revolutionary potential in the 1930s looked quite different when deployed in a 'domesticated' post-war context. Phillips characterizes Steichen's 'operating procedure' as follows:

> To prise photographs from their original contexts, to discard or alter their captions, to recrop their borders in the enforcement of a unitary meaning, to reprint them for dramatic impact, to redistribute them in new narrative chains consistent with a predetermined thesis ... [23]

Phillips and Sekula agree that Steichen's methods ripped the photographs out of the contexts of their production and imposed meanings upon them, but the implications of this characterization can also be read another way. Whereas earlier inclusions of photographs in the background had been intended to provide historical and social context within museum display and exhibitions, Steichen's innovation was to amplify the contextual power of photographs. If, indeed, Steichen removed photographs from the context of their production and thus redacted their historical authenticity, he also corralled photographs into a context of his own making in order to exaggerate and extend their reception in an exhibitionary complex which combined multiple possible collective memories. In his earlier, wartime propaganda exhibit, 'The Road to Victory' (1942), the same large-format photograph exhibit style was deployed, with Herbert Bayer's help, to render all military personnel potentially the viewer's own family member, and American landscape as 'this land is your land'. Inspired by Bayer, Steichen crafted a patriotic message by tilting the photographs at angles as well as hanging them on vertical walls. The 12 × 40-foot mural that concluded the exhibit, composed of soldiers marching in formation and displayed on a curved wall, virtually wallpapering the installation, was supplemented by photographs of pairs of American parents (a motif Steichen returned to in 'The Family of Man').[24] Viewers essentially were invited to interpolate themselves and their own families into the national drama, and this contributed to the huge popularity of the exhibit as well as its positive reception in print media. The photographs were used generically to reference familiar categories of identity – especially the most essential of all human groups, the family – and thereby opened up the exhibit to audiences beyond photography connoisseurs. But whereas some critics argue that the ideological connotations of this universalizing tendency in either 'The Road to Victory' or 'The Family of Man' reek of Cold War paranoia, American jingoism or escapism, the perpetual popularity of the exhibit suggests that multiple kinds of responses, rather than a single, politically charged imperative, have persisted among audiences. Tellingly, the UNESCO 'Memory of the World' project website classifies the significance of the exhibit as not itself pacifist, but rather as emblematic of a time in which many people may have felt that peace was dramatically important: the exhibit 'may be regarded as the memory of an entire era, that of the Cold War and McCarthyism, in which the hopes and aspirations of millions of men and women throughout the world were focused on peace'.[25] If Steichen's goal was to promote peaceful international understanding via photographs representing the human condition without historical, social, economic or any other specific context, audiences' responses were never necessarily pacifist, politically uniform or universalist. The open-endedness of potential meaning-making, and therefore of memory, is the signal contribution of Steichen's extension of photographic exhibition practice and collective memory – even if unintentionally.

The exhibition of large-format photographs in the decades following 'The Family of Man' lent itself particularly well to what historian Cornelia Brink calls 'arguing with photographs': making a political or ideological 'case' through visual evidence.[26] The use of this format to invite audiences to feel themselves implicated, included or mirrored in the depictions of humanity and inhumanity, appears to have been particularly successful – and to what extent this is because the format draws on totalitarian propaganda and aesthetics is worth considering. Whereas earlier museum and exhibition curators had hoped that the use of photographs could inculcate a sense of context, after Steichen exhibits let the photographs 'speak for themselves', and in particular, offer damning arguments. Brink documented exhibitions of Holocaust atro-city images which appeared in 1963–64 at St. Paul's church in Frankfurt, West Germany. The symbolic choice of venue (the church had played a role in the democratic revolutions of 1848, in addition to its continuing religious functions) indicated the seriousness with which the West German government responded to public concerns about recent events related to the memory of the Holocaust – the belated trials of Auschwitz personnel; recent upswings in occurrences of anti-Semitic graffiti at cemeteries and elsewhere; and a concern that the younger generation of West Germans lacked historical understanding of the Third Reich. The first exhibition, 'The Warsaw Ghetto', comprised photographs and documents related to the ghetto's history and experiences; the second, in the winter of 1964, was titled 'Auschwitz: Photos and Documents' and had a similar format. The exhibits were mounted as temporary installa-tions on wall-sized boards with either half or the entire display space filled with enlarged photographs. Both exhibits were intended to inform and instruct, and critics voiced concerns in national and local newspapers about whether such exhibitions could succeed in the face of entrenched unwillingness to accept national responsibility for the crimes of the Third Reich. In the 'Warsaw Ghetto' exhibit brochure, German journalist Erich Kuby wrote that the success of the exhibit depended on the self-recognition of its viewers:

> If the exhibit viewers discover themselves in the mirror of these documents, or, insofar as they did not live through the Third Reich, discover their own people [*Volk*], [that would be a success]. But I would call it a failure, if the viewers say to themselves: that's what the Nazis were like, and then speak as if an invading army of aliens from Mars had occupied Germany from 1933–45.[27]

The photographs were not displayed merely for their aesthetic value, or to honour the skill of the photographers, or to admire the technical sweetness of the cameras. Rather, the photographs had evidentiary, documentary value that carried the burden of prosecution as well as education. Some of the photographs may have already been familiar to their audiences: Germans had been witness to the Allied Signal Corps documentaries immediately following the end of World War II, which recorded the atrocities of post-Liberation concentration camps for international condemnation and viewing – and these were seen as related tasks. Additionally, the first 'picture book' of the Holocaust had been published in 1960. *Der Gelbe Stern* (*The Yellow Star*) was produced by a journalist, Gerhard Schoenberner, using photographs he collected from European archives and museums: primarily images produced by the Nazi propaganda corps, military and occasionally by private citizens and soldiers.[28] Some of the famous Warsaw ghetto images from the Stroop Report, used at the Nuremberg Trials, appeared in the book. But the exhibit targeted younger audiences, those born 'with the blessing of the later birthdate', as Helmut Kohl said – those for whom the images were not yet the icons they would become. In turn, the exhibit and the audiences helped create iconicity through this exposure. The memory of the Holocaust thus transmitted visually entered into public discourse through multiple media simultaneously. Large-format photographs and recirculated iconic images alike helped form public memory, just as they did with the exhibit and book of 'The Family of Man'.

Large-format photographs filtered into museum design display more frequently throughout the 1960s and 1970s, until by the 1980s it would have seemed strange not to see them. By 1995, the 50th anniversary of the end of World War II, Smithsonian curator Steven Lubar could argue that the ubiquity of photographs made it imperative *not* to use them in the exhibit 'World War II: Sharing Memories'. The entrance to the exhibit was marked with the words, 'We all remember World War II'. Assuming memory, and then building on it, relieved Lubar and his team from the necessity of addressing the complications of multiple collective memories associated with events such as the bombing of Hiroshima, which caused so many problems on the other side of the Washington Mall, at the National Air and Space Museum.[29] Lubar's goal was to offer both histories and memories as museum objects: 'We wanted our visitors to think not only about the war but also about how we know the past, about the ways that memory and tradition relate to history and historic artefacts.'[30] In an interesting reversal of the earliest Smithsonian photographic display practices, they decided to use paintings, rather than photographs, for this purpose because photographs were deemed too familiar:

> ... most of them seem either too specific or too general. That is, some are pictures of specific scenes that mean everything to those who were there but little to those who were not. Others (the flag-raising on Iwo Jima, say) have a meaning that has become so enmeshed in our national memory that it's hard for people to see beyond the 'official' story.[31]

Rather than try to make new arguments with the photographs, which were either too specific to personal memory or too iconic in collective memory, the curators chose objects and images that they felt would allow visitors to draw from their own memories of the event, and then share them, through visitor books. The choice not to use photographs signals both public familiarity with iconic images and the normality, by the end of the century, of seeing photographs as contextualizing elements of exhibition.

'Where photography is not the theme, but the medium'

In 1947, financier Nelson Rockefeller was a member of the board of the Museum of Modern Art in New York and an enthusiastic supporter of Edward Steichen. Rockefeller believed that Steichen was able to get 'the best work being done throughout the world, and to employ it creatively as a means of interpretation in major Museum exhibitions where photography is not the theme but the medium through which great achievements and great moments are graphically represented'.[32] His comments anticipated the successful foundations of 'The Family of Man' exhibit, and highlight photography's trajectory from museum object to museum display element in the twentieth century. Since the 1970s, the photographic medium has become an essential component of increasingly contextualized museum exhibit design, and as such played an important role in stimulating collective memories. Virtually every photograph is potentially an illustration that can serve a contextualizing purpose. In this newer capacity as 'not the theme but the medium' of exhibition, the photograph has taken on a new relevance in contemporary museum practice. Although many kinds of museums continue to present stand-alone photographic exhibitions, photographs serving as illustration of historical context or to provide a sense of place have become standard means of invoking history and memory. 'The theme' they can visualize for audiences remains, however, tantalizingly beyond complete curatorial control.

As elements of museum display design, photographs offer a distinctive challenge to curators: they present multiple contexts of production and viewing, most of which will be neglected in their chosen representation. As Lubar realized, iconic images' familiarity works against their inclusion in museum exhibits that have other agendas. But the plurality of meanings and memories available through photographs also mitigates against the intention to constrain their presentation. Art historian Terry Barrett suggests that the 'external context' as well as elements internal to the photograph condition the possible meanings available to viewers. The external context comprises 'the photograph's presentational environments: how and where it is being presented, has been presented, received, how other interpreters have understood it, and where it has been placed in the history of art'.[33] The photograph's receptions over time, through recirculation, as well as its apparent ability to represent the past in which it was made, create multiple sets of external contexts for viewers. As Barrett notes, a shift in external context happens when, for instance, photographs are labelled or appropriated, as either art or evidence. A debate has raged almost endlessly since the creation of the camera about whether photographs are art or documentary, and without going into the details of that debate here, it is worth paying attention to the ease with which photographs transcend categories, which makes the shift in external context all the more significant. As Barrett wrote, 'with the addition of surrounding or superimposed texts, images are switched from the category of news to a moral indictment; by transferring a photograph from a laboratory file drawer to an oversized book, science becomes art'.[34] Not only does it matter what caption or file label is attached to the image; it also matters how the photograph is turned into a component of the 'presentational environment' and functions as part of the argument being presented. The photograph's function in establishing the validity of a designated external context depends on an assumption of its documentary, evidentiary capacity, regardless of the purposes for which it was made, kept or remembered. Thus the photograph becomes the medium of memories designated for it, rather than the ones for which it was made or recirculated.

Consider one striking example, created in the 1990s in the United States Holocaust Memorial Museum in Washington, DC, of a translation of context: four walls of photographs soaring three storeys above the viewer create a photo album of family and village memory in the 'Tower of Faces', a permanent exhibition.[35] The portraits and snapshots of village life recall a single, eradicated community, the Jews of the Lithuanian town of Eisiskes. Individual photographs on exhibit are not captioned. Instead, the visitor gets the cumulative effect of seeing people and place as enmeshed in one another, and in the site of their exhibition. The photographs are both documentary evidence and background, creating context through proximity to each other, and relying upon their powerful recollection of absence to create a sense of visual presence – even though many of the images are difficult to discern, since they are mounted high above the viewer. In the external context created by museum display, these intimate images are rendered representative, documenting losses indicative of genocide. They can also remind viewers of the lost family albums, storage boxes and frames from which these remnants have been recovered, and propagate emotional responses to love and loss. The photographs compiled as a 'tower' have been stripped of the original contexts of their meaning- and memory-making, and placed in a format that highlights the evidentiary force of the three-dimensional reality of the photographs to represent the actual absence of their subjects: real presence witnesses and insists upon actual absence. The photographs thus profoundly evoke the background of one community lost to genocide. And yet at the same time, they are background photographs, because the subject of the exhibit is not the photographs, or the individual identities of the people they represent. Photographs of the members of the Jewish community of Eisiskes represent not only them, but also what is not depicted: what happened to them. The photographs become the medium of the theme of genocide, which was never even imagined when the images were made.

Perhaps because of the burden of memory associated with Holocaust images taken by and preserved by Holocaust surviving victims, their documentary value is over-determined. 'Arguing with photographs' about the Holocaust using perpetrator images, however, continued to generate controversy at the end of the twentieth century. In the original 'Crimes of the *Wehrmacht*' exhibit, which opened in Hamburg in 1995, a significant anniversary year for the end of World War II and the Holocaust, the arguments exploded.[36] Using many previously unpublished photographs, the exhibit exposed war crimes committed by members of the German army under the Third Reich, very much against the grain of collective memories of a 'clean' army that had only followed brutal orders and had not actively participated in the Holocaust. Encouraged by the public response, both positive and negative, the organizers sent the exhibit on tour in Germany and Austria. In the ensuing public controversy, the subjects of about half a dozen of the photographs were found to have been mistakenly identified, and the exhibit's planned American tour was cancelled as a result. The value of the exhibit lay in the authenticity of its photographs, and when this was found to be lacking in some of the images, the entire project was compromised. There is an extensive literature on the exhibition and its reception, including many interviews with audiences in both countries. However, the exhibition design has received less attention, and is worth examining for ways in which the photographs, whose ultimate value lay in their status as authentic evidence, were also presented as background.

The 'Crimes of the *Wehrmacht*' exhibition reproduced images of varying sizes and assembled them on mobile, wall-sized frames surrounded by identification captions and historical analysis. Thus viewers were not looking at any single, damning photograph as an original, but rather at a collection of evidence reproduced for display. At the centre of the exhibition, the framework was arranged in the shape of an Iron Cross, whose heavy symbolic value would not have been missed by any native German speaker. Even genuinely authentic reproductions were not accepted at face value; instead, public debate based on collective memories emerged – much as if the publics were engaging with primary sources, just as historians and curators do. As the exhibit toured, news media reported on viewers' passionate responses. Public outrage mixed with calls for engagement with the difficult truths of the exhibit, and these truths varied depending on the exhibit's location – and it indeed mattered a great deal whether the audience was from Germany or Austria. Film-maker Ruth Beckerman, the daughter of Holocaust survivors, captured the provocative give and take among viewers of the exhibit in Vienna. The resulting documentary, 'East of War' (1996), vividly captures long-buried animosities and closely held convictions about the nature of regular soldiers' participation in the atrocities of World War II. Some veterans claimed that any soldier on the Eastern front must have seen and known what happened to the Jews; others claimed that maybe a few bad soldiers had done something wrong, but that they never saw or heard about it and that it was unfair to besmirch the reputation of the rest based on those few. Relatives of military personnel, particularly those born after the war, struggled to come to grips with evidence that directly challenged their families' cherished memories of honourable service. Air Force veterans confronted the evidence of what they had never seen from the air and yet been glad to avoid on the ground (indicating knowledge of the rumours of misconduct already emerging during the war). Those with the greatest stake in the honour of their family's service to the nation were also most at risk of exposure, as relatives and veterans challenged each other to define exactly which nation they had defended when the Third Reich's annexation of Austria in 1938 brought lifelong members of the Austrian military into Hitler's army.

Tellingly, the photographs were omnipresent in the background of Beckerman's shots, and her interviewees continually looked at and referred to them as they spoke with her. Directly confronted with visual evidence, audiences did not agree about the meanings or memories associated with the photographs by the accompanying texts or each other, and they continued to look, look again, look closely and step away. Most viewers appear to have accepted that the photographs, as the foundation of evidence, were the medium of the message – that the fact of the photographs' existence compelled attention equally as much as the content or subjects of each image. But the photographs were no match for the stubbornness of meanings already committed to memory. While some well-informed observers were able to identify misattribution and thus challenge the authenticity of the entire exhibit, many others felt that the evidence was simply wrong because it did not align with their pre-existing external contexts of memory. Too much was at stake in the presence of the photographs; their presentation, their presence in front of viewers, became the necessary backdrop for public anguish over long-buried issues. If each photograph had been displayed singly, alone on a wall as a documentary photograph, with only the name (and rank?) of the photographer as caption, in an exhibit titled 'German War Photography, 1939–45', would the controversy over the 'Crimes of the *Wehrmacht*' have occurred? The external contexts of presentation inherent in museum display and the collective memories visitors bring to exhibits ultimately shape the dual roles that photographs play as historical evidence and aesthetic design element. Twentieth-century display design, particularly since 'The Family of Man', has emphasized the malleability of contextualizing photographs. Perhaps ironically, the most effective use of photographs in museum display will neglect the history of their production (the photographer, the camera, the printing process, the circulation and re-circulation of the print or prints) and their three-dimensional status as artefacts. Instead, the medium of photography is deployed as a design element to promote external contexts of historical interpretation and collective memory.

Notes

The author wishes to thank Joan Tumblety for her thoughtful comments.

1 W. Ernst, 'Ex-positionen: fotografie, historie, museum', *Fotogeschichte*, 10(35), 1990, p. 55.

2 See J.K. Brown, *Making Culture Visible: The Public Display of Photography at Fairs, Expositions and Exhibitions in the United States, 1847–1900* (Amsterdam: Harwood Academic Publishers, 2001); E. Mansfield (ed.) *Art History and Its Institutions* (London & New York: Routledge, 2002).

3 M. Haworth-Booth and A. McCauley, *The Museum and the Photograph: Collecting Photography at the V&A Museum, 1853–1900* (Williamstown, MA: Clark Institute, 1998), p. 59.

4 M. Foresta, *At First Sight: Photography and the Smithsonian* (Washington, DC: Smithsonian Books, 2003), p. 18.

5 See Haworth-Booth and McCauley, *The Museum and the Photograph.*

6 Foresta, *At First Sight*, p. 18.

7 Ibid., p. 19.

8 Ibid., p. 154.

9 W.J. Bell, Jr. et al., *A Cabinet of Curiosities: Five Episodes in the Evolution of American Museums* (Charlottesville, VA: University Press of Virginia, 1967), p. 46.

10 M. Ackerman, *Farbige Wände: zur Gestaltung des Ausstellungsraumes von 1880–1930* (Wolfratshausen: Edition Minerva, 2003), p. 32.

11 S.A. Barrett, 'Photographic and panoramic backgrounds: anthropological groups', *Proceedings of the American Association of Museums*, December 1918, pp. 75–78.

12 H. Bayer, 'Aspects of design', *Curator*, 4, 3, 1961, p. 267.

13 M.A. Staniszewski, *The Power of Display: A History of Exhibition Installations at the Museum of Modern Art* (Cambridge, MA: MIT Press, 1998), pp. 45–50.

14 For numerous examples of these designers' work, see S. Polano, *Mostrare: l'allestimento in Italia dagli anni Venti agli anni Ottanta* [Mostrare: Exhibition Design in Italy from the Twenties to the Eighties] (Milan: Ed. Lybra Immagine, 1988); see also Staniszewski, *The Power of Display*, pp. 56–57.

15 B. Gilman, *Museum Ideals: Of Purpose and Method* (Cambridge: Riverside Press, 1918), pp. 251–69.

16 Ackerman, *Farbige Wände*, p. 51.

17 For images of Bayer's exhibit designs, see R. Lohse, *Neue Ausstellungsgestaltung* [New Design in Exhibitions] (Erlenbach-Zürich: Verlag für Architektur, 1953), pp. 26–27; Staniszewski, *The Power of Display*, p. 77; G. Nelson, *Display* (New York: Whitney Publications, 1953), pp. 110–19.

18 C. Yanni, *Nature's Museums* (London: Athlone Press, 1999), p. 11.

19 For fascinating details about Wittlin's life, see H. Kraeutler, 'The museologist, writer, educationalist Alma S. Wittlin (1899–1990): a preliminary research report', http://museumstudies.si.edu (accessed 28 August 2012).

20 A. Wittlin, *The Museum: Its History and its Tasks in Education* (London: Routledge & Kegan Paul, 1949), p. 242.

21 M. Belcher, *Exhibitions in Museums* (Washington, DC: Smithsonian Institution Press, 1991), p. 135.

22 E. Steichen, *The Family of Man* (New York: The Museum of Modern Art, 1953). See also E.J. Sandeen, *Picturing an Exhibition: The Family of Man and 1950s America* (Albuquerque: University of New Mexico Press, 1995); and the excellent collection of essays in J. Back and V. Schmidt-Linsenhoff (eds) *The Family of Man 1955–2001: Humanismus und Postmoderne: Eine Revision von Edward Steichens Fotoausstellung* [Humanism and Postmodernism: A Reappraisal of the Photo Exhibition by Edward Steichen] (Marburg: Jonas Verlag, 2004).

23 C. Phillips, 'The judgement seat of photography' in R. Bolton (ed.) *The Contest of Meaning: Critical Histories of Photography* (Cambridge, MA: MIT Press, 1989), p. 28. Originally published in *October*, 22, Fall 1982.

24 Lohse, *Neue Ausstellungsgestaltung*, pp. 230–33. The June 1942 issue of *The Bulletin of the Museum of Modern Art* includes photographs of each exhibit.

25 www.unesco.org/new/en/communication-and-information/flagship-project-activities/ memory-of-the-world/register/full-list-of-registered-heritage/registered-heritage-page-3/family-of-man/ (accessed 21 June 2012).

26 C. Brink, *Ikonen der Vernichtung: Öffentlicher Gebrauch von Fotografien aus nationalsozialistischen Konzentrationslagern nach 1945* (Berlin: Akademie Verlag, 1998), p. 61.

27 Ibid., p. 74; my translation.

28 In addition to Brink, see R. Sackett, 'Pictures of atrocity: public discussion of *Der gelbe Stern* in early 1960s West Germany', *German History*, 24(4), 2006, pp. 526–61, and H. Knoch, *Die Tat als Bild: Fotografien des Holocaust in der deutschen Erinnerungskultur* (Hamburg: Hamburger Edition, 2001).

29 See S. Crane, 'Memory, distortion, and history in the museum', *History and Theory*, 36(4), 1997, pp. 44–63.

30 S. Lubar, 'Exhibiting memories' in A. Henderson and A.L. Kaeppler (eds) *Exhibiting Dilemmas: Issues of Representation at the Smithsonian* (Washington, DC: Smithsonian Books, 1997), p. 15.

31 Ibid., p. 19.

32 Quoted in Phillips, 'The judgement seat', p. 27.

33 T. Barrett, 'Teaching about photography: photographs and contexts', *Art Education*, 39(4), 1986, 35. See also T. Barrett, *Criticizing Photographs: An Introduction to Understanding Images*, 4th edn (Boston: McGraw-Hill, 2006) [orig. 1990].

34 Barrett, 'Photographs and contexts', p. 55.

35 Several illustrations of the 'Tower of Faces' exhibit are available on the United States Holocaust Memorial Museum website, www.ushmm.org.

36 See the original exhibit catalogue by H. Heer and K. Naumann (eds) *Vernichtungskrieg: Verbrechen der Wehrmacht 1941–1944* (Hamburg: Hamburger Edition, 1995). For what would have been the American version of the exhibit, see *The German Army and Genocide: Crimes against War Prisoners, Jews, and Other Civilians in the East, 1939–1944*, edited by the Hamburg Institute for Social Research, New York: New Press, 1999. See also the chapters by J.P. Reemtsma, O. Bartov and B. Boll in O. Bartov et al. (eds) *Crimes of War: Guilt and Denial in the Twentieth Century* (New York: The New Press, 2002); B. Niven, *Facing the Nazi Past: United Germany and the Legacy of the Third Reich* (London & New York: Routledge, 2002); W. Manoschek, 'Austrian reaction to the exhibition "War of Extermination: Crimes of the *Wehrmacht* 1941 to 1944"' in G. Bischof (ed.) *The Vranitzky Era in Austria* (New Brunswick, NJ: Transaction Publishers, 1999).

Part III

Between 'individual memory' and 'collective memory'

The authors in these final chapters linger in different ways on the intersections of autobiographical memory and social or collective memory. Although alive to the often quite deliberate process of construction – even manipulation – that lies within memorializing practices, they are particularly interested in the search for the meaning of the past enacted by the authors of their principal source material. In the example of Tony Kushner's examination of the migrant experience, it is perhaps more a case of documenting and accounting for silences and embarrassments in the written record, which make community memorialization particularly difficult to accomplish. If the essays in Part II emphasize concerted acts of commemoration, there is more emphasis here on how individuals have played with or tried (perhaps failed) to reshape the shared stories about the past that have enveloped them.

Jason Crouthamel shows how psychologically traumatized German First World War veterans fought back after 1918 at the medical and political authorities who tried to deprive them of military pensions and to besmirch their status as men and patriots. As Crouthamel demonstrates, at the heart of this battle lay a deeply felt resistance to the dominant stories about the meaning of – thus the 'collective memory' about – the war and its casualties. These stories were at times orchestrated from above by elites whose interests were best served by a certain interpretation of that wartime past. The source material analysed in this chapter – letters – provides Crouthamel with rich evidence for individual rebellion, although he admits that it cannot provide direct access to the men's real state of mind. Hannah Ewence considers how barely disguised autobiographical fiction in contemporary Britain has played with the idea of suburbia as a place of social conformity and ethnic homogeneity. As Ewence points out, this genre of writing provides a safer space than memoir for ethnic minority authors to tell an alternative story about the past. The novelists whose work she examines seem to buy into 'majority' ideas of suburban existence but simultaneously to revise them, in a process that knits minority experience into mainstream collective memory. It is a study that suggests the 'spatialization' of autobiographical memory; and the importance of place to personal identity.

Tony Kushner concerns himself with the silences that have emerged about and within the collective memories of one particular minority – migrants. He considers the omissions and distortions that have accrued over time, and in interlocking ways – from the xenophobic filters of civil servants and blind spots of contemporary cultural and political elites, to the memory work of communities keen to honour only the sanitized and the exceptional from their troubled pasts. In peeling away layers of silence in the archival record, he sheds light on the power relations that shape what is collectively remembered and what is not. Susan Stabile's chapter presents the encounter with things undertaken by an early nineteenth-century antiquarian whose vision of 'cultural memory' was centred on the haptic power of material objects, which he sought to harness in his own memory work. Stabile offers us a glimpse not only of an elusive collection of relics whose form (and perhaps meaning) has been recast by subsequent curatorial intervention, but of a long-lost antiquarian practice that valued the stuff of the past in ways that the intervening years have obscured. In order to convey the layering involved in this process of communicating a sense of the past through objects that build on but also occlude what was already there, she employs the metaphor of memory (and memorial practices) as a palimpsest – 'an original text that is scraped, effaced, or partially erased and then written over with another text'.

8 Memory as a battlefield

Letters by traumatized German veterans and contested memories of the Great War

Jason Crouthamel

Shell shock has gained considerable attention from historians dealing with the history of memory. As historian Jay Winter observed, shell shock was a form of 'embodied memory', as tics, tremors, nightmares and other symptoms of traumatic violence made an indelible mark on the bodies and minds of men shattered by modern war.[1] This wound, newly diagnosed during the First World War, symbolized the deeply traumatic effects of industrialized combat on not only individuals, but also European culture and society. War neurosis, as it was called by German doctors, became a central site for post-war debates over the memory of the war in a fragmented and deeply divided Germany. Historians explore a number of interrelated questions on the significance of shell shock and memory: what did the proliferation of 'hysterical men' responding to the horrors of war signify about masculinity and the effects of modern combat on male bodies and minds? How did mentally ill veterans fit into debates over the memory of the war as a brutalizing or regenerative experience for individuals and societies? The focus of this chapter is on Germany's experience with mental trauma and debates over memory. In particular, it concentrates on how mentally traumatized men constructed the memory of the war experience through the prism of psychological illness.

Letters by traumatized men provide historians the opportunity to explore dissident voices of those who rejected prevailing medical and political attempts to wield authority over their minds and memories of the war. The perceptions of military doctors and political leaders coping with the epidemic of 'war neurosis' have been well documented.[2] Doctors often characterized 'hysterical men' as weak, unmanly and a contagious threat to the nation's fighting strength and resources, and they denied men status as war victims who deserved pensions. Prejudices about traumatized men as malingerers and welfare burdens intensified in Germany's first experiment with democracy, the Weimar Republic. Though the new democracy created a progressive system of welfare for war victims, including veterans who suffered psychological injuries, the republic rarely convinced doctors, or the public, that these men were productive or even authentic victims of war. After 1933, the Nazi regime targeted 'hysterical' war victims as enemies of the nation because they allegedly tarnished the sacred memory of the war and threatened the health of the nation.[3] Nazi ideologues remembered the trench experience as a healthy, rejuvenating cornerstone on which to build masculine virtues, and the regime attacked mentally traumatized men as enemies of the 'national community'.

While memories of the war constructed by medical and political authorities are readily available to historians, individual memory proves to be more difficult to locate and analyse. The perspectives of mentally traumatized individuals are a challenge to historians because they are elusive, complex and do not neatly fit into the 'official' memories constructed by medical and political elites. Fortunately, the voices of men who claimed to be psychologically shattered by the war survive in German archives, as they wrote to doctors, political elites and welfare bureaucrats about their plight in the years after the war. After 1918, traumatized men often saw themselves as still at war over the memory of the trench experience, with the battlefield shifted from the trenches to doctors' offices, welfare lines and the streets. 'Hysterical men' who survived the trenches, armed with typewriters and driven by intense bitterness aimed at doctors, welfare officials and politicians, fiercely contested the Nazi regime's official memory of the war, and they attempted to take control over the narrative of traumatic memory. Approaching the history of mental trauma from the perspectives of German veterans highlights how the battle over the significance of shell shock was not only a contest over medical theories and economic welfare, but also a battle over the 'authentic' memory of the war experience. The often tortured voices of traumatized veterans are an essential part of the history of shell shock because they reveal that there was no 'master narrative' of German trauma. Rather, traumatic memory was fiercely contested by ordinary veterans who criticized authorities' attempts to sanctify a collective memory.

In their letters to welfare bureaucrats, doctors and politicians, it is difficult to determine where 'truth' resides regarding the origins and nature of their wounds. Instead of trying to uncover veracity in the debates between doctors and patients, it is arguably more important to analyse how traumatized men *perceived* their injuries, and how they constructed memory within the framework of at least three overlapping forces – in response to the categories and prejudices imposed by military and medical authorities, in relation to cultural attitudes about masculinity, and through the filter of competing political ideologies of the interwar landscape. They used their individual traumatic memories to articulate theories on a whole range of German society's overlapping traumas, including the experiences of militarism, class warfare, welfare and society's treatment of 'social outsiders'. In this way, the memory of the original trauma in the trenches was redefined through layers of secondary trauma, namely post-war ostracization, economic suffering and the suppression and official denial of their traumatic memories.[4] In some cases, the secondary traumas supplanted the horrors of the trenches, and informed how these men remembered their combat experiences.

Veterans' desires to attack military and political authorities and gain restitution often displaced their ability objectively to reconstruct memories of their original trauma at the front. Historian Peter Barham developed an interesting way to deal with this dilemma. Using case studies of 'forgotten lunatics' in Britain, he argues persuasively that their letters to authorities were filled with such anger and hatred of medical-political elites that they reveal as much about the emotional universe of men traumatized by war as their medical, economic and political circumstances.[5] This does not delegitimize the existence of real, terrifying wounds incurred by many of these men. However, their memories were distorted by the cultural and political tensions that dominated their environment after 1918. They directed such corrosive rage at doctors and politicians for rejecting the authenticity of their wounds, or suggesting that they were unmanly for failing to recover, that their letters cast more light on their post-war psychological condition, full of resentment and loathing, than the nature of their original trauma. In a desperate attempt to assert some control, traumatized men tried to assert authority over what they saw as the 'authentic' memory of the war, which they claimed was trampled by medical and political elites. By focusing on the perspectives of war neurotics, it is possible to reconstruct a history of trauma, memory and masculinity 'from the margins', as men contested their status as 'social outsiders' who allegedly threatened collective memories of the war.[6]

Historiographical overview of traumatic neurosis and the memory of the Great War

A common thread in the scholarship on the history of traumatic neurosis is the emphasis on how this wound is constructed within the context of existing cultural values and institutions.[7] Prevailing medical theories, military interests, gender norms and the pressures of the industrial economy closely shaped how war neurosis was defined, treated and perceived. Mental medicine became increasingly militarized and rationalized within the industrialized context of total war.[8] Imperial and Weimar Germany's psychiatrists, and their theories on mental illness, must be placed within the context of welfare state politics and the pressures of military and industrial demands for soldiers and workers.[9] Maintaining functional soldiers and military efficiency became the aim of mental medicine, and doctors who prioritized the health of the individual were pushed out by medical authorities who worked with the military to discipline and punish soldiers whom they believed were unmanly and unproductive.[10]

Historians have emphasized that economic and political tensions in Germany played a major role in shaping perceptions of 'war neurosis' and traumatized men. In examining how these pressures influenced mental medicine, Paul Lerner's scholarship has been important. Using primarily psychiatrists' diagnostic reports but also narratives by traumatized patients, Lerner demonstrates that traumatic memory was largely a contest between doctors and patients, where the former often interpreted neurotic symptoms as originating in hereditary symptoms and the lack of will-power to recover from traumatic experiences.

Furthermore, financial pressures on doctors to keep down the costs of Weimar Germany's expanded welfare system also shaped their perception that war neurotics were merely 'hysterical men'. In response, 'hysterical' veterans insisted that the mental stress of the trench experience caused their complex symptoms, including tics, tremors, depression and other forms of illness. While patients were driven by a desire to gain pensions, and were sometimes capable of constructing false narratives in an effort to win compensation, psychiatrists also had an agenda to trim pension budgets.[11] There were also political pressures to avoid diagnosing war-related trauma. Political conservatives, including many doctors, perceived the new welfare system as coddling malingerers, fakers and dependent men who refused to overcome the traumatic memory of the war.[12] Subsequently, most psychiatrists denied that these men were mentally shattered by war. This political and economic debate over whether the war actually caused these wounds was thus also a debate over the memory of the war and who had authority to diagnose the effects of trauma on men's bodies and minds.

Historians have also emphasized that in addition to economic interests and political pressures, the war neurosis question was shaped by debates over gender norms and increasing fears of 'nervousness' spreading through modern society. Andreas Killen, for example, has developed interesting ways of looking at popular perceptions of gender norms and neurosis in imperial and Weimar Germany. Examining popular media, Killen highlights how a discourse on 'nervousness' became a central narrative where fears about technological developments and urbanization led to widespread anxieties about mental and physical degeneration caused by modernity.[13] Even before the war, the medical establishment expressed fears that the pace of modern life threatened to turn strong-nerved men into effeminate and weak beings, that is, 'hysterical' men. Psychiatrists viewed hysteria as a female illness. Assuming that war would replace degeneracy and weakness with a warrior ideal, doctors expected combat to be the best medicine for 'effeminate' men. Thus men who were not able to fulfil masculine expectations of fulfilling their duty towards sacrifice and self-control were denounced as both individual failures and pathological threats to the nation, even before the advent of the Nazi state.[14]

A discourse on 'martial masculinity' intensified during the interwar period and was found especially in the rhetoric of right-wing political groups such as the Nazis who envisioned veterans as 'steel-nerved' vanguards of a new order based on comradeship and soldierly virtues of sacrifice and dedication to the fatherland. Examining veterans' letters and published memoirs, especially by men on the political right, historian Thomas Kühne has analysed how memories of 'comradeship' were largely constructed to serve post-war political interests.[15] Comradeship served as a powerful, almost quasi-religious, phenomenon in German society and it was a cornerstone of Nazi culture. Mentally ill veterans were categorically excluded from the Nazis' 'national community' as unmanly shirkers. But German war neurotics themselves attempted to redefine masculine paradigms to include men who broke down in combat, and their letters after the war highlighted the complex ways in which they defined masculinity in relation to the warrior ideal. In their letters to the Nazi regime, they attacked what they saw as sterilized memories of war that ignored its long-term consequences. As will be demonstrated in this chapter, traumatized men argued that authentic comrades possessed the inner strength to acknowledge the horrifying reality of modern war, and that civilians should express comradely virtues by supporting welfare for veterans.

Narratives produced by veterans pose a challenge to historians because they often constructed memories that were fuelled by their attempts to reconstruct these masculine identities as 'good comrades'. Jay Winter has carved useful paths for scholars to analyse how shell shock affected memory and identity. Shell shock, according to Winter, represents the moment at which 'the link between an individual's memory and his identity is severed' as a result of terrifying experiences at the front, and symptoms of shell shock are thus a flight from unbearable realities in the trenches and social and cultural norms expected of men.[16] In this context, traumatized men's narratives may contain 'false' memories as men reconstruct their individual masculine identities and assign responsibility for their economic plight. Similar to sources by doctors and politicians who theorized Germany's traumatic experience, when we turn our attention to the perspectives of traumatized men, their voices must be analysed with careful consideration of the social and cultural environment in which men constructed these narratives.

Politics, memory and war neurosis from Weimar to Hitler

Veterans of the Great War described being buried alive, enduring bombardments and machine-gun fire, and other forms of unimaginable stress that lingered and haunted their psyches. In Germany alone, where mental trauma was diagnosed as 'war neurosis' or 'war hysteria', more than 600,000 soldiers suffered from a wide range of symptoms of mental disorders.[17] Germany's new democracy, the Weimar Republic, established the National Pension Law in 1920, which officially recognized war neurosis as a legitimate war-related wound, and prescribed pensions for psychologically disabled veterans as war victims. However, despite Weimar's progressive law, war neurotics were perceived by medical authorities and the public with great suspicion. The Labour Ministry, which administered the pension system, relied upon doctors who were widely sceptical about the legitimacy of 'war neurosis' and critical of men who allegedly lacked the will power to overcome their 'hysterical' condition and return to duty or work.

Veterans organized on the political left mobilized to construct their own narrative regarding the psychological effects of the war. The Communist Party used media to disseminate their theories that 'war psychosis' actually originated in the militarism and celebration of violence sanctified by doctors and generals, whom they saw as prejudiced against working-class Germans.[18] The largest political party that dominated Germany's more moderate left wing, the Social Democratic Party (SPD), took up the cause of war neurotics as empathetic symbols of the shattering effects of war. The largest war victims' organization, the *Reichsbund der Kriegsbeschädigten* (National Organization of War Victims), which had more than 500,000 members, frequently published articles by leading Social Democrats. Though the *Reichsbund* was officially not an organ of the SPD, it was endorsed by Social Democrats as the most effective promoter of war victims' rights. While the popular press portrayed the 'shakers' and 'quiverers' on the streets as 'notorious beggars' who faked symptoms to get attention, the *Reichsbund* argued that these men were legit-imate war victims who served as visible reminders of the horrifying effects of modern war. Public prejudices, they claimed, were shaped by doctors who considered working-class men to be welfare dependants and malingerers.[19]

Mainstream print media such as the *Reichsbund* publications are easily accessible for historians trying to discern how political groups constructed traumatic memory. However, the reality of mental trauma at the grassroots level, in particular the question of whether wounds were real or simulated, is much more difficult to uncover. Competing reports from doctors and patients reveal just how difficult it is to establish who is telling the truth about mental trauma. State-employed psychiatrists, many of them ex-military doctors, appeared to display clear bias against the SPD. For example, Frau K., who lost both her son and husband in the war, appealed to the *Reichsbund* for help when, according to her letter, her doctor denied her claim that she suffered from psychological problems:

> This doctor [Dr. Burckhardt] wrote that I was completely healthy and explained himself in the following way: 'You are completely healthy and should be happy that your son died for the fatherland. At least he did something. Do not let yourself be won over by the Social Democrats. It hurts your health.' I give this information to the organization and am ready to take testimony under oath.[20]

The *Reichsbund* collected a wealth of similar narratives attacking doctors for their prejudices against left-wing war victims. In particular, doctors equated Social Democratic war victims with unmanliness. One war victim accused his doctor of denouncing him as not a 'real man' because he was represented by the *Reichsbund*. In another case of a man who appealed to the *Reichsbund* for help, a doctor allegedly judged from the male patient's sandals and flowered stockings that he was a chronic, unmanly hysteric rather than an authentic war victim.[21] However, the *Reichsbund*'s conviction that war neurotics were persecuted by biased doctors reveals more about their political agenda than the actual medical condition of the men fighting for pensions. Left-wing activists focused on the political views and cultural prejudices of the doctors rather than the medical evidence at hand. The core medical question – whether the war caused mental wounds – became obscured by the long-existing political, class-based and social tensions between doctors and patients.

The plight of traumatized men worsened with the radicalization of the political right and the Nazi 'seizure of power' in 1933. During the Great Depression and Weimar's crisis in 1930–33, war victims had to watch social programmes undergo severe economic cuts, which struck disabled men and their dependants extremely hard. The failure of the political left in assisting war victims gave the Nazis an opportunity to appeal to this disillusioned, embittered social group, and the Nazis established an organization to reach out to physically disabled veterans, whom they described as the 'first citizens' of the Reich who had been betrayed by Weimar.[22] However, men suffering from psychological wounds were portrayed by the Nazis as unmanly hysterics, burdens on the national community and enemies of the sacred memory of the war, because they failed to endure the great test of manliness and national sacrifice. The Nazis' official newspaper for disabled veterans, produced by the National Socialist Disabled Veterans Association, frequently published articles by Nazi ideologues and doctors denouncing psychologically traumatized veterans. According to SA-Stormtrooper leader Ernst Röhm, war was a psychologically healthy experience that gave men 'mental powers' and entitled them to lead the nation. Röhm insisted that if men embraced 'comradeship', the ultimate masculine experience that came out of the war, they remained steel-nerved in the face of combat. In contrast, he claimed, war neurotics betrayed their front comrades and collaborated with 'Jewish-Bolshevist forces', which he believed caused defeat in 1918.[23]

Psychiatrists who joined the Nazi party reinforced such perspectives. Dr. H. Koetzle, a military doctor in Stuttgart, argued that war neurotics were fakers and that the Weimar system served only psychopaths, welfare cheats and other 'anti-social' elements. According to doctors such as Koetzle, it was defeat, revolution and the new democracy that was the real trauma, not the celebrated war experience.[24] Nazi ideologues, doctors and bureaucrats collaborated to create the new July 1934 pension law, which completely cut the remaining 16,000 war neurotics from the welfare rolls.[25] Psychologically disabled men, even if they had once been diagnosed as war victims before 1933, faced extermination in a few short years after the Nazis developed their programmes to murder mentally disabled citizens under the T-4 'euthanasia' programme.[26]

Traumatized men denounced the regime's demonization of mentally ill ex-soldiers and its failure to provide economic assistance. In fact, the Labour Ministry and Nazi leaders were flooded with thousands of letters from men who felt betrayed by the old front veteran Adolf Hitler, whom they were certain would understand how the psychological stress of the trenches could produce real mental wounds. Unwilling to be treated as unpatriotic, unmanly enemies of the nation, they contested the Nazis' whole construction of the memory of the Great War, even if they endorsed the Nazis politically. Psychologically traumatized veterans' efforts to attach themselves to the Nazis are full of contradictions and paradoxes, as revealed by their letters. While opportunism, desperation and suspicious reasoning sometimes permeate these letters, they also highlight the complex and apparently contradictory perceptions of memory constructed by psychologically shattered veterans. For some traumatized men, there was no contradiction between their belief in the Nazi party and their experiences with psychological breakdown in the Nazi-sanctified crucible of combat. The letters written by these men reveal how at the grassroots level, traumatic memory could be malleable, as men desperately reconstructed their narratives to fit the Nazi memory of the war, defeat and revolution. At the same time, veterans' letters indicate that even under the increasing violence wielded by the Nazi regime, memory continued to be contested, as these men relentlessly insisted that their traumatic injuries were indeed real.

One of the particular challenges of interpreting letters from war victims that fill archival files is identifying the letters that were, as welfare administrators at the time observed, clearly fraudulent. One relentless writer to the Labour Ministry provided stories that became incrementally more preposterous, including his claim that he lost his furniture business in the sinking of the *Lusitania*, but he would settle for '46,799 gold dollars' from the responsible German government.[27] However, despite the evidence suggesting that many of these men were opportunists at best, their letters contain perceptions that Hitler would support men suffering from war neurosis, revealing how ordinary Germans perceived Hitler as a sympathetic front veteran and all-powerful provider for their health.[28] Friedrich S., for example, who boasted that he was a long-term member of the Nazi party and an enthusiastic anti-Semite since the 1920s, also pronounced that he suffered 'long months of mental stress' and a 'nervous breakdown' while fighting in the trenches. He claimed that he was 'punished by Jewish judges' during the Weimar years when he was denied a pension, and after 1933, assuming that Hitler would be sympathetic to his plight, he reapplied for a pension.[29] Friedrich S. provided no medical documentation to support his claims, but only letters of support from his comrades in the Nazi party who attested to his exploits as a street fighter against communists.[30] Welfare officials turned down his requests, citing evidence that he was a forger, a welfare cheat, alcoholic and 'well-known psychopath'.[31] Friedrich S. insisted that his wounds were real, and he claimed some previously unmentioned physical war wounds, but he could not locate the records because, he claimed, the enemies of the state had hidden them.[32]

Within the piles of correspondence from men who hoped to benefit from the saviour-like Führer now in power, there were also veterans with documented mental illness who struggled for recognition. Emil L., for example, characterized himself as a true believer in National Socialism, but he was shocked when his pension was cancelled by the new regime. His doctors reported since 1917 that he suffered from an 'organic brain injury causing depression and agitation', and they acknowledged that his physical and psychological problems were war induced. The Nazis initially recognized Emil L. as a war veteran who deserved their special one-time financial award for veterans, but then they revoked it in 1936 based on a doctors' conclusion that Emil L. was a 'chronic psychopath' and that his 1917 diagnosis for war-related injuries was incorrect.[33] Emil L. fired off letters directly to both Hitler and Göring personally, where he insisted '[t]hat war victims should be so unjustly handled is not in accordance with the Führer's wishes'. He blamed doctors for his persistent psychological problems, claiming that they caused his depression to worsen when they took away his pension, and that their diagnosis was based on their desires to promote their careers rather than recognize a true war victim.[34] Still hoping after 1939 for Hitler's personal attention, Emil L. wrote to Nazi leaders with his plea that he was a respected member of the community: 'I have always fulfilled my duty and certainly belong to the national community (*Volksgemeinschaft*).'[35]

Though the Nazi regime treated mentally ill veterans as 'asocial' psychopaths who drained Germany's racially pure society, letters from veterans reveal that these individuals were unwilling to be treated as powerless objects. Instead, they attempted to exert agency by taking control over the narrative of their trauma, even if it meant altering or reconstructing their memories. Realizing that even with medical documentation they were still seen as 'psychopaths' and economic burdens by the new regime, mentally disabled veterans began to modify their trauma narrative to fit the Nazis' memory of Germany's original trauma, which the Nazis characterized as defeat and revolution. Men who could persuade the regime that they were psychologically traumatized by Weimar and democracy, rather than by the war, found acceptance in the Nazis' 'national community'. Emil H., for example, who worked as an administrator and suffered a 'severe shock to the system' after an explosion at a fireworks factory where he was an army clerk, worked the system after 1933 by blaming the defeat and revolution for intensifying his psychological problems and inhibiting his ability to work.[36] Having failed to gain a pension in the Weimar years when he made the case that the fireworks factory explosion frayed his nerves, Emil H.'s local branch of the NSDAP picked up his case a few weeks after Hitler became chancellor. They claimed that while he worked 'heroically' as a nationalist against the 'Marxists and Jews' who took over in 1918, his nerves could not endure the constant struggle against social democracy.[37] Addressing his letters directly to Adolf Hitler or 'anyone at the hand of our *Führer*', Emil H. described himself as a 'sick man' whose headaches and depression were exacerbated by having to live in a world dominated by communists:

At the end of 1918 there were only a few men who considered themselves German and stood at attention for their fatherland. I could not act like everything was all right and run along with the programme. I am not a little yes-man. I can only sing the German anthem, not the International [communist anthem]. It is my natural disposition not to be guilty of or contribute to the breakdown of the fatherland.[38]

His party supporters described him as a 'front fighter' who 'fulfilled his duty as a German civil servant in 1918 for our Führer', and the Labour Ministry

ADJUSTING MEMORY TO FIT CURRENT POLITICAL SITUATIONS

agreed, granting him 36 marks per month as a pension.[39] Emil H.'s success illustrates how under National Socialism, well-connected old supporters of Hitler could gain pensions for the 'stress' they endured under Weimar. Psychologically damaged 'front fighters' actively played into this narrative by focusing on the alleged political origins of their nervous conditions. Thus they removed the stigma of breaking down during the sacred war experience, and situated themselves in the narrative accepted by the Nazi regime.

'Hysterical men' attack the Nazi memory of the war

Berlin's federal archive is also filled with letters from men who refused to accept the Nazis' sterilized memory of the war. Labour Ministry files contain individual case studies stored in separate files marked 'individual problems' by pension administrators and archivists. Some of these individual cases involved war veterans who wrote letters more than ten pages each, every month, for up to 15 years from the Weimar Republic into the Nazi years. The case of Konrad D. stands out among the cases of war neurotics who attacked the Nazi regime's treatment of mentally ill veterans. Konrad D. wrote a seemingly endless stream of letters beginning in 1929, insisting that the Nazis tried to conceal the reality of the trench experience and traumatic memory. Those characterized as 'whiners' and 'malingerers' by the Nazis, he wrote, were the real 'heroes' because they had the courage to acknowledge that even normal men break down in the face of war. Konrad D.'s battles with the state over the causes of his psychological problems stretched back to 1916. At that time, doctors diagnosed him as suffering from a 'psychopathic constitution with psychogenic nervous damage, in particular irritability, tendency towards grumbling and bouts of depression', none of which were, according to military psychiatrists, war-related.[40] Konrad D. insisted that doctors were wrong and that his problems were directly war-related. Working as a bank clerk in the 1920s, he claimed that despite his willingness, frequent mental breakdowns made it impossible for him to work: 'I am at my wits' end. My restless nerves and their depressing effects that I brought home from the war and the revolution leave me unable to hold a job ... the collapse of my nerves was singularly caused by the war and its terrifying stresses, its deprivation ... the crashing artillery fire that gave me a glimpse into death.'[41] His welfare office informed him that he was indeed able to earn a living, and did not qualify for a pension.[42] Comparing his own plight to Paul Bäumer's in the famous pacifist novel by Erich Maria Remarque, he wrote: 'I've been abandoned: the thanks of the republic is a clear reflection of "The Thanks of the Fatherland", which is as well known to us as the "Amen" in church! A front fighter might as well hang himself – It is as they say: All Quiet on the Western Front.'[43]

Disillusioned by Weimar, and on the brink of starvation during the Great Depression, Konrad D. was eager to portray himself as a kind of mad prophet whose job it was to grumble about the German government's treatment of veterans. He characterized Weimar's conservative leaders, who further cut welfare funds, in the same way that they portrayed him – as psychotic, rabid enemies of society who brutalized the population with cuts to social programmes.[44] When the conservative von Hindenburg cabinet appointed Hitler to chancellor in January 1933, D.'s rhetoric did not waiver, but actually intensified. Revelling in his role as a pariah, Konrad D. appropriated the negative terms assigned to him by medical authorities, wearing them like a badge of honour. From 1933 onward he signed his letters with variations of 'D., severely disabled veteran, pensioner, and grumbler'. With twisted irony, Konrad D. thus mocked the diagnosis levelled at him and he introduced himself to the Nazi regime as 'the nation's leading whiner'.[45]

While the Labour Ministry generally ignored him in 1933–34, D. built up confidence to write his own treatises on neurosis, the memory of the war, the responsibilities of the 'national community', and healthcare and social welfare for veterans. According to Konrad D., the Nazi portrayal of war victims as 'heroes' was a cover-up for the regime's sweeping cuts to welfare for disabled veterans.[46] He criticized the Nazi cult of the front and the glorification of violence, and propaganda that celebrated the 'storm of steel', and he argued that only a pacifist society was capable of recognizing the existence of the human costs of war.[47] True 'heroism', he argued, was showing compassion for human beings destroyed in war:

> Hitler calls us war victims 'heroes': but does one let the 'heroes' become impoverished and depraved? The most pressing task of the national community is to provide sufficient welfare to war victims. Only the heroic spirit is able to obtain state support and defend against a world of enemies … only by granting justice can the national psyche avoid becoming sick and the spirit of truth not fall into decay.[48]

The Nazi propagandists who generated an official memory of the war as a sacred experience actually had no personal experience with combat he claimed. Instead, men like himself who suffered psychological trauma were entitled to define the authentic memory of the war. Konrad D. appointed himself as an expert on veterans' issues, and in 1935 wrote a tract he titled 'The echo – a war victim's essay on the new "honorable rights of the German war disabled"', which he sent to welfare officials and insisted they adopt as their new basis for welfare. Here Konrad D. described a post-war world that extended the ideal of comradeship by giving veterans the long-term physical and psychological care they needed. Compassion for fellow human beings would be the basis for this new vision for society. 'A state that simply kills all of its sick,' he wrote, 'annihilates the spirit and preparedness of sacrifice – it digs its own grave.'[49] Konrad D. thus defined the 'national community' as one that protected its most vulnerable citizens, including the mentally ill. He took the cornerstone of the Nazi memory of the war, the ideal of 'comradeship', and accused the regime of not fulfilling this sacred bond until they showed empathy to all veterans, including those who were mentally shattered by the war. With this round of letters that included his tract 'The echo', the regime finally took notice of Konrad D. They reported that D. was a 'well-known whiner' who possessed 'an especially sensitive and nervous disposition'.[50] Archive files do not contain letters from Konrad D. past 1935. Whether he became a target of the state's persecution of 'asocials', or a victim of the T-4 'euthanasia' programme is not known.

The idea that the Nazi regime distorted the authentic memory of the war was a central theme in the writings of traumatized veterans. Erich G., another survivor of the Great War who struggled with psychological illness, accused the Nazi regime of deliberately covering up the traumatic memory of 1914–18 in order to convince Germans to wage another world war. In 1916, Erich G. was buried alive following an artillery barrage on the Eastern front, and he was treated for 'weakness of nerves'.[51] After the war, he was plagued by epileptic seizures and various nervous ailments, which his private doctors diagnosed as the result of neurological and psychological trauma inflicted in the trenches. Labour Ministry doctors, however, including one of Germany's premier specialists on war neurosis, Dr. Max Nonne, turned down Erich G.'s case as not related to war service, and Nonne noted G.'s history of petty crime, venereal disease and marital problems in the 1920s as evidence for the veteran's immoral and fraudulent character. With help from the *Reichsbund,* Erich G. hired a lawyer to sue Nonne for focusing on his character rather than medical condition, and G. amassed reports from his personal doctors testifying that his traumatic experience of being buried alive was the source of his various ailments. Like so many other desperate war victims, G. appropriated the language of state medical authorities to hurl accusations back at his opponents, calling Dr. Nonne a 'swindler and a liar'.[52]

Erich G.'s case presents a recurring problem in the writings of war neurotics that poses a dilemma for historians dealing with these sources. While he claimed to tell the truth about his personal history and war experience, he also displayed an obvious penchant for opportunism as he negotiated the political labyrinth that dominated his world. When Hitler came to power, Erich G. quickly abandoned the Social Democratic-oriented *Reichsbund* and obsequiously curried favour with letters sent directly to Hitler praising the leader's promises to pay respect to disabled veterans.[53] Despite his obvious opportunism, his construction of memory and traumatic illness is revealing. Though Erich G., like many of his mentally ill comrades, was a political chameleon, he continued to insist that normal men broke down under the strains of war, and that he was a patriotic citizen who suffered real wounds.

With the 1934 cuts to disabled veterans' pensions, Erich G. wrote to Hitler to accuse the Führer of failing to fulfil his promises to assist traumatized men. After the outbreak of the Second World War in 1939, Erich G.'s criticism intensified and he began to accuse Hitler of betraying the memory of 1914–18 and the experiences of authentic veterans like himself. Because the Nazis created an impossible image of racial perfection for soldiers to live up to, Erich G. predicted that the next generation of soldiers would also be cast aside when they broke down in the face of combat. The regime's superhuman image of the German soldier, he argued, was a myth, and the notion that Germany could win through sheer will-power was a lie. With the German army's collapse at Stalingrad in February 1943, Erich G. compared his own experience with the next generation's and saw proof in his theory that even normal men broke down under extreme stress:

> If I went to the front as a healthy man, without an inclination or disposition towards illness, then my problems must certainly have been caused by war service, or at the least, through terrible weather and stress [...] We also had to survive similar terrible conditions in 1914–18. We German soldiers are not Russians, who are able to take the stressful climate etc. without getting sick [...] Let's hope that the comrades of today's war won't have to experience what we [first] world war front fighters did, namely, to be told after the war 'the problems can't be traced back to war service'.[54]

The Nazi memory of the war suppressed the reality of the front experience, Erich G. contended. Germany lost wars because its soldiers were human, not because the nation was betrayed at home or weakened by 'hysterical' men. By destroying another generation of men the Nazis betrayed the memory of 1914–18.

Similarly to Konrad D., Labour Ministry files do not record Erich G.'s fate. His last letters in the archives end in 1943. However, the final one offers interesting language that highlights for historians the degree to which these psychologically disabled men not only emulated the medical discourse, but also tried to replace doctors as the leading authorities on trauma and the memory of the war. Erich G. shifted his writing from first to third person, describing his own case as if he were an objective observer. He recounted in detail the traumatic origins of his wounds, as he described the experience of 'this case' being buried alive under a bombardment, and the nervous disorders that followed. Shifting back to first person, he then reflected: 'Now I would like to ask you, what is your own opinion and judgment about the causes of my injuries?'[55] Erich G. appointed himself both a medical expert and a caretaker of what he perceived as the destructive reality of the war experience, and he imagined an audience that seemed to go beyond simply the bureaucrats who filed away his relentless diatribes.

Konrad D.'s and Erich G.'s letters offer a different kind of discourse for historians to analyse compared to those written by other disabled veterans. Their letters reflected an attempt on their part to bypass familiar debates over pensions. Erich G. and Konrad D. admitted bitterly that they had abandoned hope of winning pensions, and instead they concentrated on battling propagandists over the real effects of combat on human beings. Letters from these disabled men thus shifted from debates over economic restitution and more towards a desperate attempt to claim authority and control over their bodies and minds. They constructed themselves as having a new calling as the nation's 'leading whiners' who reminded the regime of the traumatic reality of modern war and warned prophetically of the nation's impending collapse.

Conclusion

The voices of mentally traumatized veterans are a vital source for historians dealing with memory, but they also pose significant challenges. Veterans adapted their memories to prevailing political environments, and evidence of opportunism and distorted realities abounded as they desperately struggled to cope with post-war economic trauma. After 1933, many of these men turned into opportunists and offered versions of their memories to suit the 'official' collective memory of the Nazi regime. As the Nazis declared that the Weimar democracy, rather than the war, was Germany's central trauma, men wrote letters tailored to satisfy this explanation for traumatic neurosis. Thus historians must be wary about locating the origins of these wounds. Determining whether the wounds actually existed is even more difficult to untangle in the fierce debates between doctors, patients and competing political interests.

At the same time, while the assimilation of personal narratives into larger collective memories makes it challenging to uncover the reality of these wounds, it is still possible to discern individual memories that resided beneath the layers of collective memory-building. In particular, veterans' voices offer a treasure-trove of insights into how men perceived the war experience and its effects on their minds and social identities. While many were willing to compromise with officially sanctioned collective memories about what caused their wounds, the vast majority of letters found in archives indicate that these men were unwilling to compromise on what they saw as a crucial point: their wounds were indeed real and did not tarnish their status as patriotic, masculine, legitimate members of the 'national community'. As veterans negotiated desperately with doctors and political leaders who considered them outsiders, they revealed their individual memories of the horrors of mass violence, their belief that 'normal' men indeed broke down, and their insistence that the fatherland owed them thanks for enduring what civilians could never imagine.

For historians of memory who try to cut through the biases of medical and political authorities to recover and define the 'German trauma', veterans' voices offer a glimpse into the complex history of memory 'from below'. Their perspectives reveal that there was no single German trauma, but rather a myriad of individual traumas narrated by damaged men who struggled to assert their vision of the authentic memory of the war experience. Individual memories did not easily fit into master narratives of trauma generated from competing political groups. Thus historians dealing with their memories must be attentive to memory as an elusive, apparently fragmented and contradictory, or even terrifying, phenomenon that individuals struggled to convey to those who did not share their experiences. The Nazis would try to enforce a unified, collective memory that fit their ideology about the war experience. However, despite the Nazi regime's attempt to annihilate the often subversive memories of individual veterans, the existence of these sources in archives remind us of the need to critically analyse collective memories if we are to reconstruct the complex ways in which societies remember modern war.

Notes

1 J. Winter, *Remembering War: The Great War Between Memory and History in the 20th Century* (New Haven: Yale University Press, 2006), p. 55.

2 For an excellent comparative study of traumatic neurosis, see M. Micale and P. Lerner, *Traumatic Pasts: History, Psychiatry and Trauma in the Modern Age, 1870–1930* (Cambridge: Cambridge University Press, 2001).

3 On Nazi Germany's attacks on the mentally ill, including traumatized veterans of the Great War, see P. Rauh, 'Von Verdun nach Grafeneck: Die psychisch kranken Veteranen des Ersten Weltkrieges als Opfer der nationalsozialistischen Krankenmordaktion T4', in B. Quinkert et al. (eds) *Krieg und Psychiatrie, 1914–1950* (Göttingen: Wallstein Verlag, 2010), pp. 54–74.

4 See J. Crouthamel, *The Great War and German Memory* (Exeter: University of Exeter Press, 2009), especially chs. 5–6; for an illuminating look at the grassroots struggles of war neurotics, see S. Neuner, *Die Staatliche Versorgung psychisch Kriegsbeschädigter in Deutschland, 1920–1939* (Göttingen: Vandenhoeck & Ruprecht, 2011), esp. Pt. III.

5 P. Barham, *Forgotten Lunatics of the Great War* (New Haven: Yale University Press, 2007), esp. ch. 19.

6 On the importance of history 'from the margins', see G. Eley, 'How and where is German history centered', in N. Gregor, N. Roemer and M. Rosemen (eds) *German History from the Margins* (Bloomington: Indiana University Press, 2006), pp. 274–75.

7 On the cultural constructions of psychological trauma in the twentieth century, see A. Young, *The Harmony of Illusions: Inventing Post-Traumatic Stress Disorder* (Princeton: Princeton University Press, 1995), esp. chs. 1–2.

8 P. Lerner, *Hysterical Men: War, German Psychiatry, and the Politics of Trauma in Germany, 1890–1930* (Ithaca: Cornell University Press, 2003), pp. 4–7.

9 Lerner, *Hysterical Men*, p. 3; for a comparison with Austria-Hungary, see H.-G. Hofer, *Nervenschwäche und Krieg: Modernitätskritik und Krisenbewältigung in der österreichischen Psychiatrie, 1880–1920* (Wien: Böhlau, 2004).

10 G.L. Mosse, 'Shell-shock as a social disease', *Journal of Contemporary History*, 35(1), 2000, pp. 1–8.

11 P. Lerner, 'An economy of memory: psychiatrists, veterans and traumatic narratives in Weimar Germany', in A. Confino and P. Fritzsche (eds) *The Work of Memory – New Directions in the Study of German Society and Culture* (Urbana: University of Illinois Press, 2002), pp. 175–88.

12 G. Eghigian, *Making Security Social: Disability, Insurance, and the Birth of the Social Entitlement State in Germany* (Ann Arbor: University of Michigan Press, 2000), pp. 245–46.

13 A. Killen, *Berlin Electropolis: Shock, Nerves and German Modernity* (Berkeley: University of California Press, 2005), p. 10; on cinematic representations of shell shock, see A. Kaes, *Shell Shock Cinema: Weimar Culture and the Wounds of War* (Princeton: Princeton University Press, 2009).

14 J. Crouthamel, 'Male sexuality and psychological trauma: soldiers and sexual "disorder" in World War I and Weimar Germany', *Journal of the History of Sexuality*, 17(1), 2008, pp. 60–84.

15 T. Kühne, 'Gender confusion and gender order in the German military, 1918–45', in K. Hagemann and S. Schüler-Springorum (eds) *Home/Front: The Military, War and Gender in Twentieth-Century Germany* (New York: Berg, 2002), p. 234.
16 Winter, *Remembering War*, pp. 52–53.
17 D. Kaufmann, 'Science as cultural practice: psychiatry in the First World War and Weimar Germany', *Journal of Contemporary History*, 34(1), 1999, pp. 125–26.
18 The German Communist Party insisted that psychiatrists were simply puppets of capitalist forces: see E. Vogeley, 'Die Psychiatrie und Neuorologie im Dienst der kapitalistischen Klass', *Internationaler Bund*, 10, October 1928, Bundesarchiv mit Stiftung Archiv der Parteien der DDR, Berlin.
19 Letter from *Reichsbund der Kriegsbeschädigten* to the Labour Ministry, 3 January 1921, Bundesarchiv Berlin-Lichterfelde (BAB) R3901/36137.
20 Letter from widow of Wilhelm K. to the *Reichsbund*, 2 March 1921, BAB R3901/36027.
21 Letter from Hartmann S., included in *Reichsbund* report, sent to Labour Ministry, 21 October 1924; and Report from *Reichsbund* member Hölter, Barmen district, delivered to Labour Ministry, 26 September 1924, BAB R3901/36027.
22 J.M. Diehl, *Thanks of the Fatherland* (Chapel Hill: University of North Carolina Press, 1993), ch. 1.
23 E. Röhm, 'Über den Frontsoldaten', *Deutsche Kriegsopferversorgung*, 2, February 1934, p. 2.
24 Dr. H. Koetzle, 'Gedanken zur Reform des Reichsversorgungsrechts', *Deutsche Kriegsopferversorgung*, 2(1), October 1933, p. 10.
25 Diehl, *Thanks of the Fatherland*, pp. 37–39.
26 Rauh, 'Von Verdun nach Grafeneck', pp. 54–74.
27 Karl Maria W. to Ministerialrat Hoppe, Reichsarbeitsministerium (Labour Ministry, henceforth RAM), 19 October 1932, BAB R3901/7011.
28 This phenomenon in which Hitler was broadly seen as a saviour-like figure by many Germans is explored in I. Kershaw's *The Hitler Myth: Image and Reality in the Third Reich* (Oxford: Oxford University Press, 1987).
29 Letters from Friedrich S. to Labour Ministry 25 and 26 April 1934, BAB R3901/37017.
30 Letter from NSDAP Kreisleitung Halensee (Berlin) to Labour Ministry, 25 April 1934, BAB R3901/37017.
31 Letter from Labour Ministry to Friedrich S., 3 September 1935, BAB R3901/37017.
32 Letters from Friedrich S. to Labour Ministry, 16 July 1935 and 22 August 1935, BAB R3901/37017.
33 Letter from Main Welfare Office Brandenburg-Pommern to Labour Ministry, signed by government representative Panse, 30 December 1937, BAB R3901/37015.
34 Letter from Emil L. to Reich chancellor, 29 January 1938, BAB R3901/37015.
35 Letter from Emil L. to Generalfeldmarschall Hermann Göring, 12 September 1939, BAB R3901/37015.
36 Letter from Reichsbund ehem. Angehöriger der Heeres-und Marine-Verwaltungen, Spandau, to Labour Ministry, 20 October 1932, BAB R3901/37014.
37 Letter from Kreisleitung der NSDAP, Siegburg, to Labour Ministry, 11 February 1933 and Letter from Main Welfare Office Rheinland to Labour Ministry, 26 April 1933, BAB R3901/37014.
38 Letter from Emil H. to 'Kanzlei des Führers und Reichkanzlers zu Händen unseres Führers Adolf Hitler', 25 May 1935, BAB R3901/37014.
39 Letter from NSDAP, Kreishauptabteilung Siegburg to Hermann Göring, 30 May 1933, BAB R3901/37014.
40 Report by private doctor Bratz, hired by Konrad D., outlined D.'s case history since the Great War in letter to RAM, 25 July 1931, BAB, R3901/37011.

41 Konrad D. to RAM, 10 and 21 July 1929, BAB, R3901/37011.
42 Hauptversorgungsamt (Main Welfare Office – HVA) Berlin, report by Oberregierungsrat Detring, to RAM, 24 January 1929, BAB R3901/37011.
43 Konrad D. to RAM, 8 June 1929, BAB R3901/37011.
44 Konrad D. to RAM, 22 September 1931 and 23 March 1932, BAB R3901/37011.
45 Konrad D. to Staatssekretär Dr. Lammers, 19 March 1933, BAB R3901/37011.
46 Ibid.
47 Konrad D. to Labour Minister Franz Seldte, including D.'s essay, 'Das Echo', 12 March 1935, BAB R3901/ 37011.
48 Konrad D. to Staatsekretär Lammers, 19 March 1933 and letter attached to report from Ministerialrat Sieler to Dr. Lammers, 5 April 1933, BAB R3901/37011.
49 Ibid.
50 Letter from Versorgungsamt (Welfare Office) V Berlin to Direktor des Hauptversorgungsamts, 13 July 1935, BAB R3901/37011.
51 Strafgericht report regarding case of Erich G. vs Prof. Dr. Nonne, includes reports from Dr. F. Zimmermann, 5 September 1931, BAB R3901/37011.
52 Erich G. to RAM, 12 Nov. 1932, BAB R3901/37013.
53 Erich G. to Adolf Hitler, 24 March 1933, BAB R3901/37013.
54 Erich G. to RAM, 21 March 1943, BAB R3901/37013.
55 Erich G.'s 'Bericht über die mutmassliche Ursache des Leidens', which appears undated in this file after his 21 March 1943 letter, BAB R3901/37013.

9 Memories of suburbia

Autobiographical fiction and minority narratives

Hannah Ewence

What is the nature of the relationship between history and memory, and how might certain writing modes mediate and articulate that relationship? In a hugely influential article 'Between memory and history: *les lieux de mémoire*', published in 1989 as a synthesis of his body of work on the topic, the French historian Pierre Nora condemned what he perceived as 'the conquest and eradication of memory by history'.[1] The 'acceleration of history'[2] (or the perception of it) throughout the nineteenth and twentieth centuries, Nora feared, had virtually obliterated global cultures of folk traditions and 'environments of memory' (*milieux de mémoire*). This had left only fragments or traces behind, scattered, as sites of memory (*lieux de mémoire*) to be retrieved and reconstructed by the eager few. While 'true' or 'real' memory – 'social and inviolate, exemplified in but also retained as the secret of so-called primitive or archaic societies' – had all but been annihilated Nora argued, a modern form of memory had taken its place.[3] 'Modern memory' is embodied within the practice of oral history, heritage, commemoration, archives and genealogy. According to Nora, its popularity reflects an insatiable appetite to remember and record what might otherwise be forgotten, as well as an anxiety to store and to catalogue the past for its possible but indeterminate use in the future. The writing of memory through the practice of history, then, is key within this process. However, within such thinking 'modern memory' appears to be a poor substitute for its 'pure' cousin, having been corrupted by its 'passage through history', becoming mechanical and 'deliberate' rather than 'spontaneous'.[4]

Yet Nora's scathing appraisal of memory in its present form is far from persuasive. The oppositions that Nora establishes between history and memory appear fabricated and unnecessarily provocative, overlooking the ways in which history and memory can, and do, successfully overlap and cross-fertilize. Nora's polemics instead call to mind the suspicions that many 'traditional' historians expressed towards the integration of memory within the discipline as source and subject from the mid-twentieth century onwards. While Nora's reluctance to embrace 'modern memory' seems to be an articulation of a rather curious nostalgia for an unburdened past rather than a resistance to the democratization of history, it nevertheless inadvertently highlights a previously insidious tendency to cast memory aside as an emblem of subjectivity and fabrication, and a direct challenge to 'truth' and 'authenticity'. For Nora, the 'mechanical' outputs of 'modern memory' are not so much inauthentic as insincere and generic, reflecting the nationalization or 'domination' of certain memory narratives and sites. There is little acknowledgement of the multiple and mutually beneficial intersections that can and do occur between national memory/history and personal memory. As Hue-Tam Ho Tai, in a review of *Realms of Memory* (the English translation of the *Lieux de mémoire* project) points out, Nora's 'distinction between history and memory is too simplistic. Even atomized memory uses the milestones of official, national history to construct or reconstruct the past.'[5] In memoirs, autobiography and life-writing, this use of history to give form, cohesion and dynamism to personal reminiscences has become an accepted part of the genre.[6] Hanging one's memories upon climactic moments of national or even global history not only infuses such memories with greater significance and broader realms of meaning and comprehension, but also demonstrates the permeation of national memories *within* individual remembrances. However these types of writing modes are not simply passive reflectors of 'history' but also produce a renegotiated version of 'the past' as it was experienced in the 'then' and re-remembered or reconstructed in the 'now'. The continued success of, and multiple uses found for *The Diaries of Anne Frank*, and indeed the ubiquity of Anne herself as a symbol of the Holocaust, is a key example of the ways in which life writing can provide a forum for the explosive and repeated convergence of history and memory – a process through which each continues to remake the other.

Fiction too (often thanks to the influence of Marxism, feminism and post-colonialism in recent decades) has been a crucial medium for uncovering obscure or forgotten pasts as well as for reproducing those that are well known. Similarly to autobiography, memoirs and memory work undertaken by historians more broadly, fiction provides an arena through which private memory can be formulated, interrogated and made distinct from (and even challenge) public memory while remaining wholly rooted within local, national and even global traditions of remembering (and forgetting). This is a particularly crucial endeavour when it brings previously marginalized histories to the fore – histories with the potential to confront and reformulate public historical narratives. Within fiction, as within social and cultural history and life writing, the macro-narrative and the micro-narrative can compete, co-exist and converge. However, fiction is not history. As a writing mode, it is not bound by scholarly conventions of, and aspirations to, accuracy and objectivity, but rather by the instinct for creativity. As a forum for memory, too, there are far fewer limits than within the genre of autobiography. Fiction can disguise, embellish and fabricate memory – and unapologetically so. It can also liberate memory, acting as a cathartic medium for mental exploration, for going 'off *piste*', providing an arena for full disclosure with a 'get out' clause.

The points of similarity between history, memory and fiction are evident, but a clear relational line running between all three is less so. Ironically Nora acknowledged this close association, noting the hybridized forms of history that were beginning to emerge as 'the boundaries between' history, memory and fiction became increasingly blurred.[7] This 'cultural turn' has gathered significant momentum since the 1980s, and is now a leading force within approaches to, and the writing of, the past. Taking a lead from these developments, this chapter explores how, even when the autobiographical dynamic of a novel is indistinct, unacknowledged or altogether absent, fiction *can* and *does* provides a space in which history and memory meet. In contrast to Nora, I want to suggest that memory is rarely destroyed by history but is, instead, frequently the means of its illumination and rejuvenation. What is more, the spatial quality of fiction is frequently at the very heart of this symbiosis. That is to say, the spaces and places within fiction can both figuratively and literally operate (to borrow from Nora) as 'sites' or 'environments' of memories.

Adherents to the 'spatial turn' (as a sub-set of the cultural turn) within human geography, cultural studies and academia more broadly have long recognized that ideas about space and place are encoded with individual and collective identity(ies), memories and histories. As the authors of a recent volume remind us, 'People give meaning to what is otherwise an abstract location, a point on a map, a structure at the intersection of coordinates, random space. But people do not simply invest a place with significance: the process is reciprocal, with place becoming a part of the identity of those who interact with it.'[8] This is particularly true of life writing in its various forms. As Steve Pile has suggested, 'narratives of the self are inherently spatial; ... they [are] spatially constituted. That is, stories about the self are "produced" out of the spatialities that seemingly only provide the backdrop for those stories or selves.'[9] In discussing the synthesis of history and fiction within sites of memory, Nora hinted at an association between space, memory, and identity, although he failed to explicitly draw out the spatial dynamic of memory. Nora conceded only that '[m]emory takes root in the concrete, in spaces, gestures, images, and objects' while 'history binds itself strictly to temporal continuities'.[10] This rather contemptuous view of history's limited, one-dimensional capabilities has thankfully been ignored by contemporaries of Nora.

Human geographers and historians have instead begun to borrow from each other's craft as a means to explore the spatial qualities of memory and history, considering how both are rooted in space as well as time. Doreen Massey in particular has skilfully drawn out the dual spatial/temporal qualities of history, demonstrating that places (as remembered in the past and conceptualized in the present) are hybridized and constantly evolving 'envelopes of time-space', constituted through layers of history as well as through interactions with the world beyond.[11]

In this chapter, I explore how memory functions within and through the conceptualization of place within three novels: Hanif Kureishi's *The Buddha of Suburbia* (1990); Zadie Smith's *White Teeth* (2000); and Naomi Alderman's *Disobedience* (2006). These three works, penned by 'minority' writers, all draw upon childhoods in post-war British suburbia to provide the backdrop for their debut novel. Significantly, then, all three novels do contain autobiographical elements, although the authors have, to varying degrees, been resistant to readings that have aligned their lives too closely with the text. Nevertheless, or perhaps because of this resistance, the line between myth, memory, public and private, history and fiction within each of the novels often appears blurred. In their representations of the London suburbs, Kureishi, Smith and Alderman all borrow from established and often deeply negative myths regarding place. The collective memory of the post-war suburbs as conformist, corrosive and stifling underscores each of their prose, which seemingly aligns minority experience with majority perception. However, these authors gradually develop their ideas of place beyond the purely stereotypical, ultimately delivering unique and personal images of life in the urban peripheries. Bound up in those images are individual remembrances of the past that intersect with, problematize and forge collective memories of suburbia.

The Buddha of Suburbia

Possibly the most iconic British suburbia novel within a flourishing Anglo-American literary sub-genre, is Hanif Kureishi's 1990 debut novel *The Buddha of Suburbia*. It is a semi-autobiographical coming-of-age story which stars Karim Amir, a young, rather naïve kid from the south London suburbs, of mixed English and Indian parentage. Set in 1970s Britain, against a climate of virulent racism and social unrest, Karim identifies as an outsider, fully conscious yet desperately anxious about his unusual position as something of an ethnic, cultural, even sexual hybrid. From the outset he declares: 'I am often considered to be a funny kind of Englishman, a new breed as it were, having emerged from two old histories.'[12] Karim's keen awareness of his racial hybridity mirrors the author's own background. Kureishi, born in Bromley in 1954, is the child of an Indian/Pakistani father and an English mother. His father, Rafiushan, came from a relatively wealthy Muslim family living in Madras, and was sent to study in Britain in 1947. Upheaval and partition of the Indian subcontinent transformed Rafiushan from an Indian to a Pakistani in his absence.[13] Hanif, his son, seems to have felt this spatial identity confusion keenly, experiencing it as an inherited trauma – a tangible sense of displacement and 'in-betweenness'. In an interview in 1997, the writer attempted to articulate this:

> I came from two worlds ... There was my Pakistani family, my uncles, aunts and so on. Then there was my English family, who were lower middle or working class. My grandfather had pigeons and greyhounds and all that. ... So, finding my way through all that ... I wrote all those books to make sense of it.[14]

Fiction, for Kureishi, is an acknowledged cathartic process – a way of working through a sense of 'otherness'. Within *The Buddha of Suburbia* – a novel accredited with being the most closely autobiographical of all of his work – Kureishi explores these remembered adolescent anxieties in spatial terms. From the beginning, Karim's sense of his racial difference is set alongside his antithetical relationship with Bromley. 'Perhaps it is the odd mixture of continents and blood, of here and there, of belonging and not, that makes me restless and easily bored', Karim muses in the opening chapter. 'Or perhaps it was being brought up in the suburbs that did it.'[15] The South London suburbs of Karim/Hanif's youth are immediately established as parochial and confining, as detrimental to living, to being fully alive. Instead, Karim craves the city 'where life was bottomless in its temptations'.[16] After the separation of his parents, and his own foray into the world of theatre, Karim finally finds himself in the big city – London and then New York – a move which he feels signifies his socio-cultural transcendence from suburban mediocrity to urban success.

This repudiation of the suburbs as an asphyxiating space for youth and creativity, and indeed as little more than a 'leaving place' for the pursuit of urban pleasures, mimics a familiar trope for representing the suburbs. As Simon Frith has demonstrated, the iconography of the metropolis as the antithesis of the suburbs has been absolutely fundamental to British rock and pop movements across the post-war decades, not least David Bowie and glam rock, who hailed from Karim/Hanif's own Bromley stomping ground, attending the same school.[17] 'Boys were often to be found on their knees before this icon,' Karim recalls, 'praying to be made into pop stars and for release from a lifetime as a motor mechanic or clerk in an insurance firm, or a junior architect.'[18] This semi-spiritual reverence for pop culture and fame weaves its way throughout *The Buddha of Suburbia*, drawing upon cultural memories of the 1970s music scene, constructing a soundtrack that is evocative and nostalgic, hedonistic and angry. In doing so, it evokes both the mood of a generation and of a location, symbolizing the commonplace derision of 1970s suburbia, and youthful rebellion against it. As a narrative device, Kureishi uses cultural memory as shorthand not only for an era, but also for a place and a mood. It is a trope for aligning personal memory rooted in place with a shared sensual memory. Just as music acts as a medium through which Karim as a school-kid seeks, and finds, acceptance, it also provides a common 'meeting place' of memories for the author and reader. It is a way for Karim to participate in, and Kureishi through him to manipulate, popular spatial/cultural stereotypes, bringing greater meaning to memories of place.

This appropriation of a familiar cultural narrative of the suburb by Kureishi is thus deeply suggestive of his own desire to identify with a sense of 'Britishness'. Kureishi's framing of the suburb as a locale that fosters small-mindedness, competitive materialism, deep-rooted unhappiness and, above all, dysfunctional families, replicates a distain for suburbia that is distinctly British, even English (whatever we understand by this distinction). As Vesna Goldsworthy has written:

Just what is it about the idea of suburbia in England that makes the choice of suburban life 'the love that dares not speak its name'? We profess to hate the suburbs but we want our gardens secluded, our parking off-street and our shops and post offices close by – but not to the point of living above them.[19]

Kureishi's novel epitomizes this strange paradox, loudly despising suburban lifestyles and suburban characters, and yet, as the place of Kureishi's childhood, it is a setting that he repeatedly (through Karim), figuratively and literally, explores, examines, deconstructs and returns to again and again. It is the site of his memories – the environment against which his adolescence is irrevocably mapped.

In this sense, then, *The Buddha of Suburbia* is encoded with both a distinctly personal and a distinctly 'British' folk memory of place. Yet, as Karim reminds us, this is a Britain of 'new breeds', a nation still struggling to emerge from underneath the rubble of its disintegrated empire and still acclimatizing to the growing racial diversity of its towns and cities. Karim symbolizes both positions: he is the Englishman surveying the devastation, and the immigrant anxious to find his place in a hostile Britain. In an early chapter, Karim pays homage to the narrative of the newcomer, recounting his own father's, Haroon's, experience.

London, the Old Kent Road, was a freezing shock … It was wet and foggy; people called you 'Sunny Jim'; there was never enough to eat, and Dad never took to dripping on toast. 'Nose drippings more like,' he'd say, pushing away the staple diet of the working class. 'I thought it would be roast beef and Yorkshire pudding all the way.'[20]

Haroon's rapid disillusionment with the 'mother country' he encounters upon his arrival in England – a 'mother country' wholly at odds with the place he had expected to find – echoes the disappointment of so many commonwealth immigrants. It is the universal migrant tale – a conventional 'race memory' that one might expect to encounter as a matter of course within post-colonial narratives. Yet, through its comic framing, Kureishi also establishes this experience as a snippet from a distinctly personal, even genealogical album of memories. This is not a lone example. The following chapter, which recounts Karim's thwarted attempts to begin a relationship with a local girl Helen, also sets public memory/national history against private experience. When Karim tries to call upon Helen, her father ('Hairy Back') bars the door, telling Karim, '"We don't want you blackies coming to the house", going on to say, "However many niggers there are, we don't like it. We're with Enoch. If you put one of your black 'ands near my daughter I'll smash it with a 'ammer! With a 'ammer!"'[21] Karim retreats, but not before deciding to let down the tyres on Hairy Back's Rover, and to urinate through the car window. This scene is a nod to an infamous episode in Britain's recent race history that saw Conservative MP Enoch Powell take a controversial (but publicly popular) stand against commonwealth immigration in a politically explosive speech in Birmingham in 1968. Kureishi's pointed reference to the episode within the text confronts the inherent, unapologetic racism of the 1970s, exploring the infiltration of the racist sentiment espoused within Powell's 'rivers of blood' speech (as the Birmingham speech became known) from politics to the social attitudes of the average suburban householder. Its use as a formative experience for Karim is a direct challenge to a time and a mood which has too frequently been subject to collective amnesia. Moreover, and more importantly, Kureishi's inclusion of this episode also gives voice and agency to those subject to British racism, overturning simplistic and lazy assumptions about Britain's minorities as a community of passive victims. It is little stretch to imagine that this episode might wholly or partially reflect an experience from Kureishi's own youth. The novel as a writing mode and a memory space thus provides a medium through which an author can embellish and reformulate the past, even constructing and playing out creative forms of revenge for persons within that past. In this sense, the novel acts as a distinctly personal backward journey, a repository but also a workshop for one's own memories. It is a space in which the past can be laid out, scrutinized, and even recrafted.

White Teeth

The much acclaimed *White Teeth*, published a decade after *The Buddha of Suburbia* in 2000, also utilizes familiar historical settings, cultural references and an eclectic array of characters to explore and fold together recognizably public, with compellingly private, layers of memory. At the time of publication and since, Zadie Smith's debut novel was praised as an eloquent celebration of multiculturalism in the contemporary London suburbs, adopting both a far more confident and a far more optimistic view of how minority communities might not only assimilate but co-exist within suburbia. The passage of ten years between Kureishi's debut novel and Smith's seems to have made all the difference. Set primarily in Willesden, north-west London, from the mid-1970s to the eve of the millennium, *White Teeth* weaves together the lives of three dysfunctional families – the Bengali Iqbals, the racially-mixed Joneses and the Anglo-Jewish Chalfens – employing a satirical style to explore the nature of roots, belonging and the post-colonial migrant experience. It sets intimate personal stories against the grand sweep of history, touching upon the Indian mutiny of 1857, the Jamaican earthquake of 1907, World War Two, Powellism, the end of the Cold War, the Salman Rushdie affair, and the millennium. As Philip Tew has observed, throughout *White Teeth*, Smith displays an acute historical consciousness.[22]

Despite the episodic 'family saga' style of the novel, reviewers were quick to point to the parallels between the novel and the young author's own life. Zadie Smith, herself the child of a racially-mixed marriage, was born in 1975 in Hampstead, and raised in Willesden. In the fictitious Joneses, are distinct echoes of her own family. Similarly to Archibald Jones, a middle-aged divorcee, and

Clara Bowden, a young second-generation British-Jamaican, her own parents were from different generations, as well as of different racial backgrounds. Similar to the Willesden community in the novel, the community in which Smith grew up was enormously diverse. It provided a home to various commonwealth migrants, to upwardly mobile minorities moving out from the inner city, and to middle class 'white' Britons amongst others. The Willesden of both Smith's childhood and of *White Teeth* is an unequivocally multiracial, even post-colonial environment. Yet Smith has been hesitant to fully embrace the apparent parallels between her life and her writing. In an interview with PBS Masterpiece Theatre, she reasoned,

> The people in *White Teeth* are immigrants. I'm not an immigrant so it's a different experience. But I was around people who had that experience, who felt separated or cut in two, who had moved from one country to another, who had that sense of leading two lives.[23]

Smith, similarly to Kureishi, has expressed discomfort at being cast in the role of spokesperson for the universal 'minority experience'. As she has rightly insisted, she has never been an immigrant. She never had to go through the process of departure, journey, and arrival. She simply 'is', and has always been 'here'. According to Smith, her sense and recollection of place is firmly rooted and unconfused, although she admits these impressions have been subject, or at least empathetic, to outside influences. Moreover, similarly to Kureishi/Karim, Smith's mixed ethnic background suggests her unavoidable hybridity or 'in-betweeness' between nations, cultures and histories. These are explicit themes which various characters within the novel, if not Smith herself, repeatedly grapple with.

Despite Smith's disavowal of autobiographical elements within *White Teeth*, the unmistakable chronological and geographical parallels between the novel's primary suburban setting and the cityscape of Smith's own childhood hints that spatial memories and ideas about place are interwoven within the prose itself. These literary sites of spatial memory form a collage of the author's own memories and impressions, but also reflect local and collective remembrances of North London particularly, and suburbia in a more abstracted sense. In her description of the North West London district of Cricklewood in 1975 on the novel's opening page, for example, she declares it to be 'no kind of place. It was not a place a man came to die. It was a place a man came in order to go other places via the A41.'[24] This satirically disdainful treatment of the London suburbs sets the scene for the rather hapless Archibald Jones' attempt, and failure, to end his own life with that most suburban of domestic appliances, the vacuum cleaner. Besides the interplay of Smith's evident local knowledge regarding the Cricklewood road system, she also draws upon popular perceptions of suburban lifestyles as consumerist and quite literally asphyxiating. However, just as Vensa Goldsworthy has suggested, Smith's attitude towards suburbia, as within British cultural discourse more broadly, is far from clear-cut.[25] After enjoying a reprieve from his untimely end,

Archie meets and marries the young Clara Bowden, finding a new home for them in Willesden Green. For Archie, the suburbs no longer signify an end but a new beginning. On moving day, as Archie and Clara travel through the suburban landscape, visited by Clara for the very first time, she reflects:

> What kind of place *was* this? That was the thing, you see, you couldn't be *sure*. Travelling in the front passenger seat of the removal van, she'd seen the high road and it has been ugly and poor and familiar ... but then at the turn of a corner suddenly roads had exploded in greenery, beautiful oaks, the houses got taller, wider, more detached, she could see parks, she could see libraries ... and, though it wasn't Morocco or Belgium or Italy, it was nice – not the promised land – but *nice*, nicer than anywhere she had ever been.[26]

Clara, the narrator informs us, comes 'from Lambeth (via Jamaica)' – the heartland of the Afro-Caribbean community in 1970s Britain.[27] Replicating the experience of many others from this community, it is marriage, rather than aspiration, which brings her to the suburbs. It is a landscape that, upon first impressions, is unfamiliar, surprising, a place of contrasts. In viewing it, Clara can only muster the rather uninspired pronouncement 'nice', reflecting a distinctly 'British' spatial ambivalence towards suburbia that resists giving oneself over fully to its allure. It is a narrative device which allows Smith to marry her personal memories of place with collective, particularly 'British' representations of suburbia.

If Smith uses Archie Jones and Clara Bowden to explore conventional ideas about suburban space, then it is through Alsana, the young, fiery Bengali wife of Samad Iqbal, Archie's best friend, that the author presents immigrant memories of 1970s North London. For Alsana, the suburbs are a place to escape to for a bit 'of peace and quiet' after life in the East End 'where that madman E-Knock someoneoranother gave a speech that forced them into the basement while kids broke the windows with their steel-capped boots'.[28] Although, observes Alsana, people in Willesden are no less bigoted and no more liberal than anywhere else, 'there was just not enough of any one thing to gang up against any other thing'.[29] The suburbs, for Alsana, are the great equalizer. Smith, who had not been born when Enoch Powell delivered his infamous 'rivers of blood' speech, imagines Alsana's confusion and bitterness at her victimization by racist thugs and her consequently favourable impression of the suburbs. For the author, it is, unlike Kureishi's directly personal recollections of this episode in British race history, an inherited 'race memory'. One wonders if its inclusion is a gesture to make Smith's exploration of the minority experience in Britain more accessible and familiar to a mainstream audience, or if the author fictionalizes collective memory as part of a cathartic process to confront a past that was her mother's, and thus, indirectly, her own.

As is evident throughout *White Teeth*, Smith continually demonstrates her awareness of tapping into what is nationally memorable. Although pop culture is not integrated within the novel as explicitly as it is within *The Buddha of Suburbia*, Smith nevertheless draws upon cultural memory to 'set the scene' for the reader. The party at which Archie and Clara meet, on New Year's Day 1975, for example, is scattered with the intoxicated, copulating or sleeping forms of young party-goers, many of whom, the reader learns, belong to a commune. Talk focuses upon politics, religion, history and morality. It is a recognizably 1970s scene.[30] When *White Teeth* was adapted for television in 2002, the director, Julian Jarrold, made full use of music to further compound the effect. It was a memory trick that Smith fully appreciated. When asked about this ploy in an interview shortly after the television adaptation was first aired, Smith insisted:

> Yeah, the music is great. The director said to me that the music sends people immediately to that place and that time, particularly British pop music, because it's a very small country and the songs get played endlessly. They're a quick and easy way to get into the seventies or into the eighties.[31]

Elsewhere in the novel, Smith herself draws upon pop culture to establish a point of reference for the reader, as well as for comic effect. In November 1989, the Joneses and the Iqbals come together to watch the fall of the Berlin Wall on television, mostly because the two families feel duty-bound to participate in what the national and international media have persuaded them to consider 'an important and educational historical moment'. Disagreements between the different generations quickly flare up. Alsana and Samad are cynical, Irie (Archie and Clara's teenage daughter) is earnest and enthralled, and Archie is bored. In a revealing exchange, Irie lambasts her fellow viewers for their apparent inattention:

> 'Jesus *Christ*. Can't any of you understand the enormity of what's going on here? These are the last days of a regime. Political apocalypse, meltdown. It's an historic occasion.'
> 'So everyone keeps saying,' said Archie, scouring the *TV Times*. 'But what about *The Krypton Factor*, ITV? That's always good, eh? 'Son now.'[32]

The clash between the weight of history and day-to-day trivialities, priorities and responses underscores this comic scene. Macro- and micro-history compete and it is the banalities of the everyday which win out. Fiction alone has the capacity, perhaps even the audacity, to challenge history in this way whilst autobiography typically prefers to 'save face'. In confronting 'historic occasions' through the genre of comic realism, *White Teeth* provides a glimpse of authentic and sincere private memory which, in other genres of memory writing, might be repressed or marginalized in a bid to 'edit out' less palatable responses or experiences.[33] Zadie Smith elevates private memory and experience to sit alongside, and even to gently mock the grand sweep of history. It is a memory narrative of, and for, the 'everyman'.

Disobedience

Naomi Alderman's *Disobedience*, published in 2006, poses a different set of challenges to the historian interested in memory. It is not, in a strict sense, a historical novel. Although it does include brief visits to the central characters' childhoods, there is little external contextualization for these episodes within a broad or familiar historical framework. Instead it is a deeply personal, insular and semi-autobiographical story set in contemporary Britain. The novel, acclaimed and denigrated in equal measure as an 'exposé' of the Jewish Orthodox community, relates the return of Ronit, a career-driven, feminist, bisexual Jewish woman, to the deeply conservative community of her youth in Hendon, North West London, after the death of her father.[34] At first, Ronit is appalled by the suffocating parochialism of the suburb, feeling 'the thin sticky strands' of the place 'encircle and engulf' her, and she longs to break free.[35] Only the hunt for her mother's Sabbath candlesticks – a thinly veiled metaphor for her own lost Jewishness – keeps her there. In her youth, Ronit had fled residential North London, rebelling against her upbringing, and striking out for New York as a place where she might be whatever type of Jew and whatever type of woman she wants to be. Her return to Hendon is fraught with difficulties as she is forced to confront her own sexuality, as well as people from her past, whose lives she judges to be 'narrow' and full of 'horror and desperation'.[36] They too are rather horrified by Ronit and her liberal outlook, conspiring to force her into a hasty departure, confirming Ronit's suspicions that although Hendon lies on the peripheries of a great city, it is essentially a village – a village where one must conform and where 'people know one another's business'.[37]

   At first glance, then, Alderman's setting is forged in the likeness of the quintessential asphyxiating suburb. It is an environment that the author knows well. Similarly to Ronit, Alderman was raised in Hendon within an observant Jewish family. As a young woman, she too felt the pull of an alternative lifestyle, leaving to work for a job in publishing in New York, before returning a few years later to settle once again in Hendon. Alderman's feminism, similarly to Ronit's, seems to have grown directly from her upbringing within the Orthodox Jewish community of Hendon. In interviews and blogs, Alderman bitterly remembers being made to listen to her male peers at school thanking God in their daily prayers 'for not being made a woman'.[38] These and other memories inform her intellectual appraisal of Orthodox Judaism as deeply misogynistic, as intent upon 'the erasing of women from public life',[39] although, as Alderman admits, confronting this truth has been a slow and difficult process:

> I probably first started questioning in my teens, but I was over thirty when I finally felt able to say, 'I'm no longer an Orthodox Jew.' It's taken thought and therapy. It's taken writing a novel. It's taken finding new friends and difficult conversations with old ones, and with family.[40]

Disobedience, then, has been for its author a cathartic medium for revisiting and re-evaluating the past. Moreover, the novel also provided a 'safe space' for Alderman to act out a set of imagined scenarios, indeed a whole revised personal history, that she would not have dared to in reality. As Alderman acknowledges in an interview with Aida Edemariam, she has never played out her own deep-seated desires to challenge the status quo, other than by the writing of her début novel – her only form of personal disobedience.[41] Writing, and more particularly fiction writing, has provided a way for Alderman to articulate very personal, private memories in a very public way. In doing so, she has overcome any attempts to erase her from national life, or, indeed, from the historical record.

In her treatment of Hendon throughout *Disobedience*, Alderman outwardly takes her lead from a long Anglo-American tradition of suburban denigration, of which other contemporary British writers such as Hanif Kureishi and Zadie Smith are a part.[42] These negative stereotypes of suburban space have also found their way into Anglo-Jewish fiction. They make an appearance in nineteenth- and twentieth-century novels as a setting indicative of wealth, greed and immorality, and as an environment that was poisonous to Jewish life, and for Jewish women particularly.[43] Indeed, so entrenched had this use of the suburbs become as a narrative device that conveyed the unequivocal message that 'small communities foster small-mindedness' that it led Dina Rabinovitch in review of *Disobedience* in the *Guardian* to ask in weary cynicism, '[w]ell, what else is new?'[44] Alderman's treatment of suburbia as emblematic of confined and confining lifestyles and realms of experience draws upon her own equation between the suppressive nature of Jewish Orthodoxy and suburban Hendon. However, it also borrows from established spatial memories and notions of place that have become so powerful that they transcend chronological, geographical and cultural constraints. *Disobedience* has no need for a historical dimension. Choosing the suburbs for its setting roots the novel within an expansive, transparent tradition whilst encoding the novel with ready layers of meaning. It is a ploy, perhaps, to open up the enigmatic world of Orthodox Judaism for a mainstream audience.

Yet although Alderman draws upon conventional and familiar ideas about, and memories of, the contemporary London suburbs, it is also a novel steeped with Jewish meaning. Each chapter is prefaced with an extract from Judaic scripture or religious life, binding together the novel's spiritual and secular themes, and setting its narrative within the impressive sweep of Jewish history and theology. There is also a powerful immediacy to these extracts that transports and transplants Jewish readers into the synagogue, around the dinner table on *Shabbat* or returns them to the *Cheder* (religious schools) of their youth. It is a narrative device that creates a space for evoking and sharing memories of Jewish life.

In her descriptions of Hendon, too, Alderman repeatedly utilizes not only Anglo-American tropes regarding suburbia, but also pointedly taps into the Jewish spatial imagination. Throughout the novel, although Hendon is ever-present, its Jewish inhabitants 'wear it lightly'; afraid to articulate affinity with place, let alone claim ownership. 'Hendon does not exist,' the narrator explains. 'It is only where we are, which is the least of all ways to describe us.'[45] Gardens are overgrown, homes are shabby and unloved, and British shops go unpatronized. Instead the Jewish community establish their own shops as an act of self-sufficiency, ready to 'depart for other shores' at a moment's notice.[46] This pervasive sense of insecurity typifies the tormented Jewish diasporic imagination. It reflects a long racial memory of imagined and inherited trauma born of persecution, dislocation and eternal wandering. Alderman articulates this through her characters' hesitancy to engage with suburban space. 'We who live in Hendon like to imagine ourselves elsewhere,' the narrator insists. 'We carry our homeland on our backs, unpacking it where we find ourselves, never too thoroughly or too well, for we will have to pack it up again one day.'[47] This heritage of painful remembrances operates to impart Alderman's depictions of Hendon with heightened significance for Jewish readers, while helping to translate and give greater meaning to Jewish life for a non-Jewish world.

Throughout *Disobedience*, conventional and minority experiences of suburbia overlap, creating a setting that is replete with two versions of the past: British and British-Jewish. This duality is made explicit in Ronit's vision of Hendon in the novel's closing chapter:

> Last night I dreamt that I flew over Hendon. ... At first, I saw its dried streets, the identical mock-Tudor houses. I saw the fitted wardrobes, the two-car families, the jobs for life in accountancy or law. ...
>
> And I said, 'Lord, can there be passion in Hendon? Can there be desire or despair, can there be grief or joy, can there be wonder or mystery? Lord', I said, 'can this place live?'
>
> And the Lord said to me, my child, if I will it, it will live.[48]

Ronit comes to recognize that 'God is in Hendon',[49] that the suburb has a spiritual core and a Jewish vitality and heritage. From the outside, however, Hendon's 'Jewishness' is masked by a conventional 'British' façade of 'mock-Tudor' housing – itself a fabrication of a cherished but long-distant past. As Doreen Massey has shown and Alderman seems to recognize here, places are 'a conjunction of many histories and many spaces'.[50] Fiction establishes a medium through which this conflation of histories and geographies can be explored.

Conclusion

For Kureishi, Smith and Alderman, a clear sense of place is fundamental within their writing as a site for exploring history, memory and identity – although the point at which autobiography stops and fiction begins is less clear cut. As a narrative device, the London peripheries are a particularly compelling choice because socio-cultural discourse regarding suburbia within

Anglo-American cultural traditions has become pervasive enough to make it feel like a 'known' place to the reader. Each novelist has been able to make use of shared ideas and assumptions about the suburbs to encode their prose and by extension their personal memories of that place, with greater meaning. 'The suburbs' in an abstracted sense quite neatly provides a meeting place for global, national, local and personal ideas about place. Similarly, too, these are ideas that transcend time (and indeed reflect present perceptions of suburbia), making Kureishi's depiction of Bromley in the 1970s just as pertinent and accessible to a twenty-first-century reader. In this way, the reader participates in a dialogue with the writer to build further layers of memories upon those that already exist within the text. The foregrounding of the suburbs in this process demonstrates the way in which fiction participates in, and contributes to, an evolving and hybridized conceptualization of place and of the past.[51]

Memory-fiction then is a mutually beneficial medium that – certainly in the case of these three novels – provides a literary space for the author to explore, work through and deposit memory. Equally, however, fiction is deeply evocative, drawing upon the reader's own repository of memories and points of shared experience. Indeed, these novels suggest the potential for fiction to represent not only the author's memories, but a spectrum of memories for a whole community. As Bart Moore-Gilbert observes of Hanif Kureishi's fiction, 'Kureishi has clearly succeeded in generalizing his own experience of the cultural "in-betweenness" faced by millions of migrants and their descendants the world over.'[52] For some, however, this is a false assumption about the representative quality of fiction. Reviews penned by those from within the communities which *White Teeth* and *Disobedience* depict have appeared affronted at what they see as a 'mis-representation' of their lives and histories.[53] Clearly the expectations placed upon fiction to achieve a measure of authenticity – especially in the case of writing that shines a light into a dark corner of national life for the very first time – are both understandable but yet, to an extent, unreasonable. One wonders if a novel can really be expected to adequately satisfy the creative rigours of fiction writing, as well as the (often politicized) motivations of the author, while simultaneously placating those it attempts to parody.

For the more detached historian, however, the landscapes (or rather, in this case, cityscapes) of public and private memories encapsulated within these three novels are nevertheless useful because they expose lives, places and histories – however imperfectly drawn – that have typically been marginalized within more formal or traditional historical sources. As Doreen Massey has written of the representation and conceptualization of places, '[t]he identity of places is very much bound up with the *histories* which are told of them, *how* those histories are told, and which history turns out to be dominant'.[54] This is equally true of the experiences and histories of people and communities, reminding us of the inherent power structures still in play that continue to dictate which histories will be told and by whom. While oral history has done much to redress this imbalance, fiction can reach into corners where oral history might prefer not to go. As Naomi Alderman has intimated, without her fictionalized treatment of homosexuality within the British Jewish Orthodox community, that subject would have remained obscure and, for some, obscene.[55] The publication of *Disobedience* forced this issue out into the open. Although the novel's revelations only mark the beginning of a very long road towards open and unimpeded discussion on this topic within the community, the text, together with media debate surrounding its publication, can now at least be added to the historical record.

Of course, the difficulty still remains that fiction is *not* history, and nor should it, or could it, pretend to be. Nevertheless, as this brief analysis of these three novels hopefully demonstrates, layers of memory – real and imagined, directly and indirectly experienced – lay beneath fictional narratives. They are implicit within the text and become explicit through better acquaintance with the author, although it is not the historical 'authenticity' of such memories that really matters. Instead, what *is* important are the ways in which history and memory are explored, deconstructed and showcased by fiction. In each of these three suburban novels, the writers – none more so than Zadie Smith – assume the role of cartographer, using their novels to plot personal memories upon the nation's mental map of remembrances. Through that endeavour to combine history and memory, fiction literally becomes a site of memories and a ready workshop for the historian.

Notes

1 P. Nora, 'Between memory and history: *les lieux de mémoire*', *Representations*, 26, 1989, p. 8.
2 Ibid., p. 7.
3 Ibid., p. 8.
4 Ibid., p. 13.
5 Hue-Tam Ho Tai, 'Remembered realms: Pierre Nora and French national memory', *The American Historical Review*, 106(3), 2001, pp. 906–22.
6 See M. Chamberlain and P. Thompson (eds) *Narrative and Genre* (London & New York: Routledge, 1998), p. 1.
7 Nora, 'Between memory and history', p. 24.
8 D. Cesarani, M. Shain and T. Kushner, 'Introduction', in D. Cesarani et al. (eds) *Zakor v. Makor: Place and Displacement in Jewish History and Memory* (London: Vallentine Mitchell, 2008), p. 1.
9 S. Pile, 'Memory and the city', in J. Campbell and J. Harbord (eds) *Temporalities, Autobiographies and Everyday Life* (Manchester: Manchester University Press, 2002), pp. 111–27.
10 Nora, 'Between memory and history', p. 9.
11 D. Massey, 'Places and their pasts', *History Workshop Journal*, 39, 1995, pp. 182–92.
12 H. Kureishi, *The Buddha of Suburbia* (London: Faber & Faber, 2009) [orig. 1990], p. 3.
13 For an introduction to Hanif Kureishi's life and writing see B. Moore-Gilbert, *Hanif Kureishi* (Manchester & New York: Manchester University Press, 2001).
14 W. Leith, 'Sex, drugs and a mid-life crisis', 'Life' section of *The Observer*, 23 March 1997, p. 8.
15 Kureishi, *The Buddha of Suburbia*, p. 3.

16 Ibid., p. 8.
17 S. Frith, 'The suburban sensibility in British rock and pop', in R. Silverstone (ed.) *Visions of Suburbia* (London: Routledge, 1997), pp. 269–79.
18 Kureishi, *The Buddha of Suburbia*, p. 68.
19 V. Goldsworthy, 'The love that dares not speak its name: Englishness and suburbia', in D. Rogers and J. McLeod (eds) *The Revision of Englishness* (Manchester & New York: Manchester University Press, 2004), p. 101.
20 Kureishi, *The Buddha of Suburbia*, p. 24.
21 Ibid., p. 40.
22 P. Tew, *Zadie Smith* (Basingstoke: Palgrave Macmillan, 2010), pp. 31–32.
23 'An interview with Zadie Smith', PBS Masterpiece Theatre (2002–3), www.pbs.org/wgbh/masterpiece/teeth/ei_smith_int.html (accessed 26 March 2012).
24 Z. Smith, *White Teeth* (London: Penguin Books, 2001) [orig. Hamish Hamilton, 2000], p. 3.
25 Goldsworthy, 'The love that dares not speak its name'.
26 Smith, *White Teeth*, pp. 47–48.
27 Ibid., p. 27.
28 Ibid., pp. 62–63.
29 Ibid., p. 63.
30 Ibid., pp. 19–26.
31 'An interview with Zadie Smith', PBS Masterpiece Theatre.
32 Smith, *White Teeth*, p. 241.
33 For a compelling study into the self-censoring processes inherent within the practice of life writing see J. Mace, 'Reminiscence as literacy: intersections and creative moments', in R. Perks and A. Thomson (eds) *The Oral History Reader* (London & New York: Routledge, 1998), pp. 393–401.
34 See, for example, C. Wides, 'Naomi Alderman interview', *Something Jewish*, 24 March 2006, www.somethingjewish.co.uk/articles/1819_naomi_alderman_inter.htm (accessed 27 March 2012); G. Alderman, 'Disobedience of an obedient girl', *Jewish Chronicle*, 3 March 2006, p. 31; and M. Shaviv, 'Hendon forbid!', *Jewish Chronicle*, 3 March 2006, p. 43.
35 N. Alderman, *Disobedience* (London: Penguin, 2007) [orig. Viking, 2006], p. 142.
36 Ibid.
37 Ibid., p. 123.
38 See, for example, A. Edemariam's interview with Alderman, '"There was really good stuff in the way I was brought up. But rubbish stuff too"', *Guardian*, G2, 20 February 2006, p. 12 and N. Alderman, 'According to your will', *Granta*, 20 May 2011, www.granta.com/New-Writing/According-to-Your-Will (accessed 27 March 2012).
39 Alderman, 'According to your will'.
40 Ibid.
41 Edemariam, '"There was really good stuff in the way I was brought up"'.
42 Some mid-century examples within American popular culture include Richard Yates' highly-acclaimed debut novel *Revolutionary Road* (1961) and Ira Levin's *The Stepford Wives* (1972), both of which were made into films: Bryan Forbes, *The Stepford Wives* (1975); Frank Oz, *The Stepford Wives* (2004); Sam Mendes, *Revolutionary Road* (2008). The recent reincarnation of these novels as successful Hollywood films is indicative of the persistence of 'suburb-phobia' within Western culture to the present day.
43 I am referring in particular to Amy Levy's *Reuben Sachs: A Sketch* (London & New York: Macmillan and Co., 1888), and Brian Glanville's *The Bankrupts* (London: Secker and Warberg, 1958), as two key examples of this Anglo-Jewish literary tradition. I have written about the position of Jewish women within the suburban settings of these two novels elsewhere. See H. Ewence, 'Placing the

other in our midst: immigrant Jews, gender and the British imperial imagination', unpublished PhD thesis (University of Southampton, 2010), pp. 242–49.

44 D. Rabinovitch, 'This is Hendon: disobedience by Naomi Alderman gives Dina Rabinovitch the small-town blues', *Guardian*, 'Guardian Review' section, 4 March 2006, p. 17.

45 Alderman, *Disobedience*, p. 216

46 Ibid., p. 124.

47 Ibid., p. 216.

48 Ibid., pp. 253–54.

49 Ibid., p. 217.

50 Massey, 'Places and their pasts', p. 191.

51 For a detailed discussion of the ways in which places are fluid and hybrid constructions, see Massey, 'Places and their pasts'.

52 Moore-Gilbert, *Hanif Kureshi*, p. 17.

53 Some examples of negative 'internal' reviews include Shaviv, 'Hendon forbid!', and A. Nair, 'White Teeth: Zadie Smith', June 2000, www.anitanair.net/reviews/review_2.htm (accessed 27 March 2012).

54 Massey, 'Places and their pasts', p. 186.

55 In an interview with Aida Edemariam, Alderman makes this very clear, going on to say that she believes 'a lid ... needs to be lifted' on the existence of homosexuality with the Orthodox Jewish community. See Edemariam, '"There's really good stuff in the way I was brought up"'.

10 Alienated memories

Migrants and the silences of the archive

Tony Kushner

This chapter explores the archive – in the broadest sense the repository of visual, oral and written traces of the past in the present – in relation to processes of both remembering and forgetting. It centres on some difficult records produced by state bureaucracy – those outlining the deportation of aliens in Britain during the first half of the twentieth century – and explores them for what they reveal and conceal about the ethnic minorities they sought to police. And it considers the resonances of the earlier, often still pervasive, unease about the figure of the immigrant in the memory work conducted by contemporary museums that seek to recuperate the migrant as a positive presence. What lies at the heart of the discussion that follows is the problem of silence in and about this archive. What remains unspoken in the original records and later museal – and other – representations of the migrant experience? What are the implications of those silences either for our national stories about the past or for memory work within ethnic minority communities? What – as historian Michel-Rolph Trouillot has asked in a different context – is the relationship between the silences of the archive, memory and power?[1] By analysing two case studies of a Jewish prostitute and a West African sex offender, the chapter asks whether it is even possible to re-establish the human agency of these 'subalterns' deported as aliens by the British state; and further how migrant history and heritage confronts such troubling pasts. It concludes by querying whether, in constructing both majority and minority narratives, the option of forgetting is morally valid in the process of carrying out memory work.

Where migrants are concerned, forgetting lies at the heart of both official and popular versions of the British 'island story'. In recent Home Office public declarations and in the formal documentation for contemporary citizenship tests in the UK, much is made of the allegedly positive reception given to those seeking asylum in the past: 'Britain is proud of its tradition of providing a safe haven for people fleeing persecution and conflict.' A narrative of generosity stretches from the sixteenth and seventeenth centuries with 'Protestant Huguenots from France [escaping] religious persecution' and continues through to the twenty-first century.[2] The Huguenot refugees especially became the model refugee group: in state and popular mythology they possess the ideal characteristics. In later memory work, they are perceived as genuine – as victims of a religiously intolerant (Catholic) state that was also the demonized enemy of Britain (France) – and they integrated well, contributing new skills (especially in business and science) and becoming loyal members of society. Ambiguities with regard to their treatment, integration and loyalty have been smoothed over to create a storyline that is flattering to both these particular refugees and the receiving society.[3] East European Jews at the turn of the twentieth century, refugees fleeing Nazism during the 1930s and, most recently, Ugandan Asians in the 1970s have been added to this reassuring narrative, which conflates Britishness with what Chancellor of the Exchequer Gordon Brown referred to in 2004 as an intrinsic British commitment 'to tolerance and fair play'.[4]

Remembering minorities in the museum

Barbara Roche, former Labour Home Office minister with responsibility for immigration and asylum, has recently campaigned for the creation of a museum of immigration to Britain to be located in the English capital. Certainly, Britain is now lagging behind France, Germany and settler societies such as America and Australia in *not* possessing such a museum.[5] If such a heritage site is created, however, it seems unlikely that it will possess the critical edge of, for example, the Melbourne Immigration Museum, which in its publicity acknowledges that '[m]ore than 9 million people have migrated to Australia since 1788. Countless others have tried and failed.' Visitors are asked directly to 'find out why'.[6] As a politician, Roche justified the 'firm but fair' asylum policies of the New Labour government (with the emphasis on the former), asserting that 'this country has a proud tradition of taking in refugees over many centuries'.[7] As chair of the Migration Museum Working Group, Roche stated in 2009 that establishing it

> would be a powerful signal that the UK has embraced the centrality of migration in our national life. Emigration and immigration are bound up with what it means to be British ... If we could understand, accept and celebrate that, we would have a stronger society and a brighter future.[8]

No doubt if this Migration Museum is created, the contributions of migrants to Britain will feature prominently alongside British hospitality towards newcomers. It will reflect the celebratory approach that is present in many ethno-religious minority heritage sites and is also dominant in what has been described as the 'most ambitious European [immigration museum] to date: the Cité nationale de l'histoire de l'immigration', which opened in Paris during 2007.[9] Whether there would be space for counter-narratives in Roche's project is debatable, so great is the need for an inclusive and mutually reassuring construction of the 'island story'.

Historian and former immigration lawyer, Louise London, is one of the few scholars to have produced a more challenging version of British responses to newcomers, in a detailed and complex study of immigration control procedures during and immediately after the Nazi era.[10] Responding to Roche's repetition of the 'proud tradition' mythology, London noted that '[s]uddenly it occurred to me to wonder what adjective Roche would propose ... to describe Britain's history of *not* taking in refugees: would that be proud too? Or would it be the opposite? Shamefaced? Hidden? Denied? Suppressed?'[11] Outlining refusal of entry, segregation and deportation, London does so '[b]ecause, even if it isn't proud, even if it doesn't fit the political message, this country also has a tradition of not taking in refugees'.[12]

Ironically, even those who want to recognize the contribution of migrants to Britain tend to support the notion of 'reasonable' and 'moderate' immigration control, that it is needed for the well-being of all concerned, including the newcomers who would face understandable fears and hostility if their numbers and activities were not kept in check. The idea of abandoning controls altogether – the dominant situation across the world until the late nineteenth century – has become an 'outrage' in public and private discourse. Thus, the late Steve Cohen, an immigration lawyer who believed in the slogan 'No One Is Illegal', noted that '[t]he reality is that opposition to controls in principle has become the programme that dare not speak its name'.[13]

Progressive memory work associated with migration to Britain is increasingly dominated by this 'reasonable' position, especially with regard to documenting generosity towards refugee entry, sensible controls and the achievements and integration of newcomers. Publications such as the Commission for Racial Equality's *Roots of the Future: Ethnic Diversity in the Making of Britain* (1996) and the work of the Museum of London in particular, with key exhibitions such as 'The Peopling of London: 15,000 Years of Settlement from Overseas' (1993) and 'Belonging: Voices of London's Refugees' (2006–7), typify this cautiously integrative approach.[14] It has been marked by a 'return' to the archive to find evidence of migrant presence but also a broadening of existing repositories by collecting new materials generated by newcomers, including the creation of oral and video histories of them. 'Belonging' was advertised as '[a] thought provoking exhibition that challenges assumptions about refugees and explores the contributions they make to London'. The visitor was urged to '[h]ear powerful personal stories and see objects, photographs, film and art that bring home tales of loss, adaptation and achievement'.[15] Accounts of persecution in the refugees' homeland were not minimized in this landmark exhibition, but in contrast the arrival in Britain was presented as a place of new beginnings and progress. Immigration controls and popular hostility to newcomers was relatively downplayed.[16] Ultimately the narrative is redemptive and progressive, even if not simplistically so:

> Being a refugee is devastating and traumatic. Refugees face huge challenges and barriers in building new lives in London, and their achievements are

hard won. Yet they make enormous contributions to the capital – politically, economically, and culturally. They help to shape the city we know today.[17]

Indeed, it is not irrelevant that the Home Office, responsible for social cohesion in Britain, was one of the sponsors of 'Belonging'.

The self-conscious construction of a new archive, one that in the case of 'Belonging' includes 'inspiring real life accounts of refugees from Africa, the Middle East, Europe, Asia and Latin America',[18] has to be contextualized in a country in which many politicians and much of the media stigmatize asylum seekers. If the representation of refugees and responses to them is overly positive in these progressive heritage displays/publications, it is an understandable (and laudable) intervention to restore the balance against a dominant discourse that highlights criminality, disease, danger (especially that of terrorism) and the animosity (real or potential) of the receiving society. There is, however, a danger that internal divisions *within* the refugee communities, as well as the voices of those who are marginal to them (including the many who find the experience of loss and dislocation overwhelming), will find no place in the 'new' archive.

Referring specifically to the 'Peopling of London' exhibition but more generally to museums tackling diversity, David Kahn has raised the dilemma this way: 'Does one – in keeping with the concept of legitimizing the group and, perhaps, providing role models – search out and exemplify extremely successful individuals to present the group's history? Or should one instead attempt to portray the experience of the average woman or man?'[19] There is a linked question of who decides upon such inclusion and exclusion. 'Belonging' was, for example, created in partnership with 25 community organizations. On the one hand, such co-operation is empowering and avoids the tendency to regard refugees as simply victims with no agency. On the other, it is normally the 'ethnic brokers' of such communities who select and shape the stories that will be told. It has been suggested that archivists and librarians are 'the stewards of the collective memory of the Jewish people. For that is precisely what our archives and libraries of Judaica are – the memory of the Jewish people.'[20] In reality, the archive is always partial, fluid and contested. As Michel Foucault stated in *The Archaeology of Knowledge*: 'The document is not the fortunate tool of a history that is primarily and fundamentally *memory*; history is one way in which a society recognizes and develops a mass of documentation with which it is inextricably linked.'[21] Indeed, the archive is not natural: it is constructed, reflecting power relations in politics, society and culture.

Home Office deportation files

Before initiatives such as those of the Museum of London and ethnic minority projects such as the Jewish Museums of Manchester and London, and Black Cultural Archives, the migrant voice has been largely suppressed in the existing archive whether in the form of state papers, newspapers or even organizations formed to 'help' newcomers. In the 'traditional' archive the migrant is either silent or her/his voice is only heard in relation to philanthropy imposed from above in an unequal power relationship. In theory, therefore, the 'old' and the 'new' archive should supplement one another. They can enable perspectives from different sides to be brought together – if not in harmony then in constructive dialogue – and thereby facilitate a more inclusive history. And yet the creation of this new positive archive of migration, underpinned with its self-affirming narrative of Britishness, however well-meaning, has, it will be argued here, made it harder to connect with the older repository. I want to illustrate this point by a case study of a particular set of records located in the National Archives (Kew) and to explore a paradox: how is it that what was the dominant discourse when dealing with 'aliens' for the greater part of the twentieth century is now largely neglected and overlooked?

The Aliens Act, 1905, was the first permanent legislation stopping the free movement of immigrants to Britain. While a relatively weak and inconsistent measure (indeed, the Home Office Permanent Under-Secretary of State responsible for it later wrote that 'from the administrative point of view [the Act] was one of the worst ever passed'[22]), a bureaucracy was created to implement it. One of the new powers under the Aliens Act was that of deportation of undesirable aliens. The Secretary of State at the Home Office was empowered to make expulsion orders under two clauses – firstly, 'in the case of convicted aliens – on a recommendation from the convicting Court', and secondly, '[i]n the case of certain descriptions of undesirable aliens – on a certificate from a Court of summary jurisdiction given after proceedings on complaint'. Under the second heading, being in receipt of parochial relief or being 'found wandering without ostensible means of subsistence, or … living under insanitary conditions' were specifically highlighted as being grounds for deportation.[23]

In 1989 Jill Pellew pointed out that while the politics of the aliens debate at the turn of the twentieth century have been well documented, still missing was 'an account by a bureaucratic historian who approaches the story of the administration of the Aliens Act, as it were, from the inside out, starting from the viewpoint of those charged with carrying it out'.[24] Yet beyond Pellew's pioneer exploration, this intricate work has not been developed further in close to a quarter of a century of subsequent scholarship. While the failure to do so perhaps reflects the unfashionable and challenging nature of bureaucratic history in contrast to the more seductive (although often more superficial) charms of cultural studies, there is also an ideological barrier in the way of such research. The belief in the innate decency of Britain, including its state apparatus, has impeded the interrogation of sources that might reveal less attractive traditions to emerge. As Colin Holmes has noted, hostility towards those of migrant origin in Britain 'cannot be wiped away as an insignificant smear of grime on the country's bright reputation'. The idea of a virtuous nation incapable of racism is, he concludes, amongst 'the most distorting celebratory myths in recent British history and act[s] as a stumbling-block against any attempt to understand and combat the various forms of hostility experienced by immigrants, refugees and minorities in Britain'.[25]

The paradox is also explained by the physical state of the Home Office's Deportation files in the National Archives, which is poor (they are crumbling and their bindings are falling apart) and their recent usage (which is minimal).[26] In essence, created from scratch with no real precedents, the civil servants responsible for documenting alien deportations were searching for administrative efficiency through a process of trial and error. It required referral to earlier cases partly because some aliens were deported more than once (or their original expulsion orders were revoked), but also through a necessity to update and improve upon a system, especially as legislation became more all-embracing and draconian as the twentieth century progressed. At a more fundamental level, those responsible for making the Aliens Act, 1905, and its successors work were learning how to do so: in 1909, for example, when Pedro Costadino was deported to Naples, one official noted that in the process a 'useful table of routes to Italy' had been obtained.[27] Since their deposit in the National Archives in 1996, these files, numbering close to 30 and covering the period from 1906 to the 1950s, have been rarely consulted and few if any historians have used them in their published work. Their state of decay, therefore, is not the fault of the modern researcher.

At a basic level, the deportation files are generally brief in their entries and do not provide the opportunities for the 'thick description' that is at the heart of modern, critically informed, interdisciplinary analysis.[28] The entries are often terse, giving just the name and nationality of the alien, his/her age, the court where the order to deport was made, whether it was carried out and, if so, to where. Yet even this detail, seemingly neutral and legal, reveals much about the categorization and indeed the racialization of aliens. It is supplemented by the occasional comment of the civil servants responsible, which provide further possibilities for interpretation.

Decisions about the expulsions of aliens were arbitrary: in 1910, for example, less than one fifth of those aliens convicted of criminal offences were deported.[29] Almost inevitably, given the vagueness of the legislation, individual prejudice on behalf of judges and magistrates about whether to implement this measure led to inconsistency. What is apparent from the deportation ledgers is that the criminalization of aliens followed a clear pattern of ethnic identification with particular crimes and offences. To read through these files is an exercise not dissimilar from investigating the popular culture of the period, whether in the form of tabloid journalism, pulp fiction (especially the genre of the detective novel) or film and theatre.[30] These ledgers indeed provide an insight into the concerns and moral panics of Britain in the first half of the twentieth century. Chinese migrants appear in the files for gambling and drugs (essentially opium) offences; Italians for crimes of violence and child exploitation; Africans for sex offences; and East European Jews for larceny, deception and prostitution/procuring. This is not to argue that the specific criminal offences committed by the individual aliens were totally invented, but it is to emphasize that they *were* socially and racially constructed (and thus self-fulfilling on behalf of the police and the courts of law).

The possibility that prejudice might be shaping the direction of policy regarding the expulsion of aliens (and, ironically, their non-expulsion) became a minor political scandal in 1909 but one that helped shape the move towards more stringent restrictionism. On 10 February 1909, Judge Rentoul, K.C., gave a public lecture in London on 'The British Empire: Its Greatness, Glory and Freedom'. According to a report in the *Daily Telegraph* the following day, Rentoul gave an account of his past week sitting at the Old Bailey. Rentoul claimed that '[t]hree-fourths of the cases tried were those of aliens of the very worst type, in their own country'. He had before him, he added, 'the Russian burglar, the Polish thief, the Italian stabber, and the German swindler'.[31] Not surprisingly, in the House of Commons, Claude Hay, an anti-alien Conservative MP, sought to make political capital of Rentoul's denunciation, forcing Liberal Home Secretary, Herbert Gladstone, to check the judge's allegations.[32] In correspondence published in a parliamentary paper, it became apparent that there was no substance to Rentoul's statistics and that the one case that could be located – that of a German army deserter – had not been deported by Rentoul even though the judge had the power to do so.[33] In an atmosphere of intensifying anti-alienism before the First World War, however, it has been noted that 'if Rentoul and Hay came off badly, Gladstone's victory was barren. The criminal alien had for the time being supplanted the pauper as the *bête noire* of restrictionists, and the next two years were to see him [sic] inflated to even blacker and beastlier dimensions.'[34]

Indeed, alongside the warped representation of migrant settlement in twentieth-century Britain, the deportation files also provide a condensed history of the peaks and troughs of anti-alienism in the country. For some groups, their skin colour alone would mark them out as undesirable. After the First World War, the deportation ledgers were organized alphabetically under nationality – Chinese, French, German, Italian, Russian and so on. A category 'Other' was added, which contained a mix of problematic nationalities – for example, stateless Armenians – but also those deemed to be beyond the nation-state itself because of their 'race'.[35] In the latter category was the 50-year-old Samuel Joseph McAuley, sentenced in Manchester in 1934 to three years for brothel-keeping and procuring. His nationality was described simply as 'Coloured'. In 1936 McAuley was deported to Sierra Leone, his story having a particularly sad ending – his entry in the ledger notes, '[c]ommitted suicide shortly after the vessel sailed'.[36] McAuley was part of a wider state intervention in the interwar period, which through measures such as the Special Restriction (Coloured Alien Seamen) Order of 1925 made it difficult if not impossible, regardless of passport, to prove oneself to be both black and British.[37]

A country that takes pride on its innate tolerance will have difficulty accepting that it has a deep tradition of deporting and expelling both individual and groups of aliens. At its most extreme, this has been in the form of the removal of whole communities, as with the expulsion of English Jewry in 1290. Slowly the heritage industry has, if only partially, confronted and represented this violent act in which all Jews (except for those who had converted to Christianity) were murderously sent from English ports to the continent. It seems that chronological distance and memory work associated with the Holocaust has enabled a growing awareness of 1290.[38] Other, more recent instances of ethnic cleansing on British soil have, however, received less attention. Indeed, there appears to be a correlation between the closeness to the present and the scale of amnesia.

Jonathan Boyarin reminds us that memory and forgetting are not 'simple opposites'. He implores us to see that '[t]he point is not to separate them, but to realize the surprising point that forgetting is also sometimes a technique of the dominated, used to enable memory'.[39] Remembering that Britain is a tolerant nation with regard to minorities (contrasting with its past enemies, whether they be Louis XIV's France or Hitler's Germany, or even its recent Allies, such as segregationist America) requires collective forgetting of both popular racism (for example the racist and anti-Semitic riots of 1919, 1947 and 1958), or state actions such as the wholesale removal of several hundred German Gypsies in 1905 and 1906. As Colin Holmes sardonically notes of the last mentioned, '[t]his small, weak, indeed powerless group, experienced nothing of the fabled toleration of the British'.[40]

The deportation files provide yet more instances of the collective removal of migrant communities by the state, some of which have remained in near total obscurity beyond a few specialist academics and community activists. After both world wars, for example, efforts were made to deport Chinese migrants in Britain, many of whom had fought loyally for the Merchant Navy and faced intense danger in so doing.[41] This especially affected the Liverpool Chinese community, a devastation only recently recognized and formalized. In this respect, the new Museum of Liverpool (2011) has played a key role.[42] While less systematic, even within idealized groups of refugees, such as the Belgians from the First World War and refugees from Nazism, deportation orders were made and implemented by the Home Office.[43]

Silences and the archive

These files within the largest archive in Britain, while superficially benign and 'factual', in fact reveal a hidden and largely denied history of the nation. It is clear from what has been briefly outlined that they are a neglected but essential source for the historian of immigration control procedures in Britain. But can they be utilized beyond this important, troubling but narrow focus? Can they, for example, be used to confront the life stories of those deported? Giving just the barest details of the deported aliens' biographies (some of whom were actually British subjects), they evoke the fundamental questions raised by Gayatri Chakravorty Spivak: 'Can the subaltern speak?' and 'What must the elite do to watch out for the continuing construction of the subaltern?'[44]

In terms of the archive itself, if the civil servant is heard (beyond recording detail) only in passing, the alien her/himself is utterly silent: she/he is an object to whom something is done. Others (such as British Italian and British Jewish organizations) might intervene to stop deportation. In 1909, for example, Mark Feldman was found to be in breach of a clause in the 1894 Merchant Shipping Act but the order of the Southampton court was not enforced because of the support of the Board of Deputies of British Jews: 'First offence, long residence, wife & 4 children.'[45] In themselves, however, the deportation ledgers imbue no agency upon the individual alien. The remainder of this chapter will explore further whether it is possible to recover the perspective of the deportee and how, if at all, subsequent ethnic minority memory work has dealt with their presence (and absence).

Two case studies from within this archive will be considered before bringing the analysis to a close. On one level they are diverse cases, covering different sexes and chronologies (the immediate pre-First World War era and the 1930s/Second World War). The origins and backgrounds of the two people are distinct – Jewish and East European in one case and black Nigerian (or more specifically Calibar) in the other. Apart from their imprisonment and subsequent deportation, however, they also have in common the sexual nature of their criminal offences. The issue of sex has often been at the forefront of both concern and fascination with migrant newcomers, hatred and desire intermingling and triggering strong emotional reactions. This has been especially acute with those regarded as racially 'other'. Sexual jealousy and a sense of ownership of 'white' women was, for example, the catalyst for the racist violence in Britain both in 1919 and in 1958.[46] In both the cases studied, there is little doubt that the crimes were committed, although their nature was totally at variance with one another – prostitution on the one hand and rape of minors on the other. Yet if the status of the prostitute was/is ambiguous in society (combining elements of both victim and transgressor), the dominant discourse at the time and subsequently has been generally negative. The two examples therefore provide challenges to subsequent representation, especially to the minorities to whom they directly or at least loosely belonged.

The first is Jane Cohen who on 26 December 1908 was found guilty of 'disorderly prostitution' and served in London with a deportation order to Warsaw. Cohen appears several times in the deportation ledgers. After this first entry she reappeared eight months later in the port of Southampton where she was found guilty of being in contravention of the order and given a month's imprisonment before being deported again. A final entry in the same ledger reveals that she had re-entered the country and was deported for a third time in December 1910 by a London court.[47] The final appearance was in March 1912 where in a subsequent ledger it was reported that she was given a six-month jail sentence by a court in Manchester and deported in August 1912.[48]

Even by the standards of the deportation ledgers, the information on Jane Cohen is abridged. She is described as Russian, aged 25 in 1908. A slightly fuller indication of Jane Cohen's circumstances is provided by an account of her Southampton court appearance in August 1909. The *Southampton Times* reported that she was 'a young married woman, who appeared in the dock with a baby in her arms'. Liable to three months in prison due to the contravention of the expulsion order, Jane Cohen was 'only' sentenced to one month's hard labour. Here the agency of the alien herself seems to have come into play, as she explained to the court that 'her husband [had] brought her back to the country', hinting perhaps at a degree of coercion on behalf of her spouse.[49]

To the established Jewish community of Britain, immigrant Jews engaged in prostitution constituted a severe embarrassment. A dilemma was presented whether to confront the problem or ignore it and hope it would disappear. The decision was made to take the former path and in 1885 the Jewish Ladies' Society for Preventive and Rescue Work (later the Jewish Association for the Protection for Women and Children) was formed by the aristocracy of the community.[50] As its leading member, Claude Montefiore, noted in 1902:

> the knowledge ... that the traffickers in girls and women were to a very large extent Jews and Jewesses became public property. The fact, however, that Jews and Jewesses were doing their utmost to combat this horrible trade would in his opinion be the best antidote for Antisemitism and against the charges levelled by the enemies of the Jews against the whole of Jewry.[51]

As in the deportation ledgers, the records of the Jewish Association do not give space for the voices of the women who were subject to their control. Indeed, in many cases the response of the Home Office and the Jewish organizations was the same – removal of the 'problem' to Eastern Europe.[52] If not repatriated, these Jewish 'girls' were retrained by the Jewish Association, normally as domestic servants. There was, however, an element of dissent within the organization to the effectiveness and justice of this solution. In 1911, the point at which Jane Cohen was re-entering Britain 'illegally', the Jewish Association's secretary and member of its 'Gentleman's Committee', Samuel Cohen (no relation), remarked that several cases brought to their attention 'had led them to believe that it would be for the welfare of some of the girls to be taught a trade, instead of being placed in service where many of them were liable to be over-worked and underpaid'.[53]

This more self-critical but troubling perspective was lost sight of within British Jewish memory work until the latter part of the twentieth century. Before then, if mentioned, the Jewish Association's activities were presented in a self-congratulatory fashion.[54] The rediscovery required the development of a new, more self-confident and inclusive historiography and heritage work. In relation to gender, at the forefront were Rickie Burman (until 2012 director of the London Jewish Museum but formerly curator at the Manchester Jewish Museum) and Lara Marks. The latter produced an article on Jewish prostitutes in a special issue of the *Jewish Quarterly* focusing on the East End.[55] It was part of the wider celebration of the Jewish East End, a coming of age of more radical approaches to British Jewish studies.[56] In her study of class, ethnic and gender power relations in Britain, Marks emphasized that it was 'very difficult for middle-class reformers to fully understand why women took up prostitution and were willing to sell their own bodies'. She added that 'Jewish prostitution was not merely the result of procurers trapping young innocent women in Eastern Europe, as has commonly been portrayed by contemporaries and subsequent Jewish historians'. While the possibility of the 'entrapment of innocent women' was not denied by Marks, she concludes that the 'image of the prostitute purely as victim ignores the social and economic conditions many women faced, and the fact that, for some women, prostitution may have been a matter of choice'.[57]

The exact circumstances of Jane Cohen's prostitution are beyond the archive. The 'illegality' of her family's status in Britain precludes a presence in official records such as the census, and what became of the Cohens is almost certainly impossible to ascertain. The information that the official record provides does reveal the fluidity of Jewish migration patterns before 1914 and the case is also a stark reminder that the ideal of the Jewish family as a site of stability and respectability (one that even the anti-alienists grudgingly accepted) does not always stand up to scrutiny. Other examples of desertion (male and female) and violence within the deportation registers confirms the need to treat the Jewish family in a more critical manner and beyond the comfortable stereotypes constructed by Jews and non-Jews alike.[58]

Consider the alternative version of the Jewish past privileged in Charles Van Onselen's remarkable psycho-biography of Joseph Silver. The biographer provides a neat alphabetical survey of his subject's staggering curriculum vitae:

> arsonist, bank robber, barber, bigamist, brothel-owner, burglar, confidence trickster, detective's agent, gangster, horse trader, hotelier, informer, jewel thief, merchant, pickpocket, pimp, policeman, rapist, restaurateur, safe-cracker, smuggler, sodomist, special agent, spy, storekeeper, trader, thief, widower, wig-maker and white slave trafficker.[59]

It is the last mentioned that is the dominant and most disturbing theme of Van Onselen's study. Yet while the detective work and interrogation of the international archive is astonishing and the methodology truly multidisciplinary, the author concludes that there are elements of his subject matter's biography and of his perverse psychological make-up that will never be recovered. Even so, a multilayered portrait of this white slave trafficker and his life story in Eastern and Western Europe, South Africa and the Americas *is* constructed by Van Onselen. Within six pages of the narrative, the location shifts from South Africa to London and then to Southampton. The south-coast port does not immediately come to mind in mental maps of international crime or, for that matter, of modern Jewish history. For Van Onselen, however, it is a key site in the complex Atlantic world of trade, migration and communications commandeered by Joseph Silver and other Jewish white slavers:

Using telegraphic codes known to merchants in the white slave trade they imported prostitutes from Europe at a rate that struggled to keep pace with the demand of local brothels. The Union and Castle shipping lines, whose ships plied the Southampton–Cape Town route, were indirect beneficiaries as pimps and *madams* escorted 'fresh goods' and 'remounts' on the journey south.[60]

On 8 June 1898, the *Ionic* left Southampton carrying Silver, his fellow white slavers, and a group of Jewish women under their charge. The secretary of the Jewish Association and an officer from Scotland Yard got on board before it sailed but failed to get the women to leave the ship: 'Scorned, they disembarked to raucous cheering, hooting and taunts from the pimps lining the upper deck.'[61]

Yet in contrast to Silver himself, the Jewish prostitutes in Van Onselen's narrative remain two-dimensional, and in contrast to the nuanced perspective provided by Lara Marks, they are only presented as victims.[62] The archive of the Southampton Jewish Association, for its part, only survives for the year 1910. They just miss covering the expulsion of Jane Cohen. They do at least, however, provide a diary of the movements into the port and present a more mundane world of prostitution transmigrancy than that of the *Ionic* in 1898. The local ledger is a reminder of ordinary stories such as that of Jane Cohen, but they remain elusive. On 11 March 1910, for example, Rosa Witrowski came back to Southampton on board the *Aragon*: 'She was rescued by the Association co-worker in BA [Buenos Aires]. She was taken away out there by her intended.'[63] While Lara Marks is undoubtedly correct in demanding the return of agency to these Jewish women, it remains that ultimately the archive has rendered them effectively mute: here the surviving record does not allow the subaltern to speak.

There are limits, too, in the representation of transmigrancy found in Southampton's Sea City Museum, which opened in April 2012, timed to coincide with the 100th anniversary of the sinking of the *Titanic*. It gives more space to the theme than any other comparable port city heritage display in Britain.[64] Even so, prostitution, a feature of any sailor town, is not mentioned. Thus, at the extreme level, the role of Joseph Silver or the more everyday stories of Jane Cohen and Rosa Witrowski are perhaps too disturbing for popular consumption and too challenging in the construction of the city's usable past. Similarly, the Jewish Museum in London, reopened in 2010 after major Heritage Lottery and Jewish funding, is also silent on prostitution.

But an even greater dilemma is provided with regard to ethnic minority representation in this chapter's final case study of the archive. The original Merchant Navy index cards for foreign seamen are located in Southampton City archives with microfiche copies available at the National Archives.[65] In 2002, encouraged by the local archivists, I went through some of these cards (there are thousands of them): the shared objective was to explore how best to use them for local display. The information, like the deportation registers, is brief and the original purpose bureaucratic – to keep track of the foreign merchant seamen. Date of birth, nationality, name, photograph and ships serviced are provided. The information, as with the deportation registers, is not neutral and the nomenclature reveals the power politics at work: the title 'Johnny African' is not uncommon, exposing the underlying and deep-seated British colonial attitude when dealing with the racial 'other'. With just the barest of information – and as the naming indicates, revealing more about civil servants than the sailors – I wondered whether it was possible to re-establish the life stories of any of these men and give them more depth than the index card would allow. Otherwise they risked being presented as mere objects; the inclusion in these documents of their photographs tends to criminalize rather than humanize these seamen.

A decade later one of these 1,000 foreign sailors whose arrival in Britain was summarized by a small oblong piece of paper has become famous, or more accurately, infamous. Okun Apanuso, or Henry Bassey as his name appears on the index card, has identity number 350580 and he was described as a fireman born in Calabar, British West Africa. His nationality was British as was his father's. There are four others with the surname 'Bassey' within these index cards.[66] They are unrelated and only one – Henry – had a connection to the legendary singer and entertainer, Shirley. Indeed, Henry was her father. It emerged, or re-emerged, in 2010, with a new biography of the diva,[67] that Henry was convicted in 1938 of raping two girls over a sustained period of time (five years), the youngest of whom was seven when the abuse began.[68] He was sentenced to eight years imprisonment with expulsion to West Africa to follow. In 1943 Henry Bassey was deported to Lagos.

The deportation registers for 1938 and 1943 provide only dates of convictions and sentences. Assize court records add the grim details of the offences. There seems little or no doubt that Henry Bassey was guilty. There are still worrying details about the case: he was denied leave to appeal and as his nationality was British, the legality of his deportation (or of that of other black British subjects recorded in these registers) is not fully clear.[69] Nevertheless, Henry was hardly a victim. It still remains that even taking the deportation registers and the legal material together, there is little to be gleaned about Henry Bassey: they add little to our knowledge of his personal biography beyond that provided by his Merchant Navy Seamen's index card. But the unearthing of these records by Shirley Bassey's latest biographer explains the silences that had earlier enveloped this most famous of Tiger Bay's residents, including the denial that she was actually born in this notorious sailor town district of Cardiff.[70] Before the disclosures, Neil Sinclair's 'insider' history of Tiger Bay had briefly incorporated Shirley Bassey's story into his autobiographical account of the district. Sinclair recognized that '[s]uch a talent as hers is the result of the West African heritage of Tiger Bay where Calabar, Kru, Igbo, Soso and Yoruba seamen met Celtic and Anglo-Saxon brides'.[71] Henry Bassey, who was famous for his music parties in the family house, was not explicitly mentioned by Sinclair but he is by another of the singer's biographers who quotes Shirley's mother: 'I think she got her singing from her father. He was always so fond of music. He never stopped playing gramophone records. Shirley used to sing with them as a tiny girl.'[72]

Conclusion

Ethnic minority historians have often employed positive role models to bolster the self-confidence and self-worth of their communities. This is not surprising in a world in which the dominant discourse often pathologizes them, emphasizing the (especially sexual) criminality of migrant communities. The deportation registers at the National Archives have only recently been in the public domain, but they reflect that dominant past discourse: Chinese, Jews, those of African descent and continental Europeans were accused, in some form or another, of subverting and literally perverting societal and cultural mores. There can thus be a shared desire, from those constructing a sanitized national 'island story' and those engaged in 'ethnic cheerleading', to avoid the difficult archive. But is this necessarily a problem?

Memory has to be selective or else it would overwhelm with the sheer size of its potential raw material.[73] The process of selection is not arbitrary, however, and what is forgotten often has an ethical dimension. As Paul Ricoeur suggests, highlighting in the same manner as Jonathan Boyarin, that the 'strategies of forgetting ... consist in more or less active interventions'; there 'cannot be a happy forgetting in the same way as one can dream of a happy memory'.[74] The archives I have focused on – public and private, national and local, heritage site and official repository, majority and minority – are partial and they have rarely if at all allowed the 'subaltern to speak'. But to ignore them, however disturbing they are, is not ultimately healthy. Ricoeur concludes by asking '[w]ould there not ... be a supreme form of forgetting, as a disposition and a way of being in the world, which would be insouciance, carefreeness?' He cannot answer affirmatively:

> under pain of slipping back into the traps of amnesty-amnesia, *ars oblivionis* [the art of forgetfulness] could not constitute an order distinct from memory, out of complacency with the wearing away of time ... It would simply add a gracious note to the work of memory and the work of mourning. For it would not be work at all.[75]

And in confronting racism and explaining the complexity of what it is to be a migrant or a minority, past and present, there is much soul-searching memory work still to be done.

Notes

1 M.-R. Trouillot, *Silencing the Past: Power and the Production of History* (Boston: Beacon Press, 1995), pp. 26–30, 51–53, 58–59.
2 Home Office, *Life in the United Kingdom: A Journey to Citizenship* (London: HMSO, 2004), pp. 43–44.

3 See T. Kushner, *Remembering Refugees: Then and Now* (Manchester: Manchester University Press, 2006), chs. 1 and 2; T. Kushner, *The Battle of Britishness: Migrant Journeys, 1685 to the Present* (Manchester: Manchester University Press, 2012), ch. 3.

4 Gordon Brown, speech to the British Council, 7 July 2004, http://politics.guardian.co.uk/labour/story/0.9061,12556550,00.html (accessed 9 July 2004).

5 For an overview of projects both in Britain and globally, see M. Stevens, 'Stories old and new: migration and identity in the UK heritage sector. A report for the Migration Museum Working Group' (London: Institute for Public Policy Research, 2009), pp. 13–35.

6 Melbourne Immigration Museum leaflet, 'Moving stories', April 2012, author visit.

7 Roche quoted by L. London, 'Whitehall and the refugees: the 1930s and the 1990s', *Patterns of Prejudice*, 34(3), 2000, p. 17.

8 B. Roche, foreword, in Migration Museum Working Group, 'A moving story: is there a case for a major museum of migration in the UK? A discussion paper' (London: Institute for Public Policy Research, 2009), p. 2.

9 Stevens, 'Stories old and new', p. 29.

10 L. London, *Whitehall and the Jews: British Immigration Policy and the Holocaust* (Cambridge: Cambridge University Press, 2000).

11 London, 'Whitehall and the refugees', p. 17.

12 Ibid., p. 18.

13 S. Cohen, *Deportation is Freedom! The Orwellian World of Immigration Controls* (London: Jessica Kingsley Publishers, 2006), p. 10.

14 M. Frow, *Roots of the Future: Ethnic Diversity in the Making of Britain* (London: Commission for Racial Equality, 1996); D. Kahn, 'Diversity and the Museum of London', *Curator: The Museum Journal*, 37(4), 1994, pp. 240–50.

15 Exhibition leaflet in the possession of the author.

16 Author visit, November 2007.

17 Exhibition website at www.museumoflondon.org.uk/English/EventsExhibitions/Special/Belonging/ (accessed 21 February 2007).

18 'Belonging' leaflet.

19 Kahn, 'Diversity and the Museum of London', p. 247.

20 C. Berlin, 'Judaica libraries and archives in the 21st century', in J.-C. Kuperminc and R. Arditti (eds) *Preserving Jewish Archives as Part of the European Cultural Heritage* (Paris: Editions du Nadir de l'Alliance israélite universelle, 2001), p. 25.

21 M. Foucault, *The Archaeology of Knowledge* (London: Tavistock Publications, 1972), p. 7.

22 Sir E. Troup, *The Home Office* (London: G.P. Putnam & Sons, 1925), p. 143.

23 Aliens Act, 1905 (11 August 1905, 5 EDW.7); N.W. Sibley and A. Elias, *The Aliens Act and the Right of Asylum* (London: William Clowes and Sons, 1906), pp. 58–59.

24 J. Pellew, 'The Home Office and the Aliens Act, 1905', *Historical Journal*, 32(2), 1989, p. 369.

25 C. Holmes, *A Tolerant Country? Immigrants, Refugees and Minorities in Britain* (London: Faber & Faber, 1991), p. 110.

26 On average, each file has been taken out less than once a year in this series of 29 documents (206 requests from 1999 to 2011). Email to the author from David Priest, National Archives, 28 August 2012.

27 In NA HO 372/4.

28 C. Geertz, 'Thick description: toward an interpretative theory of culture', in *The Interpretation of Cultures: Selected Essays* (New York: Basic Books, 2000), pp. 3–30.

29 Pellew, 'The Home Office and the Aliens Act', p. 381.

30 M. Diamond, *Lesser Breeds: Racial Attitudes in Popular British Culture, 1890–1940* (London: Anthem Press, 2006).

31 'Criminal aliens: Judge Rentoul's denunciation', *Daily Telegraph*, 11 February 1909.

32 See *Hansard* (HC) 5th series vol. 1, cols 228–29, 18 February 1909 and cols 969–73, 25 February 1909.

33 'Expulsion of aliens: correspondence between the secretary of state for the Home Department and His Honour Judge Rentoul, K.C. on the subject of the expulsion of aliens', *Parliamentary Papers*, 63, LXX (1909), 527.

34 B. Gainer, *The Alien Invasion* (London: Heinemann Educational Books, 1972), p. 205.

35 See, for example, National Archive (NA), HO 372/27 covering the period 1940 to 1945.

36 NA HO 372/10.

37 N. Evans, 'Regulating the Reserve Army: Arabs, Blacks and the local state in Cardiff, 1919–45', *Immigrants & Minorities*, 4, July 1985, pp. 68–106.

38 P. Skinner (ed.) *Jews in Medieval Britain* (Woodbridge: Boydell Press, 2003).

39 J. Boyarin, *Storm from Paradise: The Politics of Jewish Memory* (Minneapolis: University of Minnesota Press, 1992), pp. 1, 4.

40 Holmes, *A Tolerant Country?* p.19.

41 See NA HO 372/7, HO 372/8 and HO 372/11.

42 Author visit, January 2012. The museum opened in 2011 and has a large part of its permanent exhibition on the city's Chinatown and the deportations that took place in 1945.

43 See NA HO 372/20, which includes Joseph Amand, an 'Undesirable refugee who refuses to return to Belgium', and HO 372/26, which has cases from the 1930s involving Jews in the Third Reich. On the latter, see London, *Whitehall and the Jews*, p. 80.

44 G.C. Spivak, 'Can the subaltern speak?', in G. Nelson (ed.) *Marxism and the Interpretation of Culture* (Basingstoke: Macmillan, 1988), p. 294.

45 NA HO 372/4.

46 See G. Schaffer, 'Perverts and purists: the idea of Jewish sexual difference in Britain 1900–1945', in N. Abram (ed.) *Jews & Sex* (Nottingham: Five Leaves Publications, 2008), pp. 101–9.

47 NA HO 372/3.

48 NA HO 372/1.

49 *Southampton Times*, 28 August 1909.

50 The Jewish Association's records (hereafter JAPWC) are located in MS 173/2/3, University of Southampton archive, hereafter SUA. See also E. Bristow, *Prostitution and Prejudice: The Jewish Fight Against White Slavery, 1870–1939* (Oxford: Oxford University Press, 1982) and L. Gartner, 'Anglo-Jewry and the Jewish international traffic in prostitution 1885–1914', *American Jewish Studies Review*, 7–8, 1982–83, pp. 129–78.

51 Council minutes, 11 February 1902 of JAPWC in MS 173/2/3/1, SUA.

52 Ibid., minutes of 12 December 1904 where the only dispute between the Jewish Association and the Jewish Board of Guardians was over which organization would pay for 'repatriation of these girls'.

53 Ibid., Council Meeting, 22 November 1911.

54 V.D. Lipman, *A Century of Social Service 1859–1959: The Jewish Board of Guardians* (London: Routledge & Kegan Paul, 1959), pp. 247–55.

55 L. Marks, 'Jewish women and Jewish prostitution in the East End of London', *Jewish Quarterly*, 34(2), 1987, pp. 6–10.

56 T. Kushner, 'The end of the "Anglo-Jewish Progress Show": representations of the Jewish East End, 1887–1987', in T. Kushner (ed.) *The Jewish Heritage in British History: Englishness & Jewishness* (London: Frank Cass, 1992), pp. 78–105.

57 Marks, 'Jewish women and Jewish prostitution', p. 10.

58 See, for example, the case of Morris Isaacs, sentenced to four months in Glasgow for an assault on his wife and then deported to Vilna on 18 March 1914 in NA HO 372/6.

59 C. Van Onselen, *The Fox & the Flies: The World of Joseph Silver, Racketeer & Psychopath* (London: Jonathan Cape, 2007), p. 11.

60 Ibid., pp. 155–56.

61 Ibid., p. 6.

62 Ibid., p. 11.

63 Jewish Association for the Protection of Girls and Women, Southampton branch, 1910. This ledger was relocated to the organization at Hull and remained in private archives until recently. It is now in the Hull History Centre waiting cataloguing. A copy is in possession of the author. I would like to thank Nick Evans, the foremost authority on British transmigrant trade, for his assistance in locating this source.

64 Author visit, March 2012.

65 Southampton City Archives and NA BT 350 (CR10 1918–21).

66 NA BT 350 (CR10 1918–21).

67 J. Williams, *Miss Shirley Bassey* (London: Quercus, 2010), pp. 16–17.

68 The disturbing details of the case held at Glamorganshire Winter Assize, Cardiff, can be found in NA ASSI 76/25 and 26 and ASSI 71/68.

69 NA HO 372/10 and 27.

70 N. Sinclair, *The Tiger Bay Story* (Cardiff: Butetown History & Arts Project, 1993), p. 114.

71 Ibid., p. 58.

72 M. Burgess, *Shirley* (London: Century, 1998), p. 8.

73 See the essays in S. Della Sala (ed.) *Forgetting* (Hove: Psychology Press, 2010).

74 P. Ricoeur, *Memory, History, Forgetting* (Chicago: University of Chicago Press, 2006), pp. 502, 503.

75 Ibid., p. 505.

11 Biography of a box

Material culture and palimpsest memory

Susan M. Stabile

'Memory, or the power of recalling images once impressed upon the mind, is a faculty of great usefulness, but is by no means equally dispensed,' explains American antiquarian John Fanning Watson in *Mnemonika* (1812). Subtitled *Chronological Tablets*, the sweeping catalogue indexes 'the most remarkable occurrences from the creation of the world to the present period'. What makes these events 'remarkable' is not intrinsic, however, but rather Watson's antiquarian taste for 'everything that inquiry could learn, or industry collect'. His haphazard collection recycles and Americanizes the popular European compendium, *The Tablet of Memory*, but with a constantly shifting end point: 'If sections of the original work be omitted,' Watson explains, 'they are supplied by other matter more interesting and important to the American reader.'[1] Manipulating what is important for future publics to remember, he erases the past to make room for the present.

In revising *The Tablet of Memory* to include what he interprets as uniquely 'American' moments, John Fanning Watson manufactures an antiquity (i.e. the cultural memory of an ancient past) for an emergent nation established only 19 years earlier, a nation without a recorded past.[2] He retains the word 'tablet' in his revision's subtitle, revealing his materialist taxonomy of memories collected, arranged, and displayed. A tablet, originally made of clay or wax-covered wood and later of ivory, cardboard and parchment, is a reusable surface, a palimpsest: an original text that is scraped, effaced, or partially erased and then written over with another text. Imagine the flowing S-curve of an italic script, suddenly truncated mid-sentence. Or an anonymous reader's marginalia interrupted at the page's periphery; or a punctuation mark, once a full stop, hidden beneath an unknown secretary's cross-hatched hand. Bumps of dust congeal in ink on the palimpsest's surface, sedimented centuries stippled in layers defying visible chronology.

A palimpsest, I will argue in this essay, is both a material object and a metaphor for memory.[3] On the one hand, an earlier inscription is erased and forgotten. Lived experience becomes a memory (*deposition*); and that memory is recollected through narrative (*reposition*).[4] But memory changes with each iteration, shaped by the moment in which it is recalled. That recollection will be overwritten at a future moment, shadowed by a new memory. The past, therefore, persists only as a synecdoche, a piece of something larger – a shadow, a feeling, a fragment, a remnant, a relic, a ruin. On the other hand, a figure's trace might survive in what contemporary archaeologists call a 'cumulative palimpsest': 'the successive episodes of *deposition*, or layers of activity, remain superimposed one upon the other without loss of evidence, but are so re-worked and mixed together that it is difficult or impossible to separate them out into their original constituents'.[5] The hodgepodge of artefactual remains contract historical time into a single, undifferentiated moment.

An antiquarian palimpsest

'*Our history*, which may perhaps be applied in general to most other early history', argues Watson in his *Annals of Philadelphia* (1830), has 'but few and difficult' chances 'for a true account of the *origins of things*'.[6] Rejecting the Scottish Enlightenment model of 'stadial' history in which all societies at all times evolve through the same prescriptive stages, antiquarians accumulated and classified artefacts and texts on a descriptive basis, regardless of chronology.[7] A precursor to archaeology's development as a formal discipline in the 1840s, antiquarianism was an aesthetic practice rather than an organized method. Aesthetic judgement, or 'taste', since the eighteenth century was understood as the body's perception of the physical world through the five senses instead of a rational science.[8] An object's beauty was not inherent in its physical properties (i.e. size, shape, proportion, variety); it existed only in the perceiver's mind. Subject to individual predilections, aesthetic taste was not universal, but particular and relative.

Defining an object's value by its mnemonic associations, Watson adapted his antiquarian tastes to the principles of 'associationism': material objects stir physical sensations; sensations prompt ideas; and ideas trigger streams of associations.[9] Aesthetic judgement was both physical (rooted in the nervous system and five senses) and mental (transformed into ideas, amplified by the imagination and influenced by the emotions). A materialist mode of memory, associations recur with successive experiences of an object. Philosopher Friedrich Nietzsche later described this antiquarian sensibility: 'Feeling his way back, having a premonition of things, a scent of almost lost tracks, an instinctively correct reading even of a past which has been written over, a swift understanding of the erased and reused parchments, which have, in fact, been erased and written over many times – these are his gifts and his virtues.'[10] Using touch and smell (rather than the higher order senses of sight and hearing) as well as instinct (an intuitive rather than tactile 'feeling'), antiquarians favoured their more immediate senses, which require proximity to artefacts. Knowing the past meant touching it directly. Antiquarians did not track a narrative of cultural progress, but arrested history in immediate and palpable artefacts.[11] Those artefacts, Nietzsche warned, are vulnerable to change if not complete erasure. Thus the very objects that the associationists required to stimulate memory might very well disappear.

Equally deliquescent, memory also decays. 'The impression of an important event, or the qualities of a conspicuous individual, may be vivid upon the mind,' writes Watson, but 'the period when the former occurred or the latter flourished are often forgotten.'[12] Artefacts (i.e. objects made, modified, or used by humans) and the natural environment (i.e. trees, dirt, fossils and ruins) are more reliable than the brain, he reasoned. To possess an object is to be transported into the past: the 'relics of our forefathers' that are so 'earnestly sought and sedulously preserved ... are "full of local impressions" and transfer the mind to "scenes before"'.[13] But layered with the affective impressions of artefacts, which project the relic collector into the past and establish future associations, the brain itself was imagined as a 'deep memorial palimpsest'. As essayist Thomas De Quincey explained, it resembles a tablet's 'membrane or roll cleansed of its manuscript by reiterated successions'.[14] The vertical layers of buried correspondences anticipate what neuroscientists call 'palimpsest memory'. Switching the register from wax and paper membranes to neural circuits and synapses, they contend that episodic memory is stored in the brain's hippocampus. However, anterograde functions (existing memories hindering the processing of new ones) and retrograde functions (new memories overwriting information about old ones) can hinder recollection.[15] The archaeological model of human memory – then and now – reveals a lingering cultural anxiety about forgetting.

Preoccupied with 'prospective memory', or how the past and present would be remembered in the future, Watson believed that material objects would forestall cultural amnesia. Artefacts, then, are a kind of associative text, a citation, an allusion, a footnote referencing its historical antecedent – a person, place, or event that resonates in both its former and current contexts.[16] This context is what contemporary social scientists call 'the social life of things' or the ways in which human-made objects shape human life. People invest symbolic power in objects; objects, in turn, prompt particular thoughts, emotions, and memories. Social objects and their evocations, moreover, form a 'biography'.[17] But unlike human biographies following a progressive lineage from birth to death, origin to end, the biography of things is a palimpsest. It accumulates the social associations ascribed to an object over time, transferring 'the mind to "scenes before"'.

As an antiquarian, John Watson understood the unstable yet resonant nature of social artefacts especially when they persisted only in pieces. In collecting remnants of the colonial past, he approached cultural memory as a form of synecdoche (where a part represents the whole object), a ruin that carries with it its entire biography. Ruin is both a noun and a verb denoting an object and the process of its tenuous survival. An artefact that cheats time's destruction, a ruin also draws attention to what is no longer there, to what has been forgotten.[18] Fearing the dissolution of America's antiquity before it had even been established, Watson found historical immediacy in an artefact's transitory nature: 'my mind has been instinctive in its perception of matters and things in their state of *transitu*'.[19] Ruins, as objects *in transitu* (i.e. Latin for 'in passage'), are a kind of living history, an evolving palimpsest. To explain his predilection for *disjecta membra* (i.e. scattered ruins), Watson quotes associationist Archibald Alison: fragments offered him 'a thousand sources of imagery, provide[d] him with an almost inexhaustible field in which his memory and his fancy may expiate'.[20] Layered and incomplete, a ruin resists traditional historiography's authoritative order by materializing a memory practice that engages the imagination.[21]

Watson engaged in what we might call salvage archaeology: he collected artefacts *in transitu* that captured the emergent antiquity of the United States, inventing a public memory of its mythic founding. 'The very newness of our history and country,' writes Watson in his *Annals*, 'increases our interest in contemplating the passing events.' Watson accordingly dug up the past. He excavated city blocks, graveyards and historic landmarks throughout Philadelphia, America's first capital city, measuring what he called 'Sub-terrene and Alluvial Remains'. He found relics of the Revolutionary War just five feet beneath the western wall of the State House (i.e. Independence Hall) – a sword, musket, cartouche box, a keg of flints, an army sergeant's uniform and a dozen bomb shells filled with powder. He hung the cannon balls in his bedroom windows. He scavenged the beams, doors and windows of old buildings; he dragged rotting boards from colonial wharfs. He saved and restored dilapidated furniture – chairs, clock cases and tea tables; escritoires, benches and pier glasses. He squirreled away maps and textiles, colonial and continental currency, and 'autographs of the Pilgrim Fathers'.[22] He accumulated snuffboxes and shoe buckles, dress swatches and buttons, silk threads and tanned leather scraps, Indian hemp skeins and wax seals. He saved glass beads, native arrowheads and shards of exhumed coffins. He even stole as a souvenir two of the ball feet from William Penn's stately William and Mary desk and bookcase at Pennsbury.

Objects 'in transitu': a case study

The remainder of this chapter is a case study of John Watson's salvage aesthetics and his perpetuation of colonial ruins through a peculiar relic box (see Figure 11.1). In order to illustrate the social biography of this box and its contents, I employ methods of material culture studies. Material culture examines the relationship between people and everyday objects.[23] It considers the provenance of an object – its maker, materials and place of origin; its use, adaptation and changing functions; its circulation, displacement and recovery over time. More than artefactual, material culture is also experiential and affective, rooted in human practices and rituals, desires and associations, symbolic and contingent meanings. Broken and repaired, adapted and reused, collected and hoarded, gifted and archived, material culture is a palimpsest – the literal things that people leave behind. It sustains the marks of how people lived in and perceived the world and how we situate ourselves in reference to the past through them. In short, material culture embodies and evokes memory.

Figure 11.1 John Fanning Watson, relic box. Courtesy of the Winterthur Museum, Delaware.

Made in 1830, this unusual relic box has a rectangular body (8in high × 11in wide × 8.5in deep) made of elm wood, foraged from the apocryphal Treaty Tree in Kensington, Pennsylvania under which William Penn negotiated with the Lenni Lenape Indians. The walnut veneered edges framing the box show the last of a panoramic cluster of trees near Independence Hall after the turn of the nineteenth century. And the mahogany stars, inlaid in the box's front and top, are wooden beams from Columbus' house in Santo Domingo obtained by Watson in 1824. Adding to its imperial gravitas, the box has ornamental, brass hardware typical of Empire Style furniture, inspired by Napoleon's ravaging rampages in Egypt and popular in the US from 1815 to 1840. The four cast brass paw feet strangely animate the box. The paws stand firm, yet suggest mobility. Inviting its portability, the box has circular brass ring handles on each side, and a decorative ring clasped in a scowling lion's mouth on its lid. One has only to grab the proverbial brass ring to open the box and peer at its secret treasures, which are locked by the scrolling brass keyhole.

Despite its impressive decorative details, the box is a collected ruin of scrap wood (see Figure 11.2). It presents what literary critic Sophie Thomas calls an aesthetic of 'reassembly'. Since an antiquarian ruin is 'something to be simultaneously done, undone, and redone', it is never complete(d), but rather

Figure 11.2 Example of relic wood from Watson's collection. His annotation reads 'the Cotton tree in St. Salvador, under which Columbus reposed at his landing – Bro[ught] by M[ajo]r Dennis in 1835.' The pencilled sequence in the bottom right-hand corner of the label (80.171.4) is the museum's cataloguing number. Courtesy of the Winterthur Museum.

'a continuous act'.[24] Salvaging the wood from dilapidated buildings, fallen trees, old furniture, and historical sites linked to the nation's founding, Watson created palimpsestic objects (i.e. relic boxes, picture frames, chairs, tables, desks) that grafted the seventeenth to the eighteenth and nineteenth centuries. Because the decaying wood fragments 'left the impression of what they had once been', he recast 'departed and altered things' into mnemonic talismans through the process of *bricolage*.[25] *Bricolage* is an adaptive mode of being in the world that combines, reconstitutes and restages commonplace and cast-off objects.[26] It confounds a singular provenance of any of its constituent parts while at the same time retaining a sense of its previous articulation.

Lifting the box's lid, we see Watson's glass-enclosed watercolour from 1823 (see Figure 11.3). He inscribes an explanatory note in the bottom right corner: '[t]he great Elm Tree of Kensington, an emblem of the unbroken Faith of Wm Penn, who held his Treaty with the Indians under its shadow'. The annotation goes on to detail the box's composite relic wood: 'the box is made of its wood of yr 1810. The *Walnut* shows the *last* Forest-tree in City. It stood

Figure 11.3 Interior of relic box illustrating Watson's watercolour, pigeonholed storage compartments and a selection of the relics housed in the box. Courtesy of the Winterthur Museum.

vis a vis the State House'. The wood's afterlife bookends British imperial claims on the eastern seaboard (i.e. elm) and the Declaration of Independence (i.e. walnut), signed inside and read from the steps of the State House a century later. With the cityscape of Philadelphia sprawling across the background and a lone fisherman at the pier's edge in the mid-ground, the Treaty Tree dominates the painting's foreground. The painting – and the pitch-forked crack in the glass's lower right corner – thus reflects a landscape *in transitu* and the limits of antiquarianism – a growing city; a fading idyll; the felled tree, its gradual ruin.

Watson's watercolour is an adaptation of previous paintings of the famous site by Benjamin West (c. 1771), John James Barralet (c. 1796), William Russell Birch (c. 1800) and George Cooke (1812).[27] But viewed in tandem, the recycled images gradually de-people the treaty site. Watson restores Kensington's 1823 waterfront to an earlier time, to Pennsylvania's Golden Age *before* settlement. He extols the tree as a metonym (i.e. where one thing is named for its association with another thing or concept) for the union of William Penn and the Delaware Indians in 1682. But he removes the Indians from the landscape at the same time that President Andrew Jackson negotiated so-called treaties with south-eastern tribes, which divested them of their land in exchange for lands in the west. In the larger context of Indian removal, the tree becomes a strained synecdoche.[28] Rather than memorializing the absent Indians as a ruin would, the painted tree *replaces* them: 'Ironically, the very monumentality of monuments might have undercut the monument's memorial effect, standing in for memory rather than provoking it.'[29] The landscape in Watson's watercolour, while haunted by the phantom Indians, becomes an unintended site of forgetting.

The absent Indians beg an alternative interpretation, however. Watson observes that 'a single life in this rapidly growing country, witnesses such changes in the progress of society as would require a term of centuries ... in full grown Europe'. Might their disappearance in the watercolour signal a naïve and nostalgic preference for what he imagined as a simpler past? As comparative literary critic Andreas Huyssen explains, 'speed destroys space and it erases temporal distance. In both cases, the mechanism of physiological perception is altered.' Memory, it follows, requires distance from and forgetting the experience it will recall, the very things that undermine its stability and reliability.[30] Might the erased Indians, then, illustrate the necessary aesthetic distance to forget in order to remember? 'The public in general have very little conception of the really pleasing character of olden time inquiries,' Watson complains. 'They wholly overlook the real *poetry* of the subject ... by opening to itself the contemplation and secrets of a buried age.'[31] Cultural memory is not historiographic, but poetic; like a watercolour, it is an imaginative art. As Watson writes: 'facts enough of the primitive scene have descended to us, E'en to replace again/The features as they knew them then.'[32] Adapting the received painting traditions to restore the 'primitive scene' *before* the European encounter, Watson envisions America's prehistory, imagining its fading Indian antiquity.

In addition to preserving the Treaty Elm through his watercolour, Watson initiated an arboreal campaign to preserve, graft, cultivate and memorialize elm trees throughout greater Philadelphia after the famed tree fell in 1810. The roots of the 283-year-old tree were wrenched from the ground and the trunk broken off. Citizens swarmed by the hundreds, grabbing slivered souvenirs from the new ruin. One Miss Eyre dug up roots and placed them on her parlour mantle as a 'What-Not', and their curious appearance attracted the attention of visitors. Fellow antiquarians participated, 'visit[ing] the Treaty Elm as it lay in ruins and removed a limb'. Watson's contemporary, Judge Richard Peters, even justified the pillage in a poem: 'Let each take a relic from that hallowed tree,/Which, like *Penn*, whom it shaded, immortal shall be.' Yet he overlooks the relic as a synecdoche for the Lenne Lenape, too. In an apostrophe to the elm, another poem's speaker asks: 'Hast thou no record left/Of perish'd generations, o'er whose heads/Thy foliage droop'd?' In both instances, the poems personify the tree. As 'a stately witness of the solemn covenant' (to use Watson's words), 'the tree inherited the burden of cultural memory'.[33] An eyewitness, it alone could remember the exchange; it alone could sustain the apocryphal treaty and its continuous memorialization of both Penn and the

Indians. Aestheticizing the tree's ruination as well as its mnemonic ruins, Watson thus echoes Hudson River School landscape painter Thomas Cole: '[t]rees are like men, differing widely in character'.[34]

When the tree's ruins were broken off and taken as souvenirs, they immediately transformed into relics. A relic, according to Watson, is 'the remains of what was once memorable and peculiar'.[35] Unlike the Catholic cult of saints' relics, where incorruptible corpses or body parts (i.e. bone fragments, withered fingers, fingernails, hair or teeth) are intercessors for plaintive believers, an imitative path to salvation, Watson's elm wood relics offer contiguity with the nation's imagined antiquity. In possessing a relic of the country's 'Forefathers', one not only 'sees the *same* unaltered objects, which they had once seen and considered', but also 'enters in the spirit and feels their sympathies'. The tree's secular relics are synecdoches that conveyed the spirit of the deceased person. But they are also an oddly corporeal palimpsest – getting beneath the skin and entering the spirit, one body suffuses another. Associative and interceding, relics are 'a means to connect the imagination to the heart'. Likening secular to corporeal relics, Watson writes: 'the perishing, or rescued remains' of 'by-gone times' preserve 'the impersonation and ideal presence'. Rescued objects, in other words, are 'witnesses' to history, which 'speak out to our arrested and excited senses, and recite to us … the long tale of its notices and observations on men and things'.[36] Personified as witnesses, relics have *aura*: the ability to look back at us from a distance, 'however near it may be'.[37]

A relic's aura makes it mnemonic: it 'consistently evokes from the store-house of his memory the ideal presence, and is at all times ready "to walk and talk" with men of other days'.[38] Here Watson anticipates what cultural historian Alison Landsberg has coined as 'prosthetic memory' – the ability to assimilate as personal experience historical events through which they themselves did not live. Much like Watson's 'store-house', prosthetic memories become part of 'one's personal archive of experience'.[39] Thus the Treaty Tree's amputated 'limbs' ensured a vicarious experience (i.e. 'ideal presence') that stimulates the imagination (i.e. walking and talking with the dead) and consequent associations (i.e. amassed in the memory's storehouse) of an irretrievable past (i.e. 'of other days'). Without a historical reference, these memories are *prehistoric* in the sense that they exist *before* history (i.e. antiquity).[40] Watson's manufacture of American antiquity accordingly presents an associative aesthetic of memory divorced from experience or witness. The tree's relics, therefore, resemble phantom limbs that offer imagined continuity with the social body and its shared memory.

John Watson not only preserved old relics, but he also cultivated new ones for posterity by transplanting scions grafted from the Treaty Elm's 'parent stock'. He relocated two elm trees in the front courtyard of the Kensington Town House and another near the Pennsylvania Hospital. He did the same at his own home at 122 Price Street in Germantown and then again at his home 'on Main Street below Shoemaker's Lane, which flourished for some time there before disappearing'. Watson hoped the scions, as 'successors', 'might incite respect for an offshoot of the original elm ... with nourishing earth and due watering'. Because trees were 'living monuments' that 'link one generation with another', he imagined each grafted scion would 'speak forth the tree's solemn and soothing lessons, as from fathers to sons and the sons of sons'. His evolutionary rhetoric foretells the late nineteenth-century theory of 'organic memory', which considered memory and heredity as one and the same. Just as bodies were reproduced from generation to generation, so were thoughts and memories. Like relics carrying a human imprint, antiquarian history was located in the body. People *contained* history.[41]

More than a horticultural process, however, a graft (from the Greek *graphion*, meaning 'stylus, writing implement') is an inscription – 'the points of juncture and stress where one scion or line of argument has been spliced with another'.[42] Memorializing the Treaty Elm through wood relics, John Watson also commissioned a monument to be built over the site of the Treaty Tree. Constructed in 1827, the granite memorial commemorated the tree's social biography. Each side of the five-foot obelisk had a different epitaph. Read directionally from north, south, east and west, the inscriptions remember the 1682 Indian treaty, William Penn's birth and death dates, Pennsylvania's founding in 1681 and the monument's placement by the antiquarian Penn Society in 1827.[43] Much like the relic box, the monument is a *transitu* melding together disparate events. It structurally and rhetorically grafts a lasting attachment between four historical moments as well as between those moments and the early national era.

Imagined as permanent and unchanging during the nineteenth century, a monument was a valued technology for preserving the past existing in what literary theorist Mieke Bal calls 'monumental time'. It 'aspires to eternity'. At the same time, its 'constant visibility' fixes those historical moments in what Watson described as *in transit*: too often overlooked, unrecorded and forgotten.[44] Documenting the present moment as a sculptured gerund as 'history-in-the-making', a monument delays forgetting.[45] However, its imperative to remember consequently risks freezing memories and alienating future publics from associative experiences relative to and relevant for their cultural context.[46] Seen from this perspective, the Treaty Tree monument contradicts Watson's practised aesthetic of association; it undermines the unmediated and imaginative contact with a persistent past embodied by the wood relics. Unlike the tree's shards, the obelisk dictates *what* but also *how* future publics will remember.

In contrast to the monument's fixity, Watson's bricolaged relic box combines some of the same historical moments, though in an improvised and portable form. Inside the box, moreover, are related artefacts that further materialize the capricious process of cultural memory (Figure 11.3). Collecting what were called 'natural' and 'artificial' (or human-made) curiosities, Watson carefully labelled each artefact with a neatly handwritten tag. The labels provide a descriptive rather than factual provenance, however, unsystematically noting the date, location and person associated with each object. But there is no extant evidence of *how* (if at all) he arranged the collected objects within the box. Or whether he routinely discarded or replaced objects with newly found artefacts; or whether he ever considered his collection to be complete. Self-collected, Watson's artefacts are doubly autobiographical: their associations reveal as much about his aesthetic and emotive impulses as about the objects themselves.[47] Yet the box and its relics have had a curious afterlife since Watson's death in 1860.

The afterlife of relics

When curator Charles Montgomery purchased the relic box for the Winterthur Museum in Delaware in 1958, he bought only 19 of the extant artefacts, including: buttons belonging to painter and museum owner, Charles Willson Peale; more buttons of Thomas Willing, President of the 1st Bank of the United States and member of the Continental Congress; swatches of native- and Chinese-spun silk; a sweet bag and knife sheath from Queen Elizabeth I's court; glass beads from the Great Fire in New York in 1835; a shoe buckle of Miss Mary Donaldson from the Treaty of Peace Ball in 1793; Colonel Alexander Fanning's snuffbox; two Indian arrowheads; and a drawer handle from William Penn's desk and bookcase at Pennsbury. However, Montgomery refused to buy almost half of the box's contents, which were later gifted to the museum in 1980 by Katherine Cole, the widow of a local collector. The rejected relics include: a wax seal; a wood fragment taken from the Cotton tree in San Salvador under which Columbus reposed at his landing; a specimen of Indian hemp excavated beneath the Arch Street Prison wall; a small, round box containing sand from the Sahara Desert; another box containing a piece of an exhumed coffin, along with shards of bone and hair, from the Quaker burial ground on Arch Street;[48] a wood fragment of a schooner that plummeted over Niagara Falls in 1827 and another from an old wharf at Franklin Place and Chestnuts Streets in Philadelphia; a scrap of leather tanned for Washington's Centennial Procession in Philadelphia; and my arboreal favourite, a manuscript book of 'Family Trees'.

While the human remains and coffin remnant are the most literal relics, embodying Watson's aesthetic principle of *ideal presence*, the remaining items are essentially a collection of raw materials – wood fragments, hemp skeins, sand grains, silk threads and scrap leather. Watson valued these artefacts as the rough material for his bricolaged antiquity. But Charles Montgomery viewed them a century later as useless rubbish unbefitting a decorative arts museum. He dismissed the artefacts as what anthropologist Michael Thompson defines as 'transients' – objects having finite life spans and decreasing in market value over time.[49] Unlike 'durables', which are endowed with infinite life spans and both historical and market value, Watson's antiquarian relics *in transitu* (once prized for their vulnerability to decay) devolved into contemporary trash. Charles Montgomery consequently dismantled Watson's relic collection that spanned almost 400 years of British and Native American antiquity, from 1492 to 1865. His decision generates a host of questions. What other interventions have compromised the collection between Watson's death in 1860 and Montgomery's acquisition in 1958? Through how many hands did the relic box pass? How many other artefacts have been misplaced, discarded or plucked from the relic box? Along with lost objects, which cultural memories are subsequently irrecoverable? What version of Watson's selective antiquity have we actually inherited?

In disassembling Watson's collection, Montgomery jeopardized if not destroyed its historical authenticity. He reduced Watson's salvage archaeology to mere antiquarian fetishism. And he ignored the historical aesthetic of associationism. More than material artefacts, a collection is 'a mental realm over which [the collector] hold[s] sway, a thing whose meaning is governed by [him]self alone', according to Jean Baudrillard.[50] When Charles Montgomery held sway over the collection, he 'governed' it by the rules of connoisseurship typical of American art museums in the 1950s. Connoisseurship is 'the attributes of artefacts to particular hands, or times, or places'. That is, an artefact's style indicates its origin. An aesthetic archaeology, connoisseurship understands style as 'the feature that identifies an assemblage, stratum, or find-spot'.[51] Montgomery's taxonomy overlooked this palimpsest, however, with its 14 points of connoisseurship – overall appearance, form, ornament, colour, analysis of materials, techniques employed by the craftsman, trade practices, function, style, date, attribution, provenance, condition and evaluation.[52] There is no place for memory in his comparatively formulaic method. No acknowledgement of *ideal presence*. No appreciation of the artefacts as *in transitu*. No room for haptic associations. No auratic status granted as relics. Though Watson's collection exists precisely *because* it is mnemonic, an imagined antiquity created for prospective remembrance, it lost its resonance when it entered the museum's collection.

As with a monument, lived experience becomes frozen timelessness in a museum. Encased in glass, arranged in tableaux, and narrated in labels, objects are distanced from us and the history they represent. As theorist Didier Maleuvre argues, a museum marks 'an age of dislocations' that 'replaces historicity with historiography'.[53] Similar to associationism's 'law of contiguity' (i.e. things occurring close to each other in space and time get linked together in the mind) that dictated an object's meaning, a museum collection is adamantly contextual. When an artefact enters the collection, its social biography is overwritten with a new narrative.[54] Curated objects have relevance – and mnemonic resonance – only in relation to the other objects in the museum's collection. Despite their mission to preserve cultural memory, museums often have the unintended effect of rewriting it. While they make historical artefacts accessible to a contemporary audience, their 'presentist' approach to memory obscures the changing cultural significance of those objects.

Notice, for example, Winterthur's sequential acquisition numbers for Watson's relics, which are printed in pencil beneath his annotations. The relic box, for example, is: 1958.0102.001. '1958' marks the year the museum purchased the box. The second number indicates that the box was the 102nd object to be acquired in 1958. And the third number identifies it as the first of multiple items in that acquisition. The other 19 objects read sequentially – 1958.0102.002, 1958.0102.003 and so on. The discarded relics, however, follow a different sequence. As the label in Figure 11.2 shows, the relic wood from San Salvador is catalogued as 80.171.4. The variable acquisition numbers thus account for the 22-year hiatus since the collection's dissolution and reassembly. But the item numbers (.001, .002, .003 ...) enumerate the order in which the objects were catalogued in the museum collection rather than the chronology or arrangement of Watson's acquisitions. Thus each white label – combining Watson's annotation and the museum's taxonomy – visualizes two distinctive memory practices for preserving the same collection of relics.

At the same time, however, the museum's continued storage of the catalogued relics inside the box strangely preserves Watson's archaeological aesthetic. Each time I have placed the white gloves on my hands and removed the box's contents, one by one, I am struck by its cumulative palimpsest, measuring 8.5in deep. As Figure 11.3 illustrates, the two-tiered box has a removable, compartmentalized shelf for holding the miniature and fragmented items. Each artefact is wrapped in neutral-pH tissue paper, placed alongside and layered above other artefacts without any particular thematic grouping or chronological order. The delicate strata synthesize the objects separated by Charles Montgomery in 1958, blending again almost four centuries of transatlantic history. I wonder who originally decided how to layer these objects? Have decades of curators, conservationists, students and scholars maintained some semblance of that order after removing, restoring and analysing the artefacts? Since associations are formed by contiguities in space and time in Watson's aesthetic, what histories do the box and relics collectively preserve? Has our continued interaction with the relics had the happy effect of experiencing the objects *in transitu*? With no definitive answers, I defer to John Watson, who appreciated an artefact's auratic distance: 'the less we really *can know* of its history, the deeper & more intense, is the interest we feel' in a relic or artefact.[55] Though an object's *ideal presence* collapses historical time and space into a shared instant, its antiquarian value comes ultimately from its remoteness. It is their 'felt remoteness, their lack of consequence for the present that lends preserved things so much of their charm'.[56] The relics' continued aura of remoteness authenticates the long-ago and far-away past that John Fanning Watson spent a lifetime collecting.

A mirror with a memory

By way of conclusion, I turn to one final object in Watson's relic collection – a half-plate daguerreotype (5.5in × 4.1in) dated between 1850 and 1868. Daguerreotypes were a popular form of memory-making in Philadelphia from 1839 through the last decade of Watson's life.[57] A posed and frozen moment, the staged image is a chemical palimpsest – a copper plate coated with silver iodide, polished to mirrored finish, sensitized in a dark room with the chloride of iodine or bromine, placed in a camera obscura, slowly exposed to sunlight, and developed in mercury vapours until the image became visible. By washing the remaining silver iodide in hyposulfite of soda solution, the image was made permanent. Painter and inventor Samuel F.B. Morse compared the resulting composition to an aquatint engraving, 'for they are in simple *chiaro-oscura* [sic] and not in colours'.[58] A technique that contrasts light and dark, *chiaroscuro* creates texture and depth. The grey-white deposit of silver-mercury amalgam creates the daguerreotype's lighter areas, while the polished surface produces its darker and shadowed areas. Some daguerreotypists further enhanced the likeness by applying watercolour tints.[59]

But Watson's daguerreotype (presently in Winterthur's conservation laboratory) defies the technology's intended permanence in its blurred reflections, buried images and refracted outlines. Vulnerable to temperature and humidity as well as to chemical corrosion, the daguerreotype risks constant degradation. The silver's natural oxidation, along with the dust and scratches it accumulated over the past 150 years, make its deliberate tableaux difficult to discern. The domestic scene is a set piece choreographed in a daguerreotypist's studio featuring an anonymous woman and man respectively seated on the left and right side of the frame. Staying stock still for the three to 15 minutes in which the copper plate recorded their image, she averts her eyes from the camera, parting her perfectly horizontal lips into a reluctant smile. The homespun textile draped over her hands mirrors the vertical folds in her cap and dress. An unidentifiable jumble of objects sprawls at her feet. Perhaps it is a child, rounding out the familial scene. Or maybe it is balls of yarn from which she pretends to pull and knit into the fabric. Also formally dressed, the man looks downward, reading a book balanced over his opened and upturned palms. Staring longer at the tarnished surface, I see a phantom, a shadowed figure beside and behind the man. Or is it scratches on an overexposed palimpsest, light escaping from the corroded metal? What I do know is that the daguerreotype is an invented memory. It is a 'memorial' picture.[60]

Much like the popular parlour *tableaux vivant*, or 'living picture', in which costumed people enacted a mythical or historical event, the daguerreotype is a captured, museal moment.[61] It is a fiction of living history, of Watson's moments *in transitu*. A prospective memory, it signifies a private instance, yet indexes a larger historical context for future viewers. The staged technology neither reflects an authentic history nor a credible memory generated by lived experience. This daguerreotype may even be *reenactment*: the Victorian couple appear to be in colonial costume. As textiles and design historian Beverly Gordon argues, Americans participated in a colonial revival from 1850 to 1890 by posing in colonial dress. Their 'colonial' was not historical, however; it represented an 'antique' phase of American history, a *bricolage* in which the seventeenth, eighteenth and nineteenth centuries were 'mixed together freely under the "colonial" rubric'.[62]

The daguerreotype's fusion of history invites the method of 'palimpsestuous' interpretation I have used throughout this chapter, of reading an object's structure 'as a result of that process, and the subsequent reappearance of the underlying script'.[63] The daguerreotype's laterally-reversed composition reflects its mirrored surface. 'A mirror with a memory', as Oliver Wendell Holmes famously called it, the daguerreotype reverses its forward/backward axis (i.e. a raised right arm appears as a raised left arm in the mirror). As part of John Fanning Watson's relic collection, the daguerreotype is a temporal palimpsest: its forward (left) movement anticipates the future, while its backward (right) orientation mirrors the past. It produces an 'uncanny reality … a closer approximation of the thing itself'.[64] And it captures the *ideal presence* of the deceased sitters, whose gaze returns our own. Look closely. They will 'speak out to our arrested and excited senses, and recite to us … the long tale of its notices and observations on men and things' – just as Watson promised.[65]

Notes

1 A derivative of *The Tablet of Memory* (republished ten times between 1774 and 1800), *Mnemonika* is also indebted to Samuel Blodget's *Economica* (1806). John Fanning Watson, *Mnemonika* (Philadelphia: John F. Watson, 1812, and Baltimore: Edward J. Coale, 1812), pp. iii, v, vi. I cite from the latter edition.

2 See Watson's *Annals of Philadelphia* (published in 1830 and reissued more than 25 times during the nineteenth century alone). Subtitled a 'Collection' of 'Memoirs, anecdotes, and incidents … intended to preserve the recollections of olden time', the *Annals* are a haphazard collection of curiosities (organized thematically rather than chronologically) to preserve memory and trigger recollection.

3 G. Genette, *Palimpsests: Literature in the Second Degree* (Lincoln: University of Nebraska Press, 1997); S. Dillon, *The Palimpsest: Literature, Criticism, Theory* (New York: Continuum, 2007); A. Huyssen, *Present Pasts: Urban Palimpsests and the Politics of Memory* (Palo Alto: Stanford University Press, 2003); M. Vitale, 'Palimpsest of history and memory', *Annali*, 8(1–2), 2004, pp. 125–46.

4 On material memory practices see Stabile, *Memory's Daughters: The Material Culture of Remembrance in Eighteeenth-Century America* (Ithaca: Cornell University Press, 2004) and B.J. Mills and W.H Walker, 'Introduction: memory, materiality, and depositional practice', *Memory work: archaeologies of material practices* (Santa Fe: School for Advanced Research Press, 2008), pp. 3–24.

5 G. Bailey, 'Time perspectives, palimpsests and the archaeology of time', *Journal of Anthropological Archaeology*, 26(2), 2007, p. 204.

6 Watson, *Annals of Philadelphia and Pennsylvania* (Philadelphia: E. Stuart, 1899), pp. 2, 14. Hereafter I will cite from this edition by volume and page number.

7 S. Thomas, 'Assembling history: fragments and ruins', *European Romantic Review*, 14(2), 2003, pp. 177–86. On the stadial model of history, see M. Salber Phillips, *Society and Sentiment: Genres of Historical Writing in Britain, 1740–1820* (Princeton: Princeton University Press, 2000). On women and antiquarianism, see C. Winterer, *The Mirror of Antiquity: American Women and the Classical Tradition, 1750–1900* (Ithaca: Cornell University Press, 2007) and S.M. Stabile, 'Female curiosities: the transatlantic female commonplace book', in H. Brayman Hackel and C.E. Kelly (eds) *Reading Women: Literacy, Authorship, and Culture in the*

Atlantic World, 1500–1800 (Philadelphia: University of Pennsylvania Press, 2009), pp. 217–43.
8 J. Coote and A. Shelton (eds) *Anthropology, Art and Aesthetics* (Oxford: Clarendon Press, 1992); C. Gosden, 'Making sense: archaeology and aesthetics', *World Archaeology*, 33(2), 2001, pp. 163–67; and D. Howe (ed.) *Empire of the Senses: The Sensual Culture Reader* (Oxford: Berg, 2005).
9 D. Hume, *Treatise on Human Nature*, Book I, Part II, Section V (Oxford: Clarendon, 1896) [orig. 1739]; D. Hartley, *Observations On Man, His Frame, His Duty, and His Expectations*, 2 vols. (London: Samuel Richardson, 1749); T. Reid, *An Inquiry into the Human Mind on the Principles of Common Sense*, ed. Derek R. Brookes (University Park: Pennsylvania State University Press, 1997) [orig. 1764]; J. Stuart Mill, *A System of Logic* (New York: Harper & Brothers, 1848); A. Bain, *The Senses and the Intellect*, 3rd edn (New York: Appleton, 1872) [orig. 1855]; F. Hutcheson, *An Inquiry into the Original of our Ideas of Beauty and Virtue*, 2nd ed. (London: printed for J. Darby, 1726) [orig. 1725]; A. Alison, *Essays on the Nature and Principles of Taste*, 2 vols. (Edinburgh: J. Bell and J. Bradfute,1790).
10 In 'The uses and abuses of history' (1873–76), Friedrich Nietzsche distinguished antiquarian historical methods from the monumental (i.e. extolling exemplary models for future generations to imitate) and the critical (i.e. 'history which sits in judgement and passes judgement').
11 R. Sweet, *Antiquaries: The Discovery of the Past in Eighteenth-Century Britain* (London: Cambridge University Press, 2004); S. Pearce (ed.) *Visions of Antiquity: The Society of Antiquaries, 1707–2007* (London: Society of Antiquaries of London, 2007).
12 Watson, *Mnemonika*, pp. iii–iv.
13 Watson, *Annals*, 2, p. 1.
14 T. De Quincey, 'The palimpsest of the human brain', in *The Collected Writings of Thomas De Quincey*, vol. 13 (London: A&C Black, 1897).
15 C. Savin, P. Dayan and M. Lengyel, 'Two is better than one: distinct roles for familiarity and recollection in retrieving palimpsest memories', *Proceedings of the Neural Information Processing Systems Foundation*, 2011, pp. 1–9.
16 On the textual theory of citation, see J. Derrida, 'Signature, event, context', in *The Margins of Philosophy* (Brighton: Harvester, 1982), pp. 307–30.
17 I. Kopytoff, 'The cultural biography of things: commoditization as process', in A. Appadurai (ed.) *The Social Life of Things* (Cambridge: Cambridge University Press, 1986), pp. 64–94; A. Huyssen, *Twilight Memories: Marking Time in a Culture of Amnesia* (New York: Routledge, 1995), p. 249; and C. Knappett, *Thinking Through Material Culture* (Philadelphia: University of Pennsylvania Press, 2005).
18 D. Maleuvre, *Museum Memories: History, Technology, Art* (Palo Alto: Stanford University Press, 1999), p. 273.
19 Watson, *Annals*, 2, p. 15.
20 Ibid.; A. Alison, *Essays on the Nature and Principles of Taste* (Edinburgh: Bell and Bradfute, 1790).
21 V. Liska 'Elusive pasts', in P. Vermeulen et al., 'Dispersal and redemption: the future dynamics of memory studies – a roundtable', *Memory Studies*, 5, 2012, pp. 225, 230–31.
22 Watson, *Mnemonika*, p. iv; *Annals*, 2, p. 1. See also Watson, *Annals*, 1, pp. 441, 396, 435, 402.
23 J. Prown and K. Haltman (eds) *American Artefacts: Essays in Material Culture* (East Lansing: Michigan State University Press, 2000); D. Miller (ed.) *Materiality* (Durham, NC: Duke University Press, 2005); F. Myers (ed.) *The Empire of Things: Regimes of Value and Material Culture* (Santa Fe: School of American Research Press, 2001); D. Kingery (ed.) *Learning from Things: Method and Theory of Material Culture Studies* (Washington, DC: Smithsonian Institutions Press, 1996); B. Brown, 'Thing theory', *Critical Inquiry*, 28, autumn 2001, pp. 1–16.

24 Thomas, 'Assembling history', p. 178.

25 Watson, *Annals*, 1, p. 443.

26 C. Lévi-Strauss, *The Savage Mind*, trans. J. and D. Weightman (London: Weidenfeld & Nicolson, 1966) [orig. French edn, 1962], pp. 16–17; B. Herman, 'The Bricoleur revisited', in A. Smart Martin and J. Ritchie Garrison (eds) *American Material Culture: The Shape of the Field* (Knoxville, Tenn.: University of Tennessee Press, 1997), pp. 37–63; A. Dezeuze, 'Assemblage, bricolage, and the practice of everyday life', *Art Journal*, 67(1), 2008, pp. 31–37.

27 In 'Fancy history: John Fanning Watson's relic box', *Common-Place*, 10(1), 2009, Yvette Piggush discusses the inhabited and dis-inhabited spaces in the paintings by Birch and Watson. www.common-place.org/vol-10/no-01/lessons/. See www.penntreatymuseum.org/treaty.php for a description of the other paintings and related relic boxes.

28 The treaties from 1810 to 1824 culminated in the Indian Removal Act of 1830. Stephen Bann discusses the dangers of what I am calling the antiquarian synecdoche: taking the part for the whole offers an immediate – but limited – perception of the past, running the risk of fetishism. See S. Bann, 'Clio in part: on antiquarianism and the historical fragment', *Perspecta*, 23, 1987, pp. 24–37.

29 A. Landsberg, *Prosthetic Memory: The Transformation of American Remembrance in the Age of Mass Culture* (New York: Columbia University Press, 2004), p. 6.

30 A. Huyssen, 'Monument and memory in the postmodern age', *Yale Journal of Criticism*, 6(2), 1993, pp. 253, 250. See also Huyssen, *Present Pasts: Urban Palimpsests and the Politics of Memory* (Stanford: Stanford University Press, 2003).

31 Watson, *Annals*, 2, pp. 1, 12.

32 Watson, *Annals*, 1, p. 130.

33 Watson, *Annals*, 1, pp. 134, 145.

34 Thomas Cole, 'Essay on American scenery', *American Monthly Magazine*, 1, January 1836.

35 Watson, *Annals*, 2, p. 13.

36 Watson, *Annals*, 2, p. 13; 1, p. 494; 2, pp. 13–14.

37 W. Benjamin, 'The work of art in the age of its reproducibility', trans. E. Jephcott and H. Zohn, in H. Eiland and M.W. Jennings (eds) *Walter Benjamin: Selected Writings, Volume 3, 1935–1938* (Cambridge, MA: The Belknap Press of Harvard University Press, 2002), pp. 104–5.

38 Watson, *Annals*, 2, p. 13.

39 Landsberg, *Prosthetic Memory*, pp. 25–26.

40 W. Benjamin, 'A short speech on Proust', in R. Tiedemann and H. Schweppenhüser (eds) *Gesammelte Schriften*, 7 vols. (Frankfurt, 1989), vol. 2, p. 1064.

41 Laura Otis examines the theory of organic memory, which emerged between 1870 and 1918, a period of intense nationalism, in *Organic Memory: History and the Body in the Late Nineteenth and Early Twentieth Centuries* (Lincoln: University of Nebraska Press, 1994), p. ix.

42 J. Culler, *On Deconstruction: Theory and Criticism after Structuralism* (London: Routledge & Kegan Paul, 1983), p. 135.

43 M.G. Lolla, 'Monuments and texts: antiquarianism and the beauty of antiquity', *Art History*, 25(4), 2002, pp. 431–49. On the relationship between Native Americans, the landscape, and monuments see P.E. Rubertone, *Archaeologies of Placemaking: Monument, Memories, and Engagement in Native North America* (Walnut Creek, CA: Left Coast Press, 2008).

44 M. Bal, *Narratology: Introduction to the Theory of Narrative* (University of Toronto Press, 1997), p. 77.

45 I. Karp, *Museum Frictions: Public Cultures/Global Transformations* (Chapel Hill: Duke University Press, 2006), p. 215.

46 R.S. Nelson and M. Olin (eds) *Monument and Memory, Made and Unmade* (University of Chicago Press, 2004); K. Savage, *Monument Wars* (Berkeley: University of California Press, 2009); and E. Doss, *Memorial Mania: Public Feeling in America* (Chicago: University of Chicago Press, 2012).

47 J. Baudrillard, 'The system of collecting', in J. Elsner and R. Cardinal (eds) *The Cultures of Collecting* (London: Reaktion Books Ltd., 1994), p. 12.

48 Though Watson's label and the Winterthur Museum's registrar records do not list the body fragments, he had interest in and access to such relics. In addition to him exhuming several bodies and relocating them in Laurel Hill Cemetery, Watson knew of a collection of bones and relics from desecrated graves near Penrose's Ferry and the mouth of the Schuykill River, which are detailed in a letter from fellow antiquarian Deborah Norris Logan to John Fanning Watson, 15 December 1827, 'Letters and communications', John Fanning Watson, Coll. 697. Am. 30163, Historical Society of Pennsylvania.

49 M. Thompson, *Rubbish Theory: The Creation and Destruction of Value* (Oxford: Oxford University Press, 1979); J. Scanlan, *On Garbage* (Chicago: University of Chicago Press, 2004).

50 Baudrillard, 'The system of collecting', p. 7.

51 R. Neer, 'Connoisseurship and the stakes of style', *Critical Inquiry*, 32(1), 2005, pp. 1–26.

52 C. Montgomery, 'Some remarks on the science and principles of connoisseurship', Reprint from the 1961 Walpole Society *Note Book*, pp. 9–20.

53 Maleuvre, *Museum Memories*, pp. 277, 57. See also S. Crane (ed.) *Museums and Memory* (Palo Alto: Stanford University Press, 2000); G. Anderson, *Reinventing the Museum* (Walnut Creek, CA: Altamira, 2004); S. Dudley (ed.) *Museum Materialities: Objects, Engagement, Interpretations* (New York: Routledge, 2006); and S. Conn, *Do Museums Still Need Objects?* (Philadelphia: University of Pennsylvania Press, 2010).

54 Baudrillard, 'The system of collecting', p. 8. See also S. Stewart, *On Longing: Narratives of the Miniature, the Gigantic, the Souvenir, the Collection* (Chapel Hill: Duke University Press, 1993); S. Pearce, *Museums, Objects, and Collections* (Washington: Smithsonian, 1993) and *Interpreting Objects and Collections* (New York: Routledge, 1994).

55 Watson, *Annals*, 2, p. 494.

56 D. Lowenthal, *The Past is a Foreign Country* (New York: Cambridge University Press, 1985) and 'Material preservation and its alternatives', *Perspecta*, 25, 1985, p. 71.

57 See related exhibit at www.librarycompany.org/catchingashadow/.

58 Quoted in S.Prime, *The Life of Samuel F.B. Morse* (New York: Appleton and Co., 1875), pp. 400–1.

59 B. Laurence Scherer, 'Early photographs: daguerreotypes', *The Magazine Antiques*, 24 June 2009, www.themagazineantiques.com/news-opinion/the-new-collector/2009-06-24/early-photographs-daguerreotypes/.

60 A. Trachtenberg, *Reading American Photographs: Images as History, Mathew Brady to Walker Evans* (New York: Hill & Wang, 1989), pp. 32–33.

61 M. Chapman, '"Living pictures": women and *tableaux vivants* in nineteenth-century American fiction and culture', *Wide Angle: A Film Quarterly of Theory, Criticism, and Practice*, 18(3), 1996, pp. 23–52.

62 Gordon divides the colonial revival into three separate, changing, but related movements (1850–90, 1890–1920, 1920–40) in 'Costumed representations of early America: a gendered portrayal, 1850–1940', *Dress*, 30, 2003, p. 3.

63 Dillon, *The Palimpsest*, p. 4.

64 Trachtenberg, *Reading American Photographs*, p. 14.

65 Watson, *Annals*, 2, pp. 2, 13–14.

Select bibliography

General

Assmann, A., *Cultural Memory and Western Civilization: Functions, Media, Archives* (Cambridge: Cambridge University Press, 2011) [orig. German edition, Verlag, 1999]

Cubitt, G., *History and Memory* (Manchester: Manchester University Press, 2007)

De Groot, J., *Consuming History: Historians and Heritage in Contemporary Popular Culture* (London & New York: Routledge, 2009)

Fernyhough, C., *Pieces of Light: The New Science of Memory* (London: Profile Books, 2012)

Green, A., *Cultural History* (Basingstoke: Palgrave, 2008)

Klein, K.L., 'On the emergence of memory in historical discourse', *Representations*, 69, 2000, pp. 127–50

Raphael, S., *Theatres of Memory*, vol. 1 (London & New York: Verso, 1994)

Schachter, D., *Searching for Memory: The Brain, the Mind, and the Past* (New York: Basic Books, 1996)

Tosh, J. (ed.) *Historians on History*, 2nd edn (Harlow: Pearson, 2009)

Tosh, J. with S. Lang, *The Pursuit of History*, 4th edn (Harlow: Pearson, 2006)

Turkle, S. (ed.) *Evocative Objects: Things We Think With* (Cambridge, MA & London: MIT Press, 2011)

Oral history and testimony

Abrams, L., *Oral History Theory* (London & New York: Routledge, 2010)

Douglas, L., *The Memory of Judgment: Making Law and History in the Trials of the Holocaust* (New Haven: Yale University Press, 2001)

Felman, S., *The Juridical Unconscious: Trials and Traumas in the Twentieth Century* (Cambridge, MA: Harvard University Press, 2002)

Langer, L.L., *Holocaust Testimonies: The Ruins of Memory* (New Haven & London: Yale University Press, 1991)

Passerini, L., 'Work ideology and consensus under Italian fascism', *History Workshop Journal*, 8(1), 1979, pp. 82–108

——*Fascism in Popular Memory: The Cultural Experience of the Turin Working Class* (Cambridge: Cambridge University Press, 1987)

——*Memory and Utopia: The Primacy of Intersubjectivity* (London: Equinox, 2007)

Perks, R. and A. Thomson (eds) *The Oral History Reader*, 2nd edn (London: Routledge, 2006)

Portelli, A., 'The peculiarities of oral history', *History Workshop Journal*, 12(1), 1981, pp. 96–107

——*The Battle of the Valle Giulia: Oral History and the Art of Dialogue* (Madison, WI: University of Wisconsin Press, 1997)

Thompson, P., *The Voice of the Past* (Oxford: Oxford University Press, 1978)

Thomson, A., 'Four paradigm transformations in oral history', *Oral History Review*, 34(1), 2007, pp. 49–70

——*Anzac Memories: Living with the Legend* (Oxford: Oxford University Press, 1994)

Wieviorka, A., *The Era of the Witness*, trans. J. Stark (Ithaca, NY: Cornell University Press, 2006)

Memorialization and commemoration

Ashplant, T., G. Dawson and M. Roper (eds) *Commemorating War: The Politics of Memory* (New Brunswick: Transaction Publishers, 2006) [orig. Routledge, 2000]

Geary, P., *Living with the Dead in the Middle Ages* (Ithaca: Cornell University Press, 1994)

——*Phantoms of Remembrance: Memory and Oblivion at the End of the First Millennium* (Princeton: Princeton University Press, 1994)

Gildea, R., *The Past in French History* (New Haven & London: Yale University Press, 1994)

Lebow, R.N., W. Kansteiner and C. Fogu (eds) *The Politics of Memory in Postwar Europe* (Durham: Duke University Press, 2006)

Lowenthal, D., *Possessed by the Past: The Heritage Crusade and the Spoils of History* (New York: The Free Press, 1996)

Nora, P., 'Between memory and history: *les lieux de mémoire*', *Representations*, 26, 1989, pp. 7–24

——(ed.) *Realms of Memory: Rethinking the French Past*, 3 vols., trans. A. Goldhammer and ed. L.D. Kritzman (New York: Columbia University Press, 1996–98)

——*Rethinking France: les lieux de mémoire*, 4 vols., trans. M. Trouille and D.P. Jordan (Chicago: Chicago University Press, 2001–10)

Radstone, S. and B. Schwarz (eds) *Memory: History, Theories, Debates* (New York: Fordham University Press, 2010)

Rothberg, M., *Multidirectional Memory: Remembering the Holocaust in the Age of Decolonization* (Stanford: Stanford University Press, 2009)

Trouillot, M.-R., *Silencing the Past: Power and the Production of History* (Boston: Beacon Press, 2004)

Winter, J., *Sites of Memory, Sites of Mourning: The Great War in European Cultural History* (Cambridge: Cambridge University Press, 1995)

——*Remembering War: The Great War Between Memory and History in the Twentieth Century* (New Haven, CT: Yale University Press, 2006)

Wolpert, A., *Remembering Defeat: Civil War and Civic Memory in Ancient Athens* (Baltimore: Johns Hopkins, 2002)

Young, J., *The Texture of Memory: Holocaust Memorials and Meaning* (New Haven: Yale University Press, 1993)

Collective memory

Confino, A., 'Collective memory and cultural history: problems of method', *American Historical Review*, 102(5), 1997, pp. 1386–1403

Crane, S.A., 'Writing the individual back into collective memory', *American Historical Review*, 102(5), 1997, pp. 1372–85

Fentress, J. and C. Wickham, *Social Memory* (Oxford: Blackwell, 1992)

Funkenstein, A., 'Collective memory and historical consciousness', *History & Memory*, 1(1), 1989, pp. 5–26

Gedi, N. and Y. Elam, 'Collective memory – what is it?', *History & Memory*, 8(1), 1996, pp. 30–50

Halbwachs, M., *On Collective Memory*, trans. and ed. L.A. Coser (Chicago: Chicago University Press, 1992)

Kansteiner, W., 'Finding meaning in memory: a methodological critique of collective memory studies', *History and Theory*, 41, May 2002, pp. 179–97

Misztal, B.A., *Theories of Social Remembering* (Berkshire: McGraw-Hill, 2003)

Novick, P, *The Holocaust and Collective Memory* (London: Bloomsbury Publishing, 2001)

Olick, J.K., 'Collective memory: the two cultures', *Sociological Theory*, 17(3), 1999, pp. 333–48

——'Collective memory: a memoir and prospect', *Memory Studies*, 1, 2008, pp. 23–27

Olick, J., V. Vinitzsky-Seroussi and D. Levy (eds) *The Collective Memory Reader* (New York: Oxford University Press, 2011)

Olick, J.K. and J. Robbins, 'Social memory studies: from "collective memory" to the historical sociology of mnemonic practices', *Annual Review of Sociology*, 24, 1998, pp. 105–40

Index

Please note that page numbers relating to notes will have the letter 'n' following the page number.

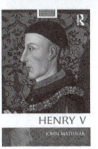

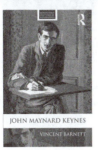